THE MAN WITH NO NAME

IAIN JOHNSTONE

CLINT EASTWOOD

Quill/William Morrow
New York

Text copyright © 1981, 1988 by Iain Johnstone
Edition copyright © 1981, revised and enlarged edition
copyright © 1988 by Plexus Publishing Limited

Originally published in Great Britain by
Plexus Publishing Limited, 26 Dafforne Road,
London SW17 8TZ England

Library of Congress Catalog Card Number: 88-64107
ISBN: 0-688-09059-1

First Revised Quill Edition
1 2 3 4 5 6 7 8 9 10

Grateful acknowledgement is made to Dave Turner of the
Clint Eastwood Appreciation Society for his endless help
with information and photographs

Book Design by Bob Burroughs
Cover design by Teresa Bonner and Chris Lower
Printed in Great Britain

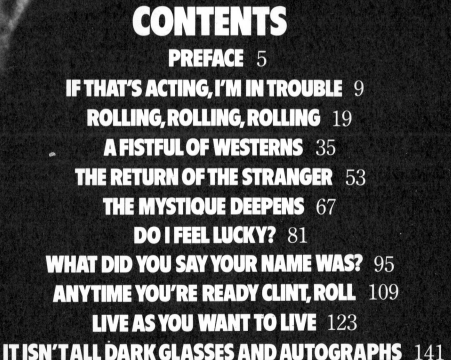

CONTENTS

PREFACE

Prefaces, although they come at the beginning of a book, are inevitably written at the end. Beneath the display of bravura that this is the most minutely researched, painstakingly written, undeviatingly planned biography ever, lies two years' self-doubt over missed opportunities, impossible mazes that have no route to their centre and unrepayable gratitude to people who have fortified one with information and, equally important, edification. So it is with this book.

It arose out of a television program shown on British Television in 1977 and called *The Man With No Name*. It consisted, in the main, of a conversation between Mr Eastwood and myself, in his back garden in Carmel, California, interrupted only by the distant barks of the sea otters, the rhythmic pounding of the Pacific surf and a few clips and quotes to throw some more light on his remarkable career. Our televised conversation lasted a mere four thousand words; now, over ten years later, with additional research and further encounters with Mr Eastwood and his colleagues, this book runs to more than sixty thousand.

The program itself came about thanks to the most straightforward command that I have ever received during fifteen years' work in television. The Controller of BBC1 told the head of presentation programs, Malcolm Walker, to make a series of profiles of 'Worldbeaters', people whose name on a marquee would guarantee a line. 'What sort of people exactly?' inquired Walker further. 'The sort of people who won't agree to be interviewed', replied his boss.

In the subsequent five years Barbra Streisand, Woody Allen, Muhammad Ali, John Wayne and Telly Savalas fulfilled the brief and so did Marlon Brando and Jack Nicholson whose four hours of filmed but not yet transmitted conversation will I hope mature like good wine as they lie incarcerated in sundry film vaults.

So that's how the Eastwood interview came about. His American press agent advised him it wouldn't be a bad idea to do a short chat with the BBC to promote his current film, *The Enforcer*, and when we met he was persuaded into a slightly longer chat.

Eastwood liked the program and told me so. Indeed, his office often shows it to visiting journalists before they get to talk to him, so I have been intrigued to read our conversation again in varying publications throughout the world, some as prestigious as Esquire, others as second-hand as the book written by two men which was peppered with familiar quotations from the television screen. I asked Eastwood for permission to write an authorised biography but he demurred saying he'd rather have a go at it himself one day. I can't wait: it should be an eye-opening piece of self-examination. In the meantime, my warmest thanks to Clint Eastwood for finding the time to read the manuscript and clarify a few points of fact.

I am myself indebted to every journalist who ever wrote about Clint Eastwood for in my research, especially in the Academy Library in Beverly Hills and the Museum of Modern Art in New York, I read every book, magazine article and press clipping that the curators deemed worth retaining and even if I

Left: Clint Eastwood today, the world's most popular film star and a man at peace with himself. Below: As Harry in Magnum Force *(1973). Right As No Name in* For A Few Dollars More *(1966).*

With Jessica Walter in Play Misty For Me *(1971).*

haven't quoted from them in the text, they have obviously contributed to my thinking on the subject. Two other interviews, one done by Arthur Knight for *Playboy* in 1974 and the other by Patrick McGilligan for *Focus on Film* in 1976, were of particular value.

I would also like to thank the following for the use of photographs from their archives and for their invaluable help in researching visual materials: Dave Turner of the Clint Eastwood Appreciation Society, (particularly for his help in identifying early films and specific scenes), Michelle Snapes of the National Film Archive Stills Library, Simon Crocker and the John Kobal Collection, Claus Borlin, Brian Burton and Nigel Messenger of Warner Bros.

The following agencies supplied pictures: Bandphoto, Camera Press, Associated Press, Syndication International, the *Daily Express, France Soir, Paris Match* and BBC Photographs. It has not been possible in all cases to trace the copyright sources and my publishers would be glad to hear from any such unacknowledged copyright holders. I should also like to thank Leonard Hirshan, Clint Eastwood's agent, and Fritz Manes, his producer, for their co-operation.

The people who worked on the television programme were unwitting contributors to this subsequent effort: not least Brian Anderson and David Myers, San Francisco's finest when it comes to camerawork, Sue Mallenson who did the research in London and Raoul Sobel who edited the film. Kerry Herman kindly did some additional research for the book in New York and is still waiting for her meal at 'The Four Seasons'. Marcia Lewis in Los Angeles cannot be discreetly thanked in print for everything she has done, but her work and encouragement in this and other projects have been enduring.

Several publishers wanted me to write a book on Eastwood when I didn't and only Sandra Wake was wily enough never to give up. She got Franny Kennett not only to edit it but to incorporate further relevant facts and figures. I'm very grateful to them both.

No name more deserves mention than Mo Hammond who sat patiently listening to the distant and irregular beat of my Olivetti when the strains of almost anything else, from Pavarotti to party chatter would have been more fun. The dictates of ego that make one isolate oneself with a typewriter for the best part of a year are more easily borne if the loved one is on your side. She was.

Finally, thanks to Clint, without whom... He gave me his time, his tale and his truth. Of these, the last is the most significant. In Hollywood, hyperbole is the order of the day. No producer, no matter how big, can resist adding a few million to the true receipts; no star, no matter how super his status, can accept the blame for a flopped film. The finger always points elsewhere; no director will admit that he lost his way half way through a film and never really found it again. But Eastwood, as I hope will emerge from this book, is unique in a number of respects and the most commendable is that from his days as a digger of swimming pools to the superstar sans pareil in world cinema he has apparently never felt the need to embellish any fact or disguise any failure.

I must thank him in another respect. I felt that after the *Dirty Harry* films and *The Outlaw Josey Wales,* he had reached the apogee of his success and would, like McQueen and Newman, quietly but opulently go into semi-retirement and be replaced by

the next generation. I was wrong. Not only have his films become more and more popular but every time there is a pleasantly silly poll in the press whether it's the *Sunday Telegraph* asking its female readers which man they fancy most, or *Life* magazine discovering the world's favourite movie star, the answer is unequivocally Clint.

Despite my continuing acquaintance with my

Above: Eastwood on the coast of Monterey, California, near his luxurious home. Below: On the set of Two Mules For Sister Sara *(1970). Eastwood admits he is almost a workaholic.*

subject, I deliberately kept him at arm's length in recounting his life and career. But one evening, and this is an impertinent claim, I suddenly realised what it was that made Eastwood tick — I could see why he reacted in various ways to various circumstances, how he had chosen to play with the unpredictable hand that life deals us afresh every morning. Eastwood started out in his career as an amiable, not remarkably gifted man, but success has made him. He has matured into fame, and it has given him confidence, increasing judgement and a growth in skill and talent. This revelation came late in the book and caused me to revise several of the suppositions I had drawn before but from then on it gave a new facility and enjoyment to the experience of writing this book. I discussed the experience with a friend who was working on a biography of Maria Callas and her eyes lit up as she recounted a parallel moment. Perhaps it happens to every biographer.

But she was writing about someone who was dead and I was dealing with a character who was vividly and vitally alive. I remembered the advice that Lord Beaverbrook once gave to a journalist on the best method of writing a profile of a living subject. 'Taking into consideration your own personality', the newspaper magnate counselled, 'write, if you like them, as if they had just died; and if you don't like them as if you wished they had just died'.

Clint Eastwood, at the time of writing, is fit and fifty. If he had just died, I wouldn't change a word of what I have written.

IF THAT'S ACTING, I'M IN TROUBLE

What was it that turned a handsome, reasonably intelligent but directionless young American into the biggest dollar-grossing star that Hollywood has ever seen? The career of Clint Eastwood is a unique success story in the American film industry. He is a self-taught, self-trained actor-producer-director who has single-handedly learnt all there is to know about the business of big film making and become a super-star, relying almost exclusively on his own native wit and judgement. What separates one man from another? A moment in Eastwood's past, from his army life in 1950, perhaps gives a clue to the character of this particular individual. . . .

Clint Eastwood was in a dilemma. He had to get back to his army camp in Monterey in a few hours before his weekend pass expired or face a certain charge of AWOL. But he was stranded in Seattle after a visit to his parents. There was no regular flight available and he did not have enough money in his pocket to buy a ticket even if there had been. He decided to head for the local navy air base to see if there was a local military flight going his way. There wasn't.

After endless enquiries he eventually tracked down a torpedo bomber that was about to leave for San Francisco. He pleaded with the pilot to let him hitch a lift. At first he was told there was no room on board. But, using every inch of his charm and his persistence, Eastwood persuaded the officer to let him ride, quite illegally, in the tiny maintenance area in the tail of the plane. It looked as if he was going to make it back in time after all.

From that moment on the trip turned into a succession of disasters. No sooner were they airborne than the pressure of his body against the door of the compartment caused it to spring open. At a height of six thousand feet it seemed certain that he was going to be sucked out of the plane. He grabbed the intercom to tell the pilot to return to base, but the intercom didn't work. Holding on for dear life with one hand he found a piece of cable and with a massive effort wound it round the door handle which he managed to pull towards him, guaranteeing himself a tenuous safety for the rest of the trip. Or so he thought.

The plane began to climb. He found himself able to receive messages over the intercom but not able to return them. The pilot instructed him to put on his oxygen mask. He did, but no air came out. Desperately he grabbed at the knobs in front of him but, being unfamiliar with the apparatus, he couldn't make it work. He shouted to the pilot through the

Left: The young Eastwood; clean-cut good looks. Above: Clint Eastwood in his youth and during his army training days.

Clint growing up in California; he reached his current height by the age of fifteen.

intercom that he had no oxygen but his cries went unheard. After a few minutes he blacked out.

Fortunately for Eastwood the pilot's own oxygen supply also proved to be faulty so he had to come down under the clouds. There, another hazard faced the two men: a dense fog enveloped the land ahead and they couldn't see the airbase where they were due to land. Eastwood knew the fuel supply was dangerously low. The pilot feared they might run out of fuel over a town or even hit a mountain so he turned the plane back out over the sea. Eastwood was afraid that if the worst came, the pilot might bail out and leave him, parachuteless, to his fate.

They flew along the coast a few hundred feet above the sea. The water was turbulent and uninviting; the fog thickened and night began to fall. After a few minutes the familiar throb of the engines came to a stop and they glided helplessly out of sight of land into what looked like a watery grave. Eastwood wondered how long the plane would float, if at all. And then more pragmatically he began to undo the cable round the door handle so that he could get out.

He barely noticed when the plane actually hit the water until the nose dipped and the tail stuck up into the air. He managed to scramble out of his potential coffin onto the wing, and so did the pilot. They made a hurried calculation as to where the shore might be and swam off together into the darkness. In the confusion they lost each other. Eastwood was a strong swimmer—his army job at Fort Ord was that of swimming instructor—and after about an hour he could dimly see the shore. But before the rocks an ominous phosphorescent glow penetrated the dusk: jellyfish. Having survived so many ordeals already he didn't particularly feel like being stung to death. He manouevred a cautious route through them but even when he reached the rocks the combination of a heavy undertow and his own exhaustion made it difficult for him to drag himself ashore.

How he succeeded in reaching safe land he cannot recall, for he passed out for the second time that day. When he regained consciousness he was lying on a flat rock. He called out to the pilot and searched the rocks and shallows for him but he was nowhere to be found. Eastwood decided that his companion had either drowned or made a landfall further up the coast.

He was now cold and hungry and far from help. The nearest sign of human habitation was the lights of a radio communications relay station in the distance, so he set out for it. Later, when he recalled this near-fatal experience, he would joke, 'I didn't mind the swim but that five mile hike to the highway really bothered me.'

When he threw open the door of the station the occupants stared at him in amazement. 'You look like a survivor from the Titanic,' one of them observed. He felt like one. But at least he had survived. The pilot made it too, having reached the shore about a quarter of a mile away from Eastwood's own landfall.

The whole nightmare adventure could have been a scene from a Clint Eastwood movie: man against the elements, facing certain death with only physical strength, fortitude, determination and sheer good luck to enable him to win through. But this accident really happened and these attributes really did help to save him. If one were to wonder why it is that one actor out of hundreds of thousands should become the biggest box office attraction in the world, then it might be worth considering whether these same attributes didn't have a greater part to play than any acting talent. Nobody pleads with a man to become a superstar: like surviving a plane crash, he has to want it, and then he has to get it himself.

At the very beginning Eastwood didn't know what he wanted. He was born during the depression, on 31 May 1930 in San Francisco. The Eastwoods were a middle-class family but class distinctions had dissolved at that time in the national economic malaise. Anyone who could find work was considered lucky. Accordingly, Clinton Senior (Clint was named after his father and was known in the family, to his ultimate annoyance, as Junior) was perpetually in search of work, sometimes as an accountant, often in as lowly a job as an attendant at a gas station.

Eastwood recalls going to ten different schools in as many years in his early life, as the family wandered from town to town in northern California. With no specific place to call home nor any constant body of friends it was hardly surprising that Eastwood developed the personality of an outsider. Sometimes it was expedient for his father to go off on his own in search of work and then Clint with his mother Ruth and sister Jeanne would stay at his grandmother's chicken farm near Livermore. The old lady was a self-sufficient person who was used to living on her own and Eastwood acknowledges that she had as much influence on his early years as either of his young parents. As well as chickens she kept horses and taught him to ride, which proved useful later in his career.

The family's peripatetic style of life came to an end when Clint's father eventually got a job with the Container Corporation of America in Oakland, near San Francisco. Clint was sent to Oakland Technical High School where one of the first boys he met was Fritz Manes, who is still a friend today: 'Clint hasn't really changed that much. He was always a tall, lanky kid and didn't necessarily dress the way the rest of the kids did. It was our first day in grammar school and it was just one of those things, we instantly identified with each other. We weren't that excited about going to school; both being sort of non-joiners, non-members of the pack. Clint had tremendous athletic ability all through school but not being a keen-spirited type guy, never really followed it through.'

To say that Eastwood was tall was an understatement—by the age of fifteen he was within an inch or so of his present height of six foot four inches. Although he was physically a natural for the basketball team and various studio biographies later emphasised his aptitude for that sport, it didn't hold any real interest for him. 'In those days I had a complex about jumping into anything with both feet, I stood back a

Clint as a teenager, enjoying his jalopy, and fishing—one of his favourite pastimes at his grandmother's farm in Livermore, California.

Top: Oakland Technical High School, where Clint was a good pupil, shy with the girls but popular. Centre: His only entry in the School Yearbook was as a member of the Banqueting Committee. Bottom: At the High School prom.

bit too much I guess; I just drew a sort of invisible coat of armour around myself. I used to pray I'd get to be an extrovert—it seemed to be an answer to most of my personal problems.'

As with any prematurely tall child at school, Eastwood felt alienated from the others, especially girls: 'I don't think there was a class I was ever in, right through from grammar, junior high and high school, where I didn't have a crush on some girl. But I was the original hang-up man. I was so much a loner, so introverted in those days that I simply couldn't express myself. It was agony for me even to ask a girl

for a date.'

Both the agony and the shyness must have been evident to the staff for although Eastwood was a conspicuous non-joiner, his English teacher, Miss Jones, conscripted him for the class play. The pain and fear of that experience remains sharp in his memory to this day. 'I hated it at the time. I was a nervous wreck and ready to cut school, I just didn't figure out that it was my bag. The part of the lead in the play was an introverted kid and I was an introverted kid so my teacher picked me for the job, figuring that I'd just act myself.'

His parents felt he needed drawing out and were anxious to come and see him perform. But the night before the first performance he went to the local drugstore with his friend, Harry Pendleton, who was cast to play his father, and together they decided that they wouldn't turn up for school the following day. The next morning a fearful Clint rang Harry: 'They'll murder us if we skip it.' Harry had come to the same conclusion and they went to face their ordeal. It wasn't as bad as they anticipated, Clint recalls: 'I remember drying up suddenly when the first laugh came. But then I realised it had come in the right place and that all the kids in the audience were laughing with me—not at me. We got through it, in fact I enjoyed doing it. But I made up my mind then that I would never get involved with anything to do with acting again.'

Eastwood made an impression on the teachers and his fellow pupils with his musical talents—he proved an accomplished pianist and trumpet player—but when he got his diploma in 1948, his only official credential in the school year book was that he had been a member of the banqueting committee. His academic record was satisfactorily average, his athletic record outstanding, but he still left school with no clear idea of what he wanted to do with his life. 'I always admired people who knew what they wanted to do, who had some kind of a focus. I had a friend, for instance, who always wanted to be a dentist, from the time he was eight years old. He went ahead and worked his way through by bartending at night and working in restaurants after school. I never saw my father in a specific profession and so I was never really raised with the idea that you grow up thinking you want to be a druggist or a physician or whatever.'

By the time Clint left school, his father was settled in a secure job and he imparted one salient piece of advice to his son: 'You don't get anything for nothing.' Eastwood Junior had done a succession of vacation jobs like hay baling in Yreka in northern California and subsequently several stints as a fire fighter in the forests near Paradise, also northern California. He was keen to find an occupation that would take him out of doors. For a year he worked as a lumberjack near Springfield, Oregon, and in the Weyerhaeuser Company pulp mill. It was a tough, man's life. At night he had little energy to do anything except collapse into his bunk at the camp, save for Saturdays when he traditionally went to town to drink a little beer with his workmates. Later, his family moved to Seattle and he followed them there, taking an even more strenuous job stoking a furnace on the 'graveyard shift' for Bethlehem Steel. During the following years, he drove a truck, worked as a lifeguard in Renton, Seattle, and then took a more mundane job in the parts department at the Boeing plant, filling in invoices and handing out equipment.

This more than anything quickened his resolve to further his education, and he decided to go back to school to major in music. Just as he was about to turn this idea into reality a superior plan was handed down to him from on high. It came in the shape of a telegram which began with the words: 'Greetings from the President of the United States'.

He found the first sixteen weeks of army basic training at Ford Ord easier than most other conscripts did. Even as a schoolboy he had worked out a regular physical training routine for himself which he maintains to this day. After the initial induction period he expected to be sent to Korea as was the case with nearly all National Servicemen at that time. But the good fortune that has remained with him throughout his life intervened. 'I was lucky. I think about ninety-nine per cent of the company I was with were sent to Korea but I just happened to hear a rumour that they needed somebody down at the pool area to teach swimming. Now I had been into swimming as a kid, my father was a very good swimmer and I, too, was a good swimmer. So I ran down to the pool and did a bit of a selling job on the captain in command. I told him I was much better than I was, of course. That often becomes the actors' lament because they're always doing that. They ask you: "Can you ride?" "Yes!" "Can you ride motorcycles?" "Yes." "Can you drive off cliffs?" "Yeah." You say anything because you want the part. This was much like that. I liked the area, I figured I'd like to stay in that kind of work so I got a job teaching swimming for two years.'

Eastwood began merely as a lifeguard but when the officers and sergeants in charge of him were sent to Korea, he stayed behind, a humble private, running the operation. 'I had the pool to myself except when they gave swimming classes to recruits. Of every twelve guys who took the swimming test, ten sank immediately. My job was to pull them out.'

He slept in a hut down by the pool and despite the apparent softness of his existence, his initiative didn't desert him. He supplemented his pay by moonlighting at night, humping sacks at the local sugar refinery and later, more legitimately, tending the bar at the non-commissioned officers' club. He needed the extra money to fund his frequent excursions with local girls.

Ever since he had filled out his six foot four inch frame, Eastwood had been the object of considerable attraction to women. His present business partner, Robert Daley, remembers that long before he became well known, 'he was always noticed by people. He was always the type that people would turn round and stare at. Of course people say today "Well, they only do that because he's a star." But I know from

experience that in the days when he was totally unknown, he was still noticed by people.' And when those 'people' turned out to be female and Eastwood was fortified by a few beers, he found himself able to overcome his basic shyness and make use of his innate charm.

But it wasn't a local girl who finally put an end to his bachelor days and ways. A friend, Don Kincaid, the one who had the ambition to become a dentist and later actually became one, was going out with a student at Berkeley. In the time-honoured tradition, he persuaded Eastwood to set aside his weekend plans and use his pass to accompany him up to San Francisco as a blind date for his girl-friend's roommate. When Clint met Maggie Johnson at the sorority house he was immediately attracted to her. 'We hit it off right away. She was the kind of girl I really liked; there was nothing phoney about her. She had natural good looks—she was blonde and fairly tall for a woman, five feet seven—and, like me, she loved the outdoors. I liked her sense of humour.'

While disclaiming any tendency towards love at first sight, Eastwood nevertheless spent many further weekends with Maggie at Berkeley until she graduated that June. It's interesting to note that Maggie, an intelligent and attractive student, much in demand amongst campus men, nevertheless was prepared to entertain the attentions of an ordinary G.I. and

Clint with his wife, formerly Maggie Johnson—'a good bathing suit type'.

former lumberjack and furnace stoker. Even then the quiet wisdom that Eastwood has subsequently exhibited in managing his own career was apparent to her.

Eastwood had plenty of time to reflect on his own life during the comparative restfulness of his army days at Fort Ord and he came to three major decisions that were to affect his future substantially. The first concerned his growing affection for Maggie, enhanced by her patent superiority to the rest of the girls he dated. The second was made on a day off when he took a trip to Carmel, which was about ten miles away. It's barely a town, but one of the most beautiful villages on the western seaboard if not in all America. After spending the morning wandering around the manicured streets and perfect white beaches he came to the conclusion, 'If I ever manage to put together a few dollars I might like to live in a place like this.' Later he did manage to put together a few dollars, indeed a few dollars more than any other actor in the world, and he built a stylish ranch-like house just outside Carmel overlooking the Pacific with a film room, gun room, gymnasium, three-car garage and a living room built around a beautiful tree that he refused to have cut down. He also acquired a considerable slab of land along the coast.

His third major decision was acting. This was a less positive decision than the other two. A unit from Universal Studios used the camp for some location shooting and an assistant director advised him that he had the right sort of looks to be in movies. He introduced him to the director who told him to ring him at the studios when he finished his army service. Another factor in his decision-making was that while he was a soldier he met David Janssen, Norman Bartold and Martin Milner who were all committed to careers in acting and, as he later drily observed, 'they all seemed to enjoy themselves.'

When he completed his time in the army he went south to Los Angeles and there, using the money he was entitled to under the GI Bill, enrolled in the LA City College to study Business Administration, a course, as he himself, with typical self-deprecation, described as being 'for any student who hasn't the faintest idea of what he wants to do when he graduates'.

In the tradition that he had established for himself he took other jobs to supplement his grant. He got an apartment in a block in Beverly Hills and bartered his rent by managing the whole building for the owners. Like his father before him he worked as a gasoline attendant at a station which was conveniently just across the street from the unemployment office on Santa Monica Boulevard. He also worked as a life guard and he dug swimming pools. That job, however, came to an end in a manner which was later to be echoed in the laconic style he adopted in many of his films.

George Fargo, who remains a friend twenty-five years later, was digging pools with him and he remembers the story: 'We were working for the United Pool Company and one day I got fired. The

boss looked over and saw Clint unbuttoning his work shirt. "What are you doing?" the guy asked Clint. And Clint just said very casually: "Well, George is my friend and he hasn't got a ride home." And he quit, just like that.'

He saw a lot of Maggie at weekends; she had moved down to Los Angeles after graduating. They would go with a crowd to Newport beach, swim, play with a basket ball and have parties and barbecues in the evenings, like many of the sun-blessed youth of Southern California. They went to a lot of jazz concerts together, and discovered a deepening mutual interest in classical music, theatre and films.

On 19 December 1953 they were married and honeymooned in Carmel. Maggie Eastwood began her married life by supporting her husband. She worked in an export firm, Industria Americana, and to supplement her income further she modelled for

Physical activity delights Clint; he is an accomplished swimmer and gymnast.

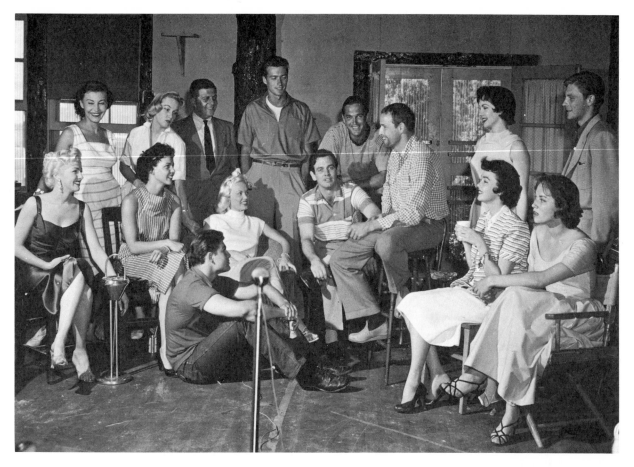

Universal's Talent School: Marlon Brando (seated centre) gives a talk to the young hopefuls. Clint Eastwood stands behind his friend, David Janssen.

Caltex and Catalina, swimsuit manufacturers. She was, as Clint readily pointed out, 'a good bathing suit type'.

A greater pressure was now on him to find a regular job, and film work seemed a likely option. There is a tangible feel of movies in the air for anyone living in or visiting the Beverly Hills district. The trade film magazines are on sale by the roadside, along with the fallacious maps of the stars' homes. The talk in the bars and drugstores inevitably turns to movies, and well-known and half-known faces from the wide screen can be seen in corner shops and restaurants. The cinema is identifiably the local industry, just as much as Boeing is in Seattle or ICI in Runcorn. Eastwood occasionally would have a drink with his former Army colleagues, David Janssen and Martin Milner who were both beginning to make headway in the competitive world of acting. More-over, people were constantly telling him that he should be in films since he was tall, well-built and good-looking in an original fashion.

One man especially, Irving Lasper, a stills photographer, and close friend of Eastwood's, urged him to try to become an actor. So using some photographs that Lasper had taken of him, Eastwood persuaded one of the Universal staff directors, Arthur Lubin, to give him a screen test. It was a bizarre experience. When I asked Eastwood about it, his memory had been refreshed by watching a film that had included just such a scene.

'It was an interview-test kind of thing. In fact I saw a movie the other night—*The Hearts of the West* —where they were doing that with Jeff Bridges. He came on and looked at the camera, turned left, turned right ... they tell you to turn this way and you stand there and they ask you what your name is and where you came from, that sort of thing. That was about the extent of it, that's all they did. They used to call them interview-type tests, as opposed to a legitimate screen test, which is working up a scene and presenting that scene.'

He wasn't optimistic about his chances. He told *Playboy* Magazine when they interviewed him in 1974: 'I thought I was an absolute clod. It looked pretty good, it was photographed well, but I thought, "If that's acting, I'm in trouble".'

However, he was elated not only by his experience but also by being in a famous studio for the first time. He returned home, called Maggie at her office and demanded that they celebrate that night. Over the bottle of wine she pointed out that this was a little premature, thousands of people were tested, she said, and few were called.

It wasn't a boom time in Hollywood. The film industry, already threatened from within by the McCarthy witch-hunts, was further threatened from without by the rise of a new adversary: television. So noxious was this competitor deemed to be that at

15

MGM, Louis B. Mayer not only refused to let his executives have televisions in their offices, but banned the sight or mention of the one-eyed devil in any MGM movies. Sponsorship from advertisers gave television a built-in revenue which studios were unable to compete with. Later, however, the studio bosses were happy enough to sell their old movies to television and this in turn provided the financial basis for the new boom in films.

Besides television, Hollywood was also beginning to lose its grip on markets abroad. Before the war, the great studios, Fox, MGM, Warner Brothers, Paramount, RKO, Columbia, Universal and United Artists had held sway and the whole of Europe sat amazed in front of visions of romance and adventure, produced by a succession of brilliant directors and studio-made personality-actors. This fascination continued during the war years, obviously helped by the presence of so many GIs in Europe and the general dominance of American culture. But after the war, there was a natural and understandable move back to nationalism in culture, and the French, Italian, and British film industries began to revive, helped not a little by the explosive experiences of the war years and a desire to comment on it in a European way. Hollywood's

Below: Eastwood learned to ride at the Universal Talent School, an ability that was to prove more than helpful in his later career. Right: A publicity shot of Clint taken at the time of his contract with Universal for Tarantula *(1954).*

reaction to this growing disinterest in its products was not very inspired: the studios continued to churn out stock films on tried and tested themes where they were sure of their way. And in time, television took up those themes and explored them with the same predictable degree of audience response. The classic example of this process is the Western, and Eastwood's career was to exemplify the ups and downs of the cinema and television industries through these years.

In 1954, when Eastwood took his screen test, audiences for films were falling dramatically and many of the studios had dropped their training programmes, which, like so many fish farms, had been created to fertilize innumerable eggs in the hope that one would eventually turn into a prize salmon. Such success often owed as much to the machinations of the publicity office as to the acting talent of the individual, but it was a system that had worked.

Having heard nothing from the director for two weeks, Eastwood ignored the traditional showbusiness maxim of 'don't call us, we'll call you', and telephoned Lubin at Universal. He couldn't get through to him on any of the three occasions he tried, nor were his calls returned. It looked as if his acting career had begun and ended with that one test and a career in business administration loomed frustratingly ahead. What a time for the legendary Eastwood luck to desert him.

But, of course, it hadn't. A few days later he was awakened from his sleep by a call from the studio. The executives had liked his test. He was in. A six month contract at seventy-five dollars a week.

ROLLING, ROLLING, ROLLING

Although the offer from Universal could potentially take him in the direction he now fervently wanted to go, towards becoming a film star, he knew that hundreds of young men and women were signed up on such six month deals and the same hundreds of young men and women were never heard of again. Maggie thought it was a bit too much of a gamble; and when they talked it over with her parents, Clint's father-in-law advised him, as any father-in-law would, that a good steady business job should be his goal. Now that he was a married man with responsibilities, maybe a qualification in business administration would be of more use to him than a six-month ego trip at Universal.

While apparently weighing up the pros and cons of the offer, in his mind there was never any real doubt. He now knew his own talent, his aim and his luck. So he gave up college and started a new education at the studio workshop school.

They didn't just try to teach him how to act; he learnt horse-riding in the Western fashion, sword-fighting in the swashbuckling fashion, table manners in the East-coast fashion and even how to dance. 'Fred Astaire never had to worry with me on the horizon: I was never that type, never that loose on my feet. But they had drama classes and I used to go to some during the day and more also in the evening with an outside group. I did that for fifteen years.' Most of the time, as he himself recalls, 'I just kept my eyes open and my big mouth shut and, as usual, I didn't mix too much.'

He would probably be surprised to learn today that anybody really noticed him, with big stars like Rock Hudson and George Lader dominating the studio, but they did. DeWitt Bodeen was working as a writer at the studio then and he recalls: 'I well remember seeing Eastwood on the lot. It was hard to miss him. His rangy height, his intense interest in anything to do with film, his wide-smiled friendliness made him stand out. . . I didn't see how Eastwood could fail.'

Initially, he didn't. After the trial six months his contract was renewed and he was given his first movie role in *Revenge of the Creature* (1955). It was a sequel to *The Creature from the Black Lagoon*—a somewhat over-the-top science fiction fantasy about a prehistoric fish-gilled man. It was directed by Jack Arnold and was actually shot in 3-D. Clint Eastwood played a character called Jennings.

'I just had this stupid scene, I had to come on as a

Left: Clint Eastwood with Myrna Hansen and Dani Crayne preparing for a scene in 'A Day in a Hollywood Star Factory.'
Above: In Revenge of the Creature *(1954).*

lab assistant—I played a lot of lab assistants in those days—and I couldn't find the white mice that were missing in the lab. So all of a sudden the guy says: "Did you look everywhere?" and I reached in my pocket and ... whoops ... there it is ... here's the white mouse. It was pretty dumb stuff but I guess they were short on time and just wanted to pad the script.

'It was one of those B-movies that Universal were making at that time. And I remember the producer liked me for the part when I went and inter-

viewed for it and I thought "Great", I was really enthusiastic. But the director hated the part, he hated the scene—it had nothing to do with me. So I went down with the producer onto the set to meet the director and they had just a knock-down, drag-out fight right in front of me, they were yelling and arguing and screaming at each other. I thought it was rather odd. And this put an added tension on the next day when I had to come in and do the scene. The director finally said: "Go ahead. I'll shoot it but I don't like it." And so, finally, when the scene was ready to

Universal's Talent Workshop included a regular course in body conditioning: Clint with Jane Howard (left), Myrna Hansen and Dani Crayne, 1955.

go I was a nervous wreck because I knew the director hated it. We did about four or five takes and he printed it. I guess it was adequate because they kept it in'—thus preserving for Jack Arnold the distinction of having directed Clint Eastwood's first screen appearance. He also directed his second, in 1955, another science fiction movie written by Martin Berkeley and starring John Agar, in which a giant spider goes crazy (as they tend to) and threatens the earth. Clint's job was to kill it.

'Another biggy that I was in . . . the second film I did was called *Tarantula*. I played the part of the jet pilot who came in and bombed this giant tarantula at the end. I was enthusiastic when I read the part because I was enthusiastic about anything that would increase my experience. But I had a helmet, goggles and a mask on so it could have been just anybody sitting there and somebody else dubbing the words.'

In the same year, 1955, he got the opportunity to don mediaeval robes as the First Saxon in *Lady*

Godiva with Maureen O'Hara and Victor McLaglen, and a sailor's uniform for *Francis in the Navy* which featured a talking mule and Donald O'Connor. 'I just played a navy buddy of Donald's. I'd come in for a line here and a line there and then got lost—part of my act.'

Francis in the Navy proved something of a triumph for Eastwood. He was listed in the credits and was sufficiently visible for various critics to call him 'handsome', 'engaging' and 'promising'. But it was, like the others, a very small part although, as Eastwood laughingly commented to *Playboy*, 'to look at some of the billings in *TV Guide* these days, you'd think I co-starred in those films'.

At the time Eastwood's salary had been raised to a hundred dollars a week and he needed it. Maggie had been continuing her job and her modelling but she had to quit both when she got hepatitis—'about as badly as you can get it without ceasing to exist' as Eastwood recalls, and the spectre of his contract not

A sequence from Tarantula, *in which Clint plays a pilot sent to bomb a giant spider.*

being renewed carried the additional burden of a succession of massive medical bills. Despite his fleeting appearances in part of the company's substantial output, he knew his position was constantly on a knife edge.

'In those days they used to have large contract groups, maybe ten to fifteen men, maybe thirty to forty women—a lot more girls than they had guys. You always hoped for a break, you always hoped for any kind of part in a picture, small, medium or, naturally, large. The big stars in those days were Rock Hudson or Tony Curtis or Jeff Chandler. Those were the studio contract actors that would play the leads in most of their films. Once in a while they'd talk about doing a biggy and go out and try to get Clark Gable. But it usually never worked out.'

Eastwood played parts too small to mention in half a dozen other Universal pictures—how small can be gleaned from the evidence that his totally disguised appearance in *Tarantula* was worth a mention—but then his career at the studio reached a new high when he was chosen to play a short scene opposite the man who was the company's hottest property—Rock Hudson. Now whether Hudson realised that the thin young man with the quiffed hair and somewhat reedy voice would achieve a fame and wealth as yet undreamed of in the realms of super-stardom, or

whether he didn't, history fails to relate. One would have expected a star of Hudson's magnitude to take barely any notice of a scene played with someone who was little more than an extra with a few words. But he did, and he felt competitive. Eastwood remains immensely amused by what happened between them.

'I'll never forget. I was a lab assistant and I had a four-line part where I'm working in an X-ray lab and Rock Hudson, who played the physician, comes in and asks me some questions. I'd been told that they wanted me to wear glasses. Well, I'd never worn glasses before and I was disappointed because I didn't think that I looked particularly good in them. But the director wanted me to wear them because I was a youthful kid and he felt it would give me a little more of an intellectual look, a physician's assistant look (if there is such a thing). So I searched around and I tried on about ten pairs of glasses. I finally found a pair that looked pretty good and I sat there looking at myself in the mirror until I got used to it. I thought, "Hey, this isn't bad at all. This may be a whole different approach." So I went on the set with these glasses and everything was fine. I got in the scene and Rock Hudson walks in and starts to say his lines, and then he looks at me, and he turns to the director and says: "Where are *my* glasses?" And the director said: "Well, you're the leading man, you don't need glasses, you don't wear them." He said: "Oh, well, I think I ought to wear some." So he went through all the ten pairs of glasses that I'd tried on and didn't find one. Then they took mine off—they fitted him perfectly. Okay. Boom. He wore them; I didn't.'

The film was called *Never Say Goodbye*—a singularly unprophetic title in Eastwood's case for this was precisely what Universal *did* say. 'Yeah, they dropped me. They were sort of dropping the whole programme slowly but surely, but they got tired of seeing me around. In those days they used to have a guy that looked like all their current guys and I didn't look like anybody who was a current contract star so they finally dumped me, figuring I wasn't heading anywhere.'

And he could have been forgiven for thinking he wasn't heading anywhere. He had no way of knowing that fourteen years later he would return to Universal, not merely as a contract star, but with his own company, Malpaso, which ironically occupied the very office blocks of those same executives who failed to renew his contract.

Even the mighty, when rejected, get pleasure out of that schoolboy sentiment, 'Just you wait, I'll show you one day.' I once made a profile of Muhammad Ali for the BBC when he was, according to his own estimate, and that of a hundred million fans, 'the king'. I went back with him to his old house in Louisville, Kentucky and as we came out, he rushed up to one of the assembled crowd that awaited him and playfully hit an overweight black man. 'I told you I'd come back one day,' he shouted with more glee than I had ever seen him display before, 'This is my friend,

Above: Clint Eastwood in Lady Godiva *(1954) with*
Maureen O'Hara. Right: The tallest guy in Francis in the
Navy *(1954).*

Samson. You used to beat me up on this street and I
said I'd come back one day and beat you up. I said I'd
come back as champion of the world, didn't I,
Samson?' Such hyperbole is very far from Eastwood's
character but one can imagine that when he arrived
back in Universal as a world star a quiet 'Hello again'
delivered in his own laid-back, very dry but well-
timed style, would have been sufficient to make the
point.

Back in 1956, however, he faced three years out
in the cold as a not-fully-fledged jobbing actor. He
wasn't alone in this; Universal had dropped his
friends David Janssen and John Saxon as well. The
girls were luckier: 'They fitted in better because
there seemed to be more bit parts for girls and they
could always open supermarkets or something in
their spare time. The guys weren't really worth
much.'

His freelance career began promisingly. In 1956
Arthur Lubin, who had directed him in *Francis in the
Navy* and *Lady Godiva* had moved to RKO. He was
going to make a comedy about a female corset
designer set at the turn of the century—*The First
Travelling Saleslady*—with Ginger Rogers and Carol
Channing. Lubin gave Eastwood 'introducing billing'
which would have been very valuable in that distinguished female company had not the picture turned

out to be quite dreadful. It can have been little solace
for him that the *Hollywood Reporter* observed: 'Clint
Eastwood is very attractive as Carol Channing's
beau.' For a time it looked as if he might get regular
parts at RKO—he was given a small role as a mad
pilot called Dumbo in Lubin's next picture *Escapade
in Japan*—but then fate intervened in the rarely-seen
shape of Howard Hughes, the owner of RKO, who
promptly closed the studios down.

In 1957 and 1958 Eastwood is said to have made
more money digging swimming pools than making
movies and parts were so few and far between that

Visiting the mule on the set of Francis in the Navy: *David Janssen, Martha Hyer, Jane Howard, Clint and Leigh Snowden.*

he seriously reconsidered whether he wanted to continue as an actor. He didn't like the process of looking for a job any more than anyone else out of work does: 'Everybody knows agents don't give a damn about young unemployed actors.'

Fortunately for him, the very medium that was causing the cinema to contract needed lots of actors to take part in its own expansion: television. Then, as now, it was considered low style for a big screen actor to appear on the small screen, but it was better than digging ditches. Eastwood played a motorcycle cop in *Highway Patrol* and various other action parts in *Navy Log* and *Men of Annapolis*. He even made a succession of appearances in another military series, *West Point*. His own army service provided him with a perfect training for the part of a West Point cadet; unfortunately the scriptwriters didn't provide much for the cadets to do. 'The trouble with that series was that practically nothing ever happens to West Point cadets in real life. They march, go to classes, play football, study, and go to bed. We'd open an episode with some strong dramatic line like: "You stole my laundry." Where do you go from there?'

However, in spite of lack of action at the Academy, he made a reputation as a tough actor who was prepared to do his own stunts and in 1957 Twentieth Century Fox offered him his first Western, *Ambush at Cimarron Pass*. It was set just after the Civil War when the Confederate and Union soldiers joined together to take on the Apaches. Eastwood played a heavy. Although it was intended for the

cinema, it was shot in ten days. Eastwood rated it a 'Z' movie. 'It was probably the worst movie ever made. When it was run at a local theatre, Maggie and I went to see it. After the first ten minutes I was so embarrassed by the cheap quality of the production and the lack of technical know-how, I slumped down in my seat and couldn't say a word. The photography was the most uneven I have ever seen. One minute it was so bright you needed sunglasses to look at the screen; the next second the print was so dark you couldn't make out anything.' The film was shot in Regalscope, a brand new colour technique which, to nobody's surprise and least of all Clint's, lasted for little more than a year.

It looked as if he was getting back into the world of major movies, a possibility that was confirmed by an offer from his first 'big-name' director William Wellman, to play in the Warner Brothers epic, *Lafayette Escadrille*. In fact this was to be his last cinema appearance for nearly seven years. Starring another Hollywood giant of that time, Tab Hunter (it's interesting to note that the studios felt obliged to invent names like 'Rock' and 'Tab' for their potential stars, whereas 'Clint' having the correct monosyllabic masculinity about it required no alteration), it was a World War One story about a famous flying unit. Eastwood and his friend David Janssen played pilots.

Despite the eminence of the director and the waterfall of publicity that Warners put out on its release, it didn't catch the public's imagination.

The spectacular hit in television at that time was a weekly cowboy adventure, *Gunsmoke,* and, imitation being the sincerest form of scheduling, the networks were anxious to make more Western series. Eastwood's agent heard that CBS were planning one and rang to see if Clint would be right for the lead. The answer was no; they needed an older man.

Having been in and around the Hollywood scene for four years, Eastwood knew a lot of people in the industry and one such particular friend of his and Maggie's was Sonia Chernus, who was then working in the script department at CBS. Emanating the usual coolness that masked his inner judgement and drive, he just happened to be passing Century City one day and dropped in to have a chat with her. She mentioned the company's intended new series and he mentioned that he'd already had a rebuff. Within minutes she was on the phone to the executive producer, Robert Sparks, and when his secretary said he was terribly busy and unavailable, she thought that no irreparable harm would be done if she and Clint were to wander across to his office anyway.

Sparks liked the look of Clint and asked him into his office to meet Charles Marquis Warren, creator of *Gunsmoke* and the doyen of the television Western. Eastwood elicited from them that there was a second lead going in their new series for a young man in his twenties. They elicited from him his previous screen credits, including, reluctantly, *Ambush at Cimarron Pass.* As he mentioned those words he felt certain that if they ever saw the film, he had no chance at all. His modesty was, perhaps, excessive; *Variety* had noted that he gave a 'fine portrayal' in the film.

But events overtook any possible viewing of his previous performances. Sparks rang him that afternoon and asked him to do a screen test. Eastwood accepted the offer readily and did the test, but he felt afterwards that it had gone badly. He had chosen to improvise some of the dialogue that was given to him and the director, who had written the part, didn't much like that. As Eastwood was leaving he saw another actor testing for the part and he heard the director saying 'Good, very good, excellent'.

A week of unendurable silence went by and then he got a call from another friend of his in the industry, a projectionist, who told him he had got the part. Eastwood asked him how he knew. The man apparently had run all the tests for the New York executives of CBS and although the director had wanted the man he had praised, the executives wanted Eastwood. The tip-off proved to be accurate: the next day CBS rang to inform him that he had been chosen to play the role of Rowdy Yates in *Rawhide.*

Eastwood was able to repay his substantial debt to Sonia Chernus some years later when he formed his own production company, Malpaso, and invited her to join it. She, perhaps more than anybody, understood the roles that suited him best and was responsible for putting many successful properties

Top: Clint in one of his early television series, Men of Annapolis. *Bottom:* Star in the Dust *(1956), a simple Western, made in twelve days.*

his way, not the least of which was *The Outlaw Josey Wales.*

Unknown to him, CBS were taking something of a risk with *Rawhide.* Neither Eastwood, nor Eric Fleming who had already been signed to play the trail boss, Gil Favor, were well-known names. The company was relying on the guiding hand of Charles Marquis Warren, who had achieved such a sure success with *Gunsmoke,* and a weekly turnover of guest stars to attract the audience. There was indecision among the ranks of executives at the network as to whether they should make a pilot and air it—as they undoubtedly would do today—or go ahead and make the first run of thirteen episodes and transmit them later. Eastwood remained uneasily at home while a decision was reached. Some weeks later he and the other members of the cast and crew were dispatched to Arizona for two months pre-filming to make ten one-hour episodes.

Eastwood loved it. Later he said they were among the happiest days of his life. The unit hired real rodeo cowboys to ensure the action was as authentic as possible and by watching and working with them Eastwood improved his own technique as a horseman. It was the outdoor life—the kind he had

Above: Rowdy Yates (Clint Eastwood) with Gil Favor (Eric Fleming), the trail boss in Rawhide. *Right: As the second man in the show, Clint played the younger, impetuous role.*

sought after leaving school—and the actors blended in with the extras, living like real cowboys. To add to his joy, not only was he getting paid for it, but he was getting a lot more lines than he ever had at Universal.

So his hopes were high and carefree when he returned to Hollywood at the end of the location period, and his chagrin was deep and inconsolable when he learnt from CBS that they had changed their minds and were not going to show the series.

The problem simply was that there were too many cowboy series on television at that time. *Wagon Train, Rifleman, Gunman, Maverick, Wyatt Earp, Gunsmoke* ... nearly thirty in all. Rather than risk more money on continuing the series, CBS decided it would be safer to shelve it. Eastwood was more than a little upset. 'I was the star nobody had ever seen. I wasn't even the actor on the cutting room floor: I was the player who was locked up in a vault.' Downhearted but not discouraged, he tried to get a part in a feature film but CBS refused to let the producer see his performance in the now-incarcerated *Rawhide.*

Yet again, the prospect of a career in business administration loomed large. His parents had moved house from Seattle to San Francisco, so Clint and Maggie set off by train to spend a less than cheerful Christmas of 1958 with them. Eastwood was twenty-eight years old and success in acting seemed as far

away as ever. However, proof that there is a Santa Claus came in the form of a telegram from his agent. Minds had been changed once more at CBS and it had been decided to schedule *Rawhide* for transmission as a replacement series in the New Year. 'Happy Christmas', the message ended. It was.

The first episode of Rawhide was shown at eight o'clock—family viewing time—on Friday 9 January 1959. Viewers were informed by the *TV Guide:* 'Eric Fleming and Clint Eastwood are the stars of a new hour-long Western series to be seen each week at this time. The stories will revolve around the Western legend of the cattle drive from Texas to Kansas.'

The pre-credit sequence began with a shout, Eric Fleming telling his fellow cowhands to 'Get 'em on, move 'em out', and then came a song, Frankie Laine singing 'Rolling, rolling, rolling, keep them dawgies rolling, keep them dawgies rolling, R-a-w-h-i-d-e ...'

The obvious parent of the series, to Western fans at least, was Howard Hawks' *Red River* with Eric Fleming playing the John Wayne role, and Clint Eastwood projecting the same type of character as Montgomery Clift had in the earlier classic. A second source was George C. Duffield's *Traildrovers Diary,* a true account by a trail boss written in the 1800s, of his experiences working the route between San Antonio and the state of Iowa. In *Rawhide,* the trek was moved from Texas to Sedalia, Missouri, and the drovers were typed as Confederate veterans. This gave the trail boss, Gil Favor, the reasoning for his reserved, highly efficient but cool handling of the men—the embryonic characterisation which Clint was later to develop into the Man With No Name in the Sergio Leone Westerns. Eastwood recalls:

'Rowdy was the second man in the show, the younger of the two leads, much more the naive guy ... or they started out that way. You saw the picture through the eyes of the younger man as he watched the more experienced man at work on the cattle drives. He was younger and more impetuous, more prone to getting involved in far-out situations as opposed to the more experienced cattle drovers. It was a fun role; I got to play some good parts.'

As is typical of a series of this type, Rowdy soon settled into a very familiar pattern of adventures, and into a standard set of relationships with the other members of the crew on that journey to Sedalia, which never ended from week to week. He performed many heroic acts, crashed off his horse several times, was allowed to become romantically entangled once or twice, and fell ill occasionally to heighten the tension for the thousands of fans who had become devoted to *Rawhide.* He tried to maintain a due deference to Gil Favor, the trail boss, but youthful (and very attractive) impatience or rebellion would sometimes break through. He also kept up a humorous running battle with Wishbone the cook (played by Paul Brinegar) about the appalling quality of the food, and in between kept that three hundred head of cattle rolling towards Sedalia. Two other permanent fixtures on the route were Jesus, who looked after the

Clint had various romantic entanglements in the Rawhide series. Above: 'Incident of the Reluctant Bridegroom', with Ruta Lee, and below, with Linda Cristal. Right: Relaxing at home with his snake-handled Colt revolver, acquired for Rawhide but later used in the Spaghetti Westerns.

Typical scenes from Rawhide's *never-ending cattle trail. Above: 'Incident of the Rawhiders'. Below: Clint gets tough in 'Incident of the Red Wind', with Neville Brand. Right: Clint said later these were among the happiest days of his life.*

horses, and Sheb Wooley, the scout. The cattle never even made it to the back lot at MGM where much of the series was filmed, but passed the same landmarks many times over in repeated shots of the much-extended trail.

The actors were joined each week by guest stars: names like Julie Harris, Lon Chaney, Peter Lorre and Victor McLaglen can be found in the cast lists. In fact the series provided the last screen appearance of Victor McLaglen, the solid sparring partner of John Wayne. Fittingly that particular episode was directed by McLaglen's son, Andrew, who went on to direct many of Wayne's finest later Westerns, such as *McLintock* and *The Undefeated*.

For Eastwood the series represented security and experience. 'It was the first steady job I had as an actor. The money was pretty good and I was getting to play a lot of good roles on television, week in, week out. Very good experience if you're selfish about it. By selfish, I mean if you take advantage of it. As soon as a lot of people get into a series that's a success they can't wait to get out of it. They think they're going to go on to bigger and better things and maybe that might be the case. But I wanted to learn just as much as I could about film and when you've done a couple of hundred shows in seven or eight years you can pick up a lot.

'I worked with a lot of directors over the years who were very knowledgeable and I learned a lot from them. I also worked with some that I didn't think were knowledgeable, and I learnt a lot from *them*. And I learned a lot about crews. When you do two hundred and fifty hours of television, you learn what makes one prop man good and another fair and another lousy, and what makes one cameraman better than another one. You learn about leadership, how one week a crew can move very fast and efficiently and the next week drag. About ninety per cent of the time, it's the fault of the director. And you just store those things up in your head.'

Eastwood stored some names up as well. When he came to make his own films, the men who impressed him from *Rawhide* found themselves with offers of work. Dean Riesner who wrote some early episodes, was later co-writer of the screenplays for *Coogan's Bluff, Play Misty For Me* and *Dirty Harry.* Ted Post directed many episodes of *Rawhide* and Eastwood gave him the chance to make his first feature *Hang 'Em High.* Post also directed the second Dirty Harry film *Magnum Force.* He was a film-maker of great practical experience, having turned out two hundred episodes of *Peyton Place,* seventy-five of *Gunsmoke,* besides many of *Rawhide, Medic* and *Wagon Train* among others.

As *Rawhide* went on, the material tended to get thinner and more repetitious. Eastwood described the problem: 'It's like writing a weekly column as opposed to a feature story, you have to fill that time every week. And a lot of the times the material isn't there, the story isn't there. We always doctored every script because on television you're just eating up vast amounts of material. So a lot of writing was done on

the set. Once in a while you have a good script. Then you really get enthusiastic and charged up.'

Off the set, he became famous. He and Maggie moved house from Sherman Oaks to a better part of Los Angeles. He got an avalanche of fan mail at the studios. He went on television chat shows and journalists besieged him with requests for interviews. Mindful, even then, of keeping his private life as private as possible, he tended not to talk about himself and Maggie, but dispensed advice on keeping fit. 'A lot of actors don't condition themselves to long periods of hard physical effort,' he told *TV Guide.* 'Towards the end of the day it shows in their performances.' He revealed that he did press-ups, worked out on Saturday mornings by running and walking alternate hundred yards along the banks of the Los Angeles River, and that he ate fruit and raw vegetables, like carrots, cauliflower and asparagus. 'The worst exercise you can get,' he warned, 'is with a knife and fork.'

Rawhide was to run for more than seven years and more than two hundred and fifty episodes, making it one of American television's most enduringly popular Western programmes. It featured in the top ten shows of the year in its second year of showing,

A publicity shot from the Rawhide *years: Eastwood with Jayne Mansfield.*

but never reappeared in the list subsequently. Abroad, however, it maintained a near fanatical level of popularity, especially in Japan. In all, *Rawhide* was sold to nearly thirty countries. (This established a pattern of success which was to continue throughout Eastwood's career, notably with the Spaghetti Westerns he made in Spain. A number of Eastwood films have received much greater acclaim abroad than in America itself.)

So Eastwood had reason to be contented. As he told *Playboy:* 'I kind of hesitated bitching about it because before you get into a series, you hear actors complaining and you think "Wow, what's this guy bitching about? He's making $50,000 a year!" So I didn't have any real beefs.' But in an untypical outburst to Hank Grant of the *Hollywood Reporter* on 13 July 1961, he did more than hint at the frustrations of being a stock character in a seemingly never-ending series. 'I haven't been allowed to accept a single feature or TV guesting offer since I started the series. Maybe they figure me as the sheepish nice guy I portray in the series, but even a worm has to turn sometime. Believe me, I'm not bluffing—I'm prepared to go on suspension if necessary, which means I can't work here, but I've open features in London and Rome that'll bring me more money in a year than the series has given me in three.'

This frustration, coming at the end of the third season's filming, was not untypical of contract actors in Eastwood's position who are tempted by offers from the outside world but hemmed in by contracts binding them to their current job. Eastwood was now a major television star: instead of suspending him, the studio accepted his wishes, permitting him to do guest shots and even feature films in his summer break if he so desired. Charles Warren, the producer had always been sympathetic to Eastwood if he complained that too many scripts in succession were favouring Fleming rather than himself. Eastwood had, on one occasion sung a song on the show and cut a disc, 'Unknown Girl,' released by Gothic records in the USA, but it didn't find its way into the hit parade.

More than anything else Eastwood wanted to direct. He had watched men of varying degrees of ineptitude arrive and direct a few episodes of *Rawhide* as part of their jobbing vocation. He and the other regular members of the unit had nursed some of the least able through their episodes, advising them and guiding them, and he knew he could direct as well, if not better, himself. He approached the matter diplomatically: 'I went to Eric Fleming and asked him "Would you be averse to my directing an episode?" He said "Not at all, I'd be for it." So I went to the producer and he said "great". Evidently he didn't say "great" behind my back but he said "great" at the time. He said: "I'll tell you what, why don't you direct some trailers for us, coming attractions for next season's shows?" I said "Terrific. I'll do it for nothing

Left: An unusually dark and mysterious cowboy image for Clint in a dream sequence in Le Streghe *(*The Witches, *1966).*

and then I'll do an episode.'"

Eastwood had seen the potential methods of making the action look more vivid and real, but had been thwarted constantly in his suggestions for shooting it that way: 'When I was on location one time, we were shooting some vast cattle scenes—about two thousand head of cattle. We were doing some really exciting stampede stuff. I was riding along in the herd, there was dust rising up, and it was pretty wild. But the shots were being taken from outside the herd, looking in, and you didn't see too much. I thought, we should get right in the middle of this damn stampede. I said to the director and producer: "I'd like to take an Arriflex, run it on my horse and go right in the middle of this damn thing, even dismount, whatever—but get in there and really get some great shots because there are some beautiful shots in there that we are missing." Well, they double-talked me. They said "You can't get in there because of union rules"—which isn't true at all, because if you're doing a shot the normal camera operator can't do, if he's not a horseman, then there's no reason in the world why you can't do it. In fact I've done it lots of times and there is no union rule against it.'

CBS let him do the trailers but, with those revolutionary ideas the management decided against making him director of an episode. 'I was set to do one but then the network reneged. They had had some problem with another actor who was in a series, directing, and so they came down with a company policy against it.'

Towards the end of his stint with *Rawhide*, Eastwood began seriously to lose interest and this was mirrored by the slow decline in public following. 'After the fifth year or so you start getting squirmy on any series and I have to admit, after seven and a half years I wasn't just nuts about it.' In a vain effort to revitalise the show, the producers dropped Eric Fleming and made Eastwood the trail boss. But this only lasted twenty-two episodes. On 8 February 1966, Frankie Laine set those 'dawgies' rolling for the last time. *Rawhide* had been one of the most long-lasting and widely-sold television series of its time, and would probably be re-run even today, were it not for the fact that it was made in black and white. An inventive and not entirely moral Italian producer later cobbled together some episodes of *Rawhide*, released the concoction in the cinema and called it *The Magnificent Stranger* (which was the shooting title for *A Fistful of Dollars*). Eastwood, though amused by their cheek, told me he was quick to put a stop to it with an injunction.

When such series die, the lead actors often find it hard to combat their type-casting and, after initial guest roles, have to face up to the reality of never being so successful again. The two principals in *Rawhide* made good starts to avoid this pitfall but tragically Eric Fleming was drowned in the Amazon while making a film in South America.

Eastwood, on the other hand, had taken out an insurance policy in the sun-baked hills of Southern Spain that was to last him a lifetime.

A FISTFUL OF WESTERNS

One man who more than any other initiated Clint Eastwood's rapid metamorphosis from TV cowboy to international film star, was Richard Harrison. He was one of a band of American actors who made a handsome living working in the Italian film industry in the sixties. When the director, Sergio Leone, decided to make his first Western, he approached several of these Americans to play in it but most were already committed for the summer. Ideally he would have liked someone like Steve Reeves, at that time one of the hottest properties in Rome, but his budget was small and Reeves was a big star. Harrison was something of a muscleman in the Reeves tradition but he, too, was busy making another film. 'Why not try Clint Eastwood?' he suggested to Leone. Leone had never heard of him.

He then approached James Coburn, whom he *had* heard of and who showed some interest in the project but wanted $25,000. This was too large a proportion of the production's slender budget, for Sergio Leone, an enthusiastic student of the Western, had spent the whole of 1963 trying to raise the cash to make his own, and through three production companies, Jolly Film (Rome), Constantin Film (Munich) and Ocean Film (Madrid) he'd succeeded in cornering a modest $200,000. Not enough for Reeves or Coburn. The search continued and, remembering Harrison's suggestion, Leone decided to find out a little more about Eastwood and ran an episode of *Rawhide*. He liked what he saw.

Left: A rare portrait of Eastwood taken in the year he went to Italy to make his first Spaghetti Western, A Fistful of Dollars *(1964). This was to become a landmark both in Eastwood's career and in the history of the Western film. Below and right: As No Name in* For A Few Dollars More *(1965).*

'I think it was called *The Black Sheep*. I didn't see a character in Rowdy Yates, only a physical figure which suited me although I later altered his appearance. Clint hardly talked in that film but what struck me was his indolent way of moving about. Clint, to my mind, closely resembles a cat. Cats are indolent, they are apparently lazy, more than laziness, it is a style of nonchalance, apparent fatigue, drowsiness.'

The first Eastwood heard of the offer was a phone call from his agent, Leonard Hirshan, in the William Morris Agency. 'He asked me if I would like to go to Europe and make an Italian-German-Spanish co-production of a remake of a Japanese film in the plains of Spain and I said: "Not particularly".'

It was the spring of 1964 and, despite his occasional feelings of frustration revealed in his comments to the *Hollywood Reporter* three years before, Eastwood was continuing with *Rawhide* at CBS and not especially ready to make a dramatic change. However his agency had promised their Rome office that they would at least get him to read the script. He too liked

what he saw. 'As soon as I started reading it, I recognised it as *Yojimbo* which I had seen with Toshiro Mifune playing the lead. From the time I saw that film I always thought it had Western characteristics; there were similar approaches in it, but I thought it was way too stylised for a Western, at least by the old standards.'

Yojimbo had been made by the famous Japanese director, Akira Kurosawa, with Mifune as a lone and lethal Samurai who comes to a town riven by two equally violent mobs, which he destroys by skilfully playing one group off against the other. Four years earlier, Kurosawa's *The Seven Samurai* had been successfully transposed to the West by the director John Sturges. It was not surprising that Leone wanted James Coburn for the lead in his own film, for Coburn had starred in *The Magnificent Seven* along with Robert Vaughn, Eli Wallach, Charles Bronson, Steve McQueen and Yul Brynner.

Although Eastwood has always made his own decisions in the final instance, there is no doubt that his wife Maggie has had a quiet influence at times in his life. This was one of those occasions. Maggie Eastwood hadn't seen *Yojimbo* but all the same she came to an enthusiastic conclusion when she read the Leone script. 'Wow, it's really interesting. It's wild.' It was also, observed her husband, unintentionally funny.

'The script was in English. It was very strange English because it had been written by a group of Italians who didn't speak English that well, especially English with what you would call Western slang. It was an Italian concept of what Western slang should be; a lot of the dialogue was a bit on the shaky side. I liked it though and I thought that maybe a European approach would give the Western a new flavour, because it had been in a very stagnant period up till then. Westerns didn't seem to have anything original or stylish done with them and I figured *Yojimbo* was a terrific idea for a remake.'

His business manager Irving Leonard was against his going to Spain for the picture; he considered it a bad move, *'malpaso'* in Spanish. (When Eastwood subsequently formed his own company ten years later he called it 'Malpaso'—perhaps an ironic reference to the best move he ever made.) But Maggie was keen and he told his agent to sign the deal, thinking he had nothing to lose because if the picture was unsuccessful, it would never find its way back to America to embarrass him. More prophetically, he said: 'I had a hunch that if it was handled well, it would work.'

Although the fee offered was low he liked the idea of travelling: 'I'd never been to Europe so it was a great opportunity for me to make the trip. So I went over there on the condition that I could change the dialogue, and I had a stunt guy go along with me, just to keep an eye on the authenticity.'

With a shrewdness and judgement well-honed by a hundred episodes of *Rawhide,* he was taking no chances of ending up in what could have been an amateur mess. He even chose his own costume in advance. 'I went down to a wardrobe place on Santa Monica Boulevard and just purchased the wardrobe and took it over there. It was very difficult because on a film you always have two or three hats of the same sort or two or three jackets of the same kind in case you lose a piece of clothing or something gets wet and you need a change. But for this film I had only one of everything: one hat, one sort of sheepskin vest, one poncho and several pairs of pants because they were just sort of Frisco-type jeans. If I'd lost any of it halfway through the film, I'd have really been in trouble.' His boots and gunbelt came courtesy of *Rawhide,* whether they knew it or not.

It is an indication of how far Eastwood had already gone in preparing the part of the Stranger in his mind that he stopped at a store in Beverly Hills to purchase a large collection of thin black cigars . . . his image of the character was developing even before he arrived in Spain.

Eight thousand miles away, on the other side of the Atlantic, the director he had yet to meet, Sergio Leone, was also at work on creating the Stranger. In what has been written about the Spaghetti Westerns, little has come from the mouth of the director who remains something of an enigmatic magus. Today he lives and works in an opulent villa in the bizarre city

The violence, the speed of action in the Leone Westerns announced a totally new European style. Left and below: A Fistful of Dollars *(1964).*

of EUR just south of Rome, a marble and stucco environment designed by Mussolini to be the head-quarters of his fascist aspirations. It still isn't finished but the elegant avenues boast grandiloquent names like Chopin, Beethoven, Art, Painting, Atlantic Ocean and Rocky Mountain. Leone lives just off Africa Avenue.

He is a heavily-built man, now in his middle fifties, with a thick dark beard, dense spectacles and an ample paunch brought on by his predilection, appropriately, for spaghetti. Despite an intellectual mien, his eyes twinkle with a saturnine humour as he speaks, haltingly, in English. He prefers to talk through an interpreter in Italian. His office is expensively decorated with *objets d'art* and framed posters and pictures from his films. He sits behind a desk of movie-mogul proportions ringed in a mist of smoke from an expensive Havana cigar.

'Clint, il personaggio, é un personaggio come ripeto che avevo chiaramente in mente. . . . Clint was the character I clearly had in mind. In my films I have more need of masks than great actors. I take the real life actor and mould the character from him. With Clint I corrected all the small physical details that didn't fit into the character. I placed that poncho on his shoulders to give him a veil of mystery. The cigar acted as a sort of pendant to those ice-cold eyes.'

The mists of time and cigar smoke have obscured the exact contribution made by each man to the creation of the Stranger but Leone is defensively

anxious that his own role should not be under-estimated. He even claimed that he was the first director to put cowboys in ponchos. 'Did you see Marlon Brando in *Southwest of Sonora*? He was wearing a poncho. Americans now copy me when they make Westerns.'

Leone had worked his way through the ranks of the Italian film industry, serving as assistant director on innumerable 'epics' and finally directing one himself, *The Colossus of Rhodes*. Given his enthusiasm for the Western he was full of excitement at the prospect of his first attempt in the genre.

Obviously with such a small budget they couldn't afford to go to America or Mexico to shoot the film, so they settled on the nearest similar territory, the hills and plains around Almería in the south of Spain. It was a poor area, infertile and had been neglected since Andalucia espoused the wrong side in the Spanish Civil War, but the burnt-out landscape and cruel, glaring Mediterranean sun gave the film an original and desolate look, unlike any previous Western.

Leone shot all three of his Spaghetti Westerns there and his choice of location gave a much needed impetus to the district which became known for a while as the 'Hollywood of Europe'. In the sixties, film makers flocked there to take advantage of the cheap labour and unspoilt settings: *Patton* was shot in the re-dressed streets of the town with its tank battles blasting away in the valleys, and David Lean shot some of the scenes of *Lawrence of Arabia* in the sun-baked plains outside the town. The hotel industry flourished and the *gitanos,* the gypsy population who lived in shacks and caves in the hills found themselves making a new and easy existence as film extras. Almería was never popular with American actors, being known variously as 'the armpit of Europe' or as the butt of the saying 'if the world ended tomorrow, Almería would have a year to go'. Eventually it was to price itself out of the market. The last time I was there, the British producer Euan Lloyd was shooting a Western in a remote valley. He indicated a farmer on top of a nearby hill, driving his tractor up and down the same furrow. 'That's the edge of his land,' explained Lloyd, 'he knows he's in shot and he wants us to buy him off.'

But when Eastwood and Leone arrived there in May 1964, no such sophistication had set in and the locals were intrigued to see a film unit at work. It would be nice to report that his encounter with Leone, historic as it was to become in film industry terms as Stanley meeting Livingstone, was marked by some prophetic exchange. As Eastwood remembers, it wasn't quite like that. 'Communication was a little rough. I knew "arrivederci" and "buon giorno" and he knew "goodbye" and "hello" and that was it. We had an interpreter the first time, then Sergio learned a little English and I learned a little Italian and we just made our way along.'

The presence of a common purpose proved more valuable than the absence of a common language. Both men realised that what they were about to do

A Fistful of Dollars *(1964). Above: The Man With No Name rides into town for the first time. Right: The Stranger's impassivity was his main attraction.*

was something quite different from the traditional Western where heroes shave daily and don't shoot until they're shot at, and those on the wrong side of the law inevitably need to visit the dentist and are usually wildly inaccurate in their firepower. What is essential in the Western is that the morality of each character should be signalled to the audience almost from the moment he enters. Eastwood was only too familiar with the traditional style and he was intrigued by the idea of challenging it.

'The typical Western done for many years was: hero rides into town, sees school marm on porch of school, sees man beating horse, he interferes, hits man who's beating horse while the school marm looks on. You know that two people are going to get together and it isn't the guy and the horse. In this one: man rides in on an ancient horse, very shabby-looking, sees man kicking kid, sees woman obviously in a distraught position at the house, obviously a prisoner of sorts and he turns and rides off. Later on he helps that woman and kid out but right away you say: "Now wait a minute, this has got to be something strange. This can't be the hero. He doesn't have a white hat and he isn't doing the normal thing."

'To me, this is what made it interesting. You couldn't predict the end of the film. But in some of the plots we were getting in Westerns for years you could pretty well predict the outcome of the story, and

when you can read the ending from the very beginning, then to me it doesn't make it very interesting.'

Leone shared this rebellious desire to tumble the old values and present the audience with a new, more mystifying piece of storytellling.

'I had seen a lot of Westerns but I hadn't liked many of them a lot. I found some interesting, especially Ford's films. Only in all of Ford's work, especially when he began, there is an abundance of optimism, whereas I have approached Western film making with a kind of pessimism. I wanted to make a Western seen by the eyes and through the eyes of a European, perhaps an unconscious criticism of the traditional kind. The reason that prompted me to start making a Western was my old theory that the greatest writer of Westerns there has ever been or will ever be, is Homer. Achilles, Agamemnon and Ajax are the archetypes of today's cowboys. I wanted also to bring back a kind of Italian *Commedia dell'Arte,* since both *A Fistful of Dollars* and *Yojimbo* were inspired by Goldoni's comedy *A Servant of Two Masters.* The Stranger in *Fistful* was a masque character, just as Arlecchino was in *A Servant of Two Masters,* who places himself between two rival factions, selling himself to either in order to emerge as the winner himself.'

A Fistful of Dollars opens with the Stranger riding slowly into a deserted town on a mule. Four gunmen attempt to shoot up the rider, but he keeps his cool and makes his way to the saloon. Here the Stranger discovers that the town is in the clutches of two warring gangs, the Rojos and the Baxters. He saunters back up the street, shoots his four aggressors (Baxter's men) and hires himself to the Rojos clan as a gunfighter. The Rojos men have just attacked a joint Mexican-American army troop, in order to steal their gold. The Baxters know of the raid, so the Rojos are eager to make a truce and prevent the Baxters from informing on them to the army authorities. The Stranger spends most of the film playing off one side against the other, and getting paid handsomely by both factions in the process. Along the way, he befriends a Mexican woman who has been kept forcibly as Ramon Rojos' mistress, and he helps her to escape with her husband and child. The Rojos family retaliate by beating up the Stranger, setting fire to the Baxter homestead and killing off the remaining Baxters. The Stranger escapes, and now more personally involved in this saga of revenge and counter-revenge because of his beating, he makes himself a bullet-proof vest and goes into the town to confront the Rojos clan. In a masterly display of gunfighting skill, he kills off all in the remaining Rojos villains. The Stranger is last seen riding out of town, presumably to return the stolen army gold, but remaining as enigmatic a figure as when he first arrived.

However high-blown the thinking was behind the film, it was patently a lift from *Yojimbo.* No attempt was made to disguise that. Just as Eastwood pretends to help both the Rojos and the Baxters, each trying to control San Miguel, so in *Yojimbo,* Mifune hired himself out to both corrupt factions in a town feud. Further, the Mifune character was actually

39

A Fistful of Dollars *(1964). Above: The Italians loved the heightened, almost unreal sequences of gunplay which were always a big feature of the Spaghetti Westerns. Right: Gian Maria Volonté co-starred with Eastwood as Rojos, the chief villain.*

called the Stranger With No Name. Early in the Japanese film, Mifune walks into a strange town past a coffin-maker, orders him to prepare two coffins, is mocked by some local thugs and kills three of them with his sword. As he returns past the undertaker he holds up three fingers and amends his order. Similarly in *A Fistful of Dollars* Eastwood walks past a coffin-maker: 'Get three coffins ready' he orders. The town heavies make fun of him, asking where his old mule is. 'You see, my mule don't like people laughing, gets the crazy idea you're laughing at him.' All four

heavies get their just deserts for such mockery and as Eastwood returns past the old man he too corrects his miscalculation: 'My mistake, four coffins.'

Leone was faithful to Kurosawa even in style. The 'coffin' shoot-out follows the Japanese original closely with the Stranger appearing in a fog of dust. The camera follows his back down the street and swirls round with the bullets when the action starts. (Here Leone had an advantage over any American director; the Hayes Office at that time still insisted that the man who shoots and the man who is shot must be in different camera cuts.) The overall pacing of the film, languid pieces of exposition punctuated by fast bouts of action, derived considerably from the Japanese original. Borrowing from Kurosawa's style also enabled Leone to achieve his stated aim of making a film unlike any previous Western. This was enhanced by the tingling operatic score by Ennio Morricone, the dissonant trills and jarring chords running counter to the usual riding-rhythm tunes of the American Western. The music served a further dramatic purpose: it emphasised the black humour of the undertaking. Eastwood knew from the outset that the film 'definitely had satiric undertones'.

But what made the film the success it was later to become was undoubtedly the character Eastwood created. He had begun in Hollywood by his purchase of the outfit and cigars—'I didn't really like the cigars but they kept me in a right kind of humour, kind of a fog. They just put you in a sour frame of mind. Those were pretty edgy cigars.' He was determined to fabricate a creature who was the antithesis of Rowdy Yates, although his performance borrowed some of its style from Eric Fleming. When he got to Spain, he went to work on the screenplay.

'The part wasn't as spare as that in the script but, to me, the more the character got into expository scenes and started explaining things, the more he dissipated the mystery of the character. So we cut it down very lean and Sergio agreed that we would try to make this guy a little bit unique. You're not quite sure who he is, you're not even quite sure he is the hero until halfway through the film.'

Eastwood has never underestimated the appeal of the mysterious as his later films demonstrated and Leone, with his wish for a classical allegorical tale, even went so far as to describe the Eastwood role as 'the incarnation of the archangel Gabriel'. Even if audiences failed to appreciate this, it did result in a clever cocktail of unreality and reality; the silent, squinting Stranger who comes from nowhere and returns there, entering a petty, squabbling world where evil vies with evil, set against an arid, dead landscape.

Both the real and the unreal invincibility of the Stranger are never better illustrated than in the final scene when the trembling Ramon pumps bullets into him—'the heart, Ramon, don't forget the heart, aim for the heart or you'll never stop me'—but the avenging angel continues his catlike approach with the bullets bouncing off him. Superman? No. Monty Python? Sort of. Ned Kelly? Well, that was the inspiration. When the Stranger throws back his serape to reveal an iron plate covering his chest, he also reveals that he has five bullets left in his gun.

Ramon, Eastwood's co-star in the film, was played by Johnny Welles, a name never to be heard of again since it was a pseudonym for Gian Maria Volonté. (*He* himself was heard of again, not just in the subsequent Spaghetti Westerns but as the Oscar-winning star of *Investigation of a Citizen Above Suspicion* in 1970.) Anxious to get an American distribution and fearful that they wouldn't be taken seriously if they had Italian names on the credits, the producers changed the names of Massimo Dallamano, the cameraman, to Jack Dalmas; Ennio Morricone to Don Savio and Sergio Leone, to Bob Robertson.

Eastwood enjoyed his summer in Spain. He was gently amused by Leone who fulfilled his own cowboy fantasies by wearing Western clothes and hats and even a holster with two toy pistols, on the set, and acting out all the parts himself in advance of each take. Eastwood noted: 'Leone is a short, heavy fellow but when he acts out roles you know he really feels himself tall and lean—a gunfighter.' He was less amused on the day he arrived on the location to find no-one else there; the crew hadn't been paid for two weeks and they went on strike until the money turned up. After the tight organisation of *Rawhide*, the chaos of a multi-national cast and crew and a director whom he later acknowledged 'was not the most planned or organised guy' was on occasion something of a nightmare.

At the end of filming, Eastwood shaved off his beard, hung up his poncho and returned to the on-going cattle drive to Sedalia not knowing whether he would ever hear of the film again. Occasionally, on television chat shows, he would entertain the audience with whimsical anecdotes about his European interlude.

The producers didn't have much faith either in the film or in Eastwood. They had told him so at the time. 'They just hated me and wanted to get rid of me they thought I was so bad. You know, in Italian movies they act a lot; they come from the Hellzapoppin school of drama so to get my effect I stayed impassive and I guess they thought I wasn't acting. But Leone knew what I was up to.'

*Fistful—Per un pugno di dollari—*was given a sneak preview in a small cinema outside Naples. The first night about fifty people turned up including a critic who wrote that no-one would ever want to see the film again. But word spread. The next night the cinema was full, by the end of the week there were queues around the block. Within months 'El Cigarillo' was a cult hero in Italy with the film outgrossing *My Fair Lady* and *Mary Poppins*.

In their detailed study, *Italian Western,* Lawrence Staig and Tony Williams suggest some cogent reasons for the success of the Spaghetti Western in Europe, and the slow response in America. Directors like Sergio Leone belonged to a truly commercial section of the Italian film industry, somewhat despised internationally: they took over old Hollywood conventions and turned them into enthusiastically popular products. Leone had himself

For A Few Dollars More *(1965). Left: No Name sizes up the situation. Above left: Always remote, uninvolved, amoral; this was the character immortalised by Eastwood and Leone. Above right: A street confrontation with the usual odds.*

been involved in what was called the 'sword and sandle' epic boom in the Roman film industry in 1964-70: he had directed Steve Reeves in a remake of *The Last Days of Pompeii,* which was one reason why he had wanted the same actor for *Fistful.* Both the imitation epic and the imitation Western bore certain characteristics which made them hugely popular in Europe: they injected a fresh approach, a knowing humour into old conventions. American audiences found this irreverence a little hard to take. Further, the Spaghetti Westerns were stronger on passionate emotions, bloody violence, (the theme of revenge, a very Italian motivation, occurs frequently) and this aspect was also totally foreign to the American tradition based on John Ford concepts of honour, bravery and romantic adventure. The Europeans have always tended to comment on the cruelty and lack of morality inherent in the American myth of the West. Apart from the Eastwood films, the school of Spaghetti Westerns, rapturously received in Italy and Spain, never caught on in the USA, except latterly as a minor cult among film buffs.

Eastwood was occupied with *Rawhide* but kept an eye on the European section of *Variety* where, one day, he read a quote from an Italian correspondent in Rome: 'Westerns have finally died out here.' Eastwood remembers, 'I thought "wouldn't you know it." Two weeks later I read another article that said the big deal in Italy was that everybody was enthusiastic about making Westerns after the success of this fantastic new film *A Fistful of Dollars.* That meant nothing to me, because the title we'd used during the shooting was *The Magnificent Stranger.* Then, about two days after that, there was another item from Rome, and it

said "*A Fistful of Dollars* starring Clint Eastwood is going through the roof here." Then I got a letter from the producer, who hadn't bothered to write me since I left even to say thank you or go screw yourself or whatever, asking about making another picture.' He agreed. This time for a few dollars more, $50,000 in all, plus a Ferrari. He returned to Europe for the Paris première where he saw for the first time the hysteria that attended his new manifestation. 'It was nice to see grown-ups behaving like a crowd of kids.'

Eastwood fever was now spreading worldwide. He was being hailed as a new Gary Cooper. In South America he was called 'El Pistolero con los Ojos Verdes'—the gunman with green eyes. But in America he remained a television cowboy. The *Fistful* producers had failed to get the US rights to *Yojimbo* and were unable to release their film there. In 1965 Sophia Loren came to Hollywood and while she was there asked to meet their biggest star, the man who was the rage of Europe. 'Who?' inquired her hosts. 'Clint Eastwood, of course,' she replied. 'Eastwood?' they repeated incredulously, just to make sure she had got the name right, 'You mean the guy in that failing television series?'

Leone circumvented any copyright problems with his second Western by writing it himself with Luciano Vincenzoni. Prudently he retained the elements that made the first one a success: Eastwood was still the nameless Stranger, Gian Maria Volonté was still the chief villain, a drug-crazed El Indio, and the title traded on the success of the original film, *For A Few Dollars More.* With an enhanced budget of $600,000, Leone was able to afford another 'name' American actor, Lee Van Cleef who, as Colonel Mortimer, competed with and then joined the Stranger in the pursuit of Indio. More money also allowed for much better action sequences and special effects. The film had more violence, which Leone had no qualms about including. 'It isn't the cinema that transmits violence to life; it is life that transmits it to the cinema. Violence belongs to ourselves because we breathe it every day. When we go out at eight in the morning the first breath of air is a breath of violence. Therefore we reproduce it faithfully.'

For A Few Dollars More sees the return of the Stranger, the Man With No Name, but this time he has a defined profession, as a bounty hunter. He is searching for a drug-addicted murderer, known as El Indio. (Volonté had also acted the part of Eastwood's main enemy, Ramon Rojos, in *Fistful*). The film opens with another bounty hunter, Colonel Mortimer (Lee Van Cleef) arriving in the town of Tucamari and with great coolness and precision killing one of his list of wanted men as the suspect attempts to flee. Mortimer then goes to the saloon where he encounters No Name, who is calmly dispatching four men at a card table. No Name saunters to the sherriff's office to collect the bounty on their heads. Having established their mutual aims and equal talents, the two men decide to team up in pursuit of El Indio. The murderer is portrayed as infinitely more evil than the two conscience-free professionals: he has a positive relish for killing.

El Indio is planning to rob the bank at El Paso, so the bounty hunters meet up there in order to waylay him. During the discussion that leads up to the showdown, it is revealed in flashback that Mortimer has a personal score to settle with the villain, because he raped and murdered Mortimer's sister some years ago. Nothing is revealed about No Name's past in this conversation, and typically in keeping with the characterisation, No Name infiltrates El Indio's gang. After several mutual double-crosses, the two bounty hunters get their prey: No Name allows Mortimer his moment of revenge in the actual killing of El Indio, while Mortimer in return hands over his own half of the bounty. No Name takes the money and is last seen loading the bodies of El Indio's gangmen into a cart, then riding out of town counting his dollars. As in *Fistful*, his motivations or preoccupations are never revealed.

This continuing challenge to the Western myth of the perfect hero and the irredeemably evil villain was spelt out in words at the beginning of the film: 'Where life had no values, sometimes death had its price.' It was a message that was repeated throughout the continuing carnage until the Stranger heaped the bodies of the dead onto a cart to go and collect his reward. Within this mayhem, Leone tried to stick to his new morality. 'I wanted to show that most heroes do what they do for money. I also wanted to prove that bad guys can sometimes have their good side. Al Capone, for instance, had a certain kind of humanity.'

Communication between the star and his director improved, not just because they had both taken a few hesitant steps into each other's language but because they were more aware of the other's strengths and weaknesses. Aware of Leone's organisational shortcomings, Eastwood appreciated his style: 'He has a very good concept of what he wants. He's very good

with composition; he has a nice eye. He's very good with humour, a very funny guy. His humour is very sardonic. He's not very good at directing actors, he's only as good as his actors are—but most directors aren't very good at directing actors. The most a director can usually do with actors is to set up a nice atmosphere in which to work.'

When I questioned Leone, he was emphatic that when he met Eastwood the latter was initially an unknown young man, who kept faithfully to the script and allowed himself to be moulded into his character by the director, as did the rest of the carefully chosen cast. Eastwood obviously has other ideas on this; he told another interviewer: 'Sergio, whom I respect very much, would never give me any credit for the style of a film I'd been in with him. This is true even though Sergio and I would hash out ideas together and toss them back and forth.' However, he concluded: 'I want to make it clear that I like Sergio, liked working with him.' And the respect was mutual.

Before he returned home after making *For a Few Dollars More,* Eastwood went to Rome to work for Vittorio de Sica, Italy's leading film director and the man who had hailed Eastwood as 'the new Gary Cooper'. Leone had been De Sica's first assistant on the acclaimed *Bicycle Thieves* and had even had a small acting part in the film. *Le Streghe—The Witches—*was a five part film, produced by Dino de Laurentiis and starring his wife, Sylvana Mangano. Clint was in the last section, 'A Night Like Any

Eastwood's character in Le Streghe *(1966) was so out of character that United Artists were said to have bought it for the vaults in America.*

Eli Wallach, the 'Ugly', played opposite Eastwood, the 'Good', for the first time in The Good, The Bad and The Ugly *(1966), and thoroughly enjoyed the experience.*

Other'. It proved less than a hit—United Artists were said to have bought it for America in order to put it in the vaults and safeguard Eastwood's new reputation. However that may be, it gave Clint and Maggie the opportunity to sample Rome surrounded by a sempiternal crush of fans. Of the film Eastwood remarked: 'It was a drawing-room thing, half reality, half fantasy. It was good to get out of my boots, though.'

He stepped into a more prestigious pair when he returned to *Rawhide* in 1965. Eric Fleming had been dropped in the war against waning ratings and went off to make a film at MGM with Doris Day, *The Glass Bottom Boat*. Eastwood now became trail boss, but only for twenty-two out of the planned thirty-nine episodes, after which the series was cancelled. Eastwood never reached Sedalia but he did reach a comfortable settlement with CBS who paid him off with $119,000.

He was by now quite a rich man. In fact he had never accepted his full fee for *Rawhide*—'I deferred part of it, figuring I was going to have a big lull after the series came to an end.' The so-called big lull began with his signing a contract for a quarter of a million dollars plus ten per cent of the western hemisphere profits to make his third Western for Leone.

The Good, The Bad and The Ugly, which started shooting in 1966, was, as *Variety* later pointed out, exactly that. It was also nearly twice as long as *A Fistful of Dollars.* With a budget of $1,200,000, Leone was determined to make an epic Western set against the backdrop of the American Civil War. He

went to the Library of Congress in Washington and made a thorough study of the period, bringing back hundreds of photographs to which he constantly referred during shooting. With a new-found confidence owing to the success of the previous two films, he boasted to Joan Marble of the *New York Times* that 'this picture is more accurate than any American Western'.

The 'Good' was, questionably, represented by Clint Eastwood's unchanging Stranger; the 'Bad' was a return appearance of Lee Van Cleef as a sadistic killer ironically named 'Angel Eyes', and the 'Ugly' was a third American actor, Eli Wallach, who didn't know he was going to be blessed with that epithet until he saw the film. The quest, as ever, was for dollars, $200,000 in gold buried in a Confederate grave in Sad Hill Cemetery.

Paradoxically, Eastwood was still a prophet without honour in his own country, for *Time* magazine in 1967 proclaimed that in Wallach, Leone had hired his 'first big-time actor'. Wallach knew otherwise: 'Clint was very helpful to me. It was my first experience with Italian movies, and Clint guided me through it. It was clear that he knew how to make films. He also proved to be more interested in the success of the film than in his own image. When he realised that the focus of the film was going to be my

In The Good, The Bad and The Ugly, *a little passing love interest for the Man With No Name; this sequence was cut out of the US and UK versions, only appearing in Europe.*

character, Tuco, instead of his, he came up with ideas and suggestions that made my character even better.' Wallach was very impressed by Eastwood and especially by the way he saved them both from possible grievous bodily harm. Eastwood recalls: 'I remember they were going to blow up a 200-metre bridge with something like 1,800 tons of dynamite. They had five cameras on it and I said to Sergio: "Where are we going to be?" and he said, "Well, you'll be down here next to this first camera. You'll crawl up here and then, just as you come up to the top, where this camera is, the bridge will blow up behind you."

'I looked at the bridge, and I looked at the distance between it and us and I knew it was going to be close. I thought it was very close, too close. But rather than say "No, I don't want to do that" I said, "Sergio, where are *you* going to be?" And he said, "Oh, I'll be right here, right behind this camera, waiting for you." I said, "Fine. If you'll be right there with us, I'll do it." He kind of did a long look at me and I took a walk back. A few minutes later I saw two guys coming up in Wallach's wardrobe and my wardrobe and I said, "Oh, you're going to use doubles instead. Why is that?" They said, "Well Sergio's decided he wants to be up on the hill so he'll get a better look."

'So anyway that's the way it kinda was and, sure enough, when the bridge did blow up—it went prematurely too which is another story, the old "any time you're ready C.B." joke—anyway when they

finally blew the bridge up the rocks and stones almost killed the assistant cameraman on the lower camera where we would have been standing. They ripped the whole back out of a Land Rover just a few feet away.'

In *The Good, The Bad and The Ugly,* the duo of Eastwood and Wallach run a complicated bounty hunters' con-game whereby Tuco (Wallach) is handed over to various authorities in return for various rewards, only to be 'rescued' (as in the film's opening sequence) by his partner. After this escape, the action shifts to the arrival in town of Angel Eyes (Lee Van Cleef), a hired killer. He promptly dispatches his intended victim, and equally skilfully guns down the man who hired him to do the job. Angel Eyes is pursuing the whereabouts of an Army cashbox which one of his recent victims has mentioned to him just before dying. No Name rescues Tuco once more from the clutches of three other bounty hunters, and the two of them continue double-crossing each other good-humouredly through most of the film. In one memorable sequence, No Name leaves Tuco in the middle of a desert miles from the nearest town. Tuco escapes from his predicament, and just as he is about to extract vengeance in a hotel bedroom by hanging his erstwhile partner, fate intervenes in the form of the Civil War. A shell bursts into the room and removes Tuco through the floor. Eventually he gets his revenge, dragging No Name at rope's end across that same desert.

This sport is interrupted when the two men come across a carriage-load of dead and dying Confederate soldiers, one of whom reveals in his last words the whereabouts of the cash-box which Angel

Eyes is still pursuing. Sad Hill Cemetery is the site for the final confrontation between the Good, the Bad and the Ugly: without the others seeing, No Name empties Tuco's gun. Angel Eyes, duped by not knowing this, is outgunned. Tuco is left with the money but no horse, once again. No Name rides off on the only available mount, minus money but as enigmatically contented as ever.

The pairing of Eastwood and Wallach was memorable for its deceit and black humour as they alternately tried to take and save each other's lives, motivated, of course, not by any Butch and Sundance comradeship but by naked greed. In the scene where Eastwood takes Wallach's horse and leaves him with a hundred mile walk through waterless scrubland to the nearest habitation, he says, 'If you save your breath I think a man like you could manage it,' with his customary dryness. Later, the roles are reversed, and with a horse and a parasol to preserve him from the lethal noonday sun Wallach leads a parched Eastwood by the neck through the dunes of the shifting Almería desert, a scene stunningly photographed by Leone's new cameraman, Tonnio Delli Colli. The agony and the ecstasy of Eastwood's trek was dramatically emphasised by Morricone's subtle score.

It was the end of Eastwood's 387-minute screen partnership with Leone but by now the apprentice had outgrown the sorcerer and was ready to consolidate his fame and his fortune in his own country. As far as critical appreciation went, the films did not get off to a good start. The American rights to *Yojimbo* were eventually and expensively cleared enabling *A Fistful of Dollars* to open simultaneously in no less

than eighty New York cinemas on Thursday 2 February 1967. Judith Crist found it 'an ersatz Western dedicated to proving that men and women can be gouged, burned, beaten, stamped and shredded to death'. Kathleen Carroll in the *Daily News* considered it 'a straining-hard-to-be-off-beat almost pop Western; not bad enough to be bad or good enough to be good' and, recognising its derivation from *Yojimbo*, deemed it 'a washed-out imitation'. Archer Winsten in *The Post* thought the producers and director had not hired a writer: 'They simply made this picture out of 1,001 Westerns they have seen and admired.' Andrew Sarris in *The Village Voice* saw that the plot was lifted from *Yojimbo* but imagined 'the dialogue must have been written between cocktails on the Via Veneto ... the movie suffers most from the dreadfully mechanical inflections of the dubbing and the wearisome "universality" of the "Mexican" set.'

They did, however, recognise the potential of Eastwood whose character was described by Bosley Crowther in the *New York Times* as 'a morbid, amusing, campy fraud'. Kathleen Carroll noted that he had 'the deadpan detachment the role demands' and Archer Winsten correctly predicted 'he should be good for many a year of hero stints'.

Thanks to the generally hostile reviews and a February snowstorm that immobilised the city of New York the film didn't take off on the scale

The classic disinterest of No Name contrasted with the real tragedy of the Civil War. In The Good, The Bad and The Ugly, *Eastwood still made his character likeable and was assured of his position as the fastest draw in the Western box-office.*

anticipated by United Artists. Americans were slow to warm to the foreign manipulation of a genre of film that was uniquely their own. Applauding this, Andrew Sarris referred to 'the superiority of mass taste in America over that anywhere else in the world. The 42nd Street crowd, in particular, is not being taken in by this *paesano* Western.'

Eastwood was sanguine about these initial notices, even then. He knew that arriving from foreign shores as a fully-fledged star was not guaranteed to endear him to anyone. 'In the old days movie actors were put on the map by Hollywood with a big press push. I came out of making these films down in Spain with an Italian company and I know that when I came back to Hollywood, people weren't really able to accept my success. I wasn't in their good graces, so to speak. A lot of movie people didn't understand those films. The only people who seemed to catch on straightaway were the public.'

In most countries of the world this popular response was immediate. In America things were slower but gradually and inevitably the cult grew, although Eastwood wasn't propelled into the megastar category of Paul Newman or Steve McQueen. Journalists were cautious in acknowledging his rapid popularity; when *Life* magazine put him on their cover in 1971 it was with the somewhat incredulous banner: 'The world's favourite movie star is—no kidding—Clint Eastwood.'

By the time *For A Few Dollars More* opened in America in May 1967, the critics had learned from the public how to appreciate the new-style Western. Writing in the *Christian Science Monitor,* Frederick H. Guidry observed 'the casual homicides that dot the film are certainly deplorable, but the audience laughter at the superheroics shows that the production is not being taken too seriously. And at least some of the time there are signs that the producers have as much regard for wry humour as for vivid violence.' Guidry acknowledged that the Europeans had taken over the leadership from America in the action-Western field. 'Italian, Spanish and German interest behind Clint Eastwood's latest films have shown extraordinary talent for the sort of blazing-guns, laconic hero melodrama that fits in with current popular taste.'

Most critics found even the shortened American version of *The Good, The Bad and The Ugly* which opened the following year too long (it ran for three hours in Italy and two hours and forty minutes in the States). But by now they had to acknowledge the impact of the trilogy and try to understand why the films were so successful. Andrew Sarris was no longer as dismissive as he had been with *Fistful.* Referring to the Eastwood-Wallach desert scene in the new film, he perceived 'the suffering becomes so intensively vivid and the framing so conscientiously poetic that the audience is subjected to a kind of Cactus Calvary ... the sheer duration of the suffering makes Eastwood a plausible lower-class hero whose physical redemption is the contemporary correlative

The Good, The Bad and The Ugly.

49

of Christ's spiritual redemption.'

This intellectualisation of the Spaghetti Westerns was not to Eastwood's advantage. Before the films were released in America Bosley Crowther went to see *A Fistful of Dollars* in Rome and warned readers of the *New York Times* that the leading character was 'just this side of a brute, long on sadistic intentions and short on heroic qualities'. Now audiences across the land were gleefully urging this killer on. It was the dean of American critics, Pauline Kael, who most perceptively articulated the cause for concern in this. Writing in the *New Yorker* she pointed out that the Spaghetti Westerns 'eliminated the morality play dimension and turned the Western into pure violent reverie. Apart from their aesthetic qualities (and they did have some) what made these Italian-produced Westerns popular was that they stripped the Western form of its cultural burden of morality. They discarded its civility along with its hypocrisy. In a sense they liberated the form; what the Western hero stood for was left out and what he embodied (strength and gun power) was retained. . .'

By turning the bullet-ridden flesh into words, Miss Kael removed the films from the area of entertainment and placed them firmly into that of social phenomenon, probably as a force for evil. To see if she still stuck to her severely moral views, I went to visit her in 1977, in the fall splendour of her peaceful home in the Berkshires, a world apart from the burnt-out plains of Spain. She is a petite lady, slightly nervous, very welcoming and vigorously intellectual. Those who have read her work over the years know that she demands a high ethical and emotional standard in a film before she deems it worthy of praise, but at the same time she is only too aware of Eastwood's box-office appeal.

'I think he does express a new mood in movies and he certainly expresses a new mood in American life. Let me see if I can put it this way: the Bogart hero felt pain. When he killed someone he suffered from it, he was a man of experience, you saw the lines of pain in his face. The Eastwood character expresses a new emotionlessness about killing that people think is the truth now. It used to be that the man who stood for high principles was also the best shot. Now we no longer believe that in order to be a great shot you

The Man With No Name leaves Tuco teetering at the end of the film. Seconds later he turns to put a bullet through the rope and cut him down.

need principles at all. And Clint Eastwood is a totally unprincipled killer.

'John Wayne and Eastwood diverge at the point of immorality and morality—or rather amorality for Eastwood. John Wayne has an iconography about him. He stood for principles that were not directly political and he's carried those principles into the right wing political position in some of the more recent movies. But Eastwood never stood for anything but the big gun.

'It seems the hero has become a psychopathic personality, his aspectlessness when he kills begins to seem like an expression of a new nihilism. Clint Eastwood seems almost like a machine for killing, he's almost stoned, he's so quiet and inexpressive.'

Surprisingly, for one who felt so strongly about the central character, Miss Kael quite liked the Spaghetti Westerns.

'I enjoyed some of them because I come from the West myself and it was so interesting to see this European version of my part of the country. I loved the fact that the Spanish locations had a different kind of light, that the sets were enormous. I think part of the reason Eastwood travels well is because people used to think the Western was such a popular form because of its morality, but really it was because of the melodrama and the action. In a sense Eastwood has removed the hypocrisy from those characters by getting rid of all the morality.'

Eastwood has an answer to the continuing allegation of violence and it's a fairly convincing one. 'I'm appalled by violence in films but you have to tell the drama and if the basis of the drama is conflict then sometimes a certain amount of violence is justified. After we did the Italian Westerns, a hundred films came out that were twice as violent and they didn't do as well. So you can't say that violence is what sells. It isn't.'

No, what sold was a character with no name and since there was no other way to describe him, he became known by the name of the actor playing him, Clint Eastwood. Equally, although John Wayne played two hundred parts each with a different name, it's improbable that anyone thinks of him in a film as any other than John Wayne. Eastwood, like the rest of his generation, grew up watching Wayne in the movies. He was never a particular Wayne fan. In fact he had no real movie heroes except possibly James Cagney, of whom he commented: 'I liked his style and energy. He was fearless. I always love to watch his early films on television.' However, we discussed the appeal of the Wayne persona.

'Wayne played, and he did it quite well, probably as good as anybody, that kind of very moral and very strict ideals type person, who won't bend too much one way or the other. I enjoyed seeing the character myself as I grew up but it's not at all the thing I'm interested in. Nowadays I think that people want other dimensions. They like to see somebody with flaws and other desires.' Having reached his present screen eminence, Eastwood is too much a gentleman to disparage the John Wayne image totally, but when he was on the wrong end of an unfair comparison, at the time the Spaghetti Westerns reached America, he was more candid.

'People don't believe in heroes. Everybody knows that nobody ever stood in the street and let the heavy draw first. It's me or him. To me that's practical and that's where I disagree with the Wayne concept. I do all the stuff Wayne would never do. I play bigger than life characters but I'd shoot the guy in the back.'

Fortunately, the film industry was big enough for both of them. Despite his scars from the critics, Eastwood had the reassurance that there was a growing number of people who would follow him from film to film. And as the superhuman character gazed down from the screen at the assortment of faces of all nationalities who were contributing to his percentage and making him a millionaire, and then a multi-millionaire, he must have known that his instincts were pretty well turning out to be right.

THE RETURN OF THE STRANGER

It was time for Eastwood to consolidate his life. He drove north with Maggie to the Monterey peninsula, the area he had fallen in love with when he was stationed at Ford Ord, the area he thought he might like to live in if he 'ever managed to put together a few dollars'. And having acquired sufficient lira, they bought some land on the coast just outside Carmel. There was an old house on the property but they laid plans for a sizeable ranch house with a gym and picture windows and their bedroom almost jutting out over the Pacific. They also made plans to start a family after thirteen years of marriage. Clint had always told reporters, half jokingly, that they had wanted to wait until they were sure of their relationship.

Professionally he wasn't exactly besieged with offers. As he told *Playboy* later: 'Even then, with three films that were very successful overseas, I had a rough time cracking the Hollywood scene. Not only was there a movie prejudice against television actors, but there was a feeling that an American actor making an Italian movie was sort of taking a step backward.' United Artists had bought and distributed the Spaghetti Westerns in America and it was pressure from their satellite companies in Europe, asking when the next Clint Eastwood movie was coming, that brought about their decision to back *Hang 'Em High*. At $1,600,000 it was a reasonably low budget film, but with a fee of $400,000 plus twenty-five per cent of the net profits Eastwood

Left and below: Eastwood has a character with a name for the first time; Jed Cooper in the Hollywood production Hang 'Em High *(1968). Right: As Walt Coogan in* Coogan's Bluff *(1968).*

immediately established himself as a highly-paid star. He was also an influential one; he persuaded Leonard Freeman, the producer of the film who had also written the original screenplay, that Ted Post, who had never made a feature but had impressed Eastwood greatly on *Rawhide,* should be the director of the project.

A sturdy cast of well-known and later to be better-known actors like Ben Johnson, L.Q. Jones, Bruce Dern and Dennis Hopper were shipped down to Las Cruces, New Mexico to support the star of Almería. The film began brilliantly and brutally with a lynch mob leaving Eastwood for dead at the end of a rope.

He is rescued, eventually cleared of suspicion, and appointed deputy by Judge Fenton (a clear copy of the famous hanging-Judge Parker). Jed (Eastwood) proceeds to clean up the worst crimes in the state, but doubting his own motives, he always avoids capturing the gang of nine vigilantes who were responsible for his near-death.

Inexorably, the confrontation comes nearer. The

leader of the gang, Captain Wilson (played by Ed Begley), returns to town and wounds Jed. This provides an encounter with another victim of the vigilantes, Rachel (Inger Stevens) who nurses Jed and reveals that the same gang raped her after murdering her husband. Jed finally hunts down the vigilantes; Captain Wilson commits suicide rather than face a shoot-out or something worse with the deputy. Revenge providing no satisfaction, Jed tries to resign, but Judge Fenton persuades him to stay on. The film remains a study of differences between public and private forms of justice, but the motivations behind both are left confused and unsatisfying.

The film was certainly a better than average Western and in portraying the carnival-like atmosphere of public hangings was unusually acute in social observation; but it had neither the magic nor the mystique of a Leone film. Despite Clint's unchanging face and broad-brimmed hat, the character he portrayed was very different from the Stranger: he had more dialogue, he had a romance of sorts, and although he was equally proficient with the gun he always waited for the court's justice rather than dispensing his own, as he readily did in the Italian Westerns. He also exhibited less of the dry humour that had characterised the Stranger, and most

Left and below: The American public loved Eastwood's first US-made Western. Hang 'Em High *covered its costs within weeks of opening in August 1968.*

sacrilegious of all, he had a name, Jed Cooper. But he had judged the taste of the American public shrewdly, for they loved the film. It covered its costs within weeks of opening in August 1968, and at one stage was United Artists' leading money-maker that season.

Twelve years after Universal had shown him the door for failing to look like any of their contract stars, they opened it again in 1967. Doubtless if they had still had their training programme they would have been searching for a Clint Eastwood look-alike. Clint made a deal with Jennings Lang, an executive producer at Universal to make his next film, *Coogan's Bluff*, before the script was even finished. He liked the idea of the story which was set in the present — the first major role he had that was. It concerned a hick Arizona deputy being sent to New York to bring home a prisoner. Eastwood himself had arrived in New York as a fairly ingenuous westerner and he remembered that although he like everyone had been bewildered by the place, once he had got his bearings he had kept his wits about him and coped. So he felt the character should show at least a 'prairie cunning'. Besides, James Stewart and other actors had already done small-town-guy-in-big-city movies. During discussions with the director, Alex Segal, and another writer, they found themselves unable to agree on a common ground for the storyline. This proved

A Westerner hits New York: Clint Eastwood as an Arizona deputy in Coogan's Bluff *(1968).*

fortuitous. It led to the departure of Alex Segal — and Clint's first meeting with Don Siegel who was to play an even more substantial part than Sergio Leone in his unfaltering rise to fame. Siegel still doesn't know why he was hired for the project: 'I think there was a computer mistake at Universal — they lived by computers there, you know. There was a chap called Alex Segal that walked off the picture in preparation and Clint wanted a very good director — Don Taylor — to take over and it went through the computer and came out Don Siegel.'

Not true. Another director, Mark Rydell, had been approached but modestly turned the movie down because he felt he couldn't prepare it in time. He recommended the only available director whom he thought could — Don Siegel. Eastwood had seen and liked Siegel's film *The Killers* with Lee Marvin and Ronald Reagan. It had originally been intended as a television film but was given a theatrical release instead. Siegel however had more of a reputation as a maker of cult films like *Invasion of the Body Snatchers* or social films like *Riot in Cell Block Eleven* than a man guaranteed to bring in a big popular hit. Nevertheless, Eastwood gambled on using him and like all Eastwood's gambles, being a combination of intuition, cunning and unbreakable luck, it paid off.

I first met Siegel when I was working on a BBC profile of John Wayne for the Bicentennial. It had not been the best of times. Siegel was directing Wayne in *The Shootist* and the Duke had fallen ill with 'flu

Above: Eastwood behind and in front of the camera in Coogan's Bluff. *This film introduced him to one of his most influential directors, Don Siegel. Right: Clint discusses a scene with Siegel on set.*

veering towards pneumonia. On his return to the Warners back lot to finish the picture, Wayne was still visibly unwell and even more visibly irascible. Siegel handled the great man with patience and good humour. As the Duke rolled around the saloon floor in his death throes instructing the director how to shoot the scene as if he had left film school the day before, Siegel reacted with commendable, if prudent, restraint.

Siegel had originally set out to be an actor. Although born in Chicago he went to England for his education at Jesus College, Cambridge and then to the Royal Academy of Dramatic Art in London. On his return to America in 1933 he worked as an assistant film librarian at Warner Brothers and drew attention to himself with a documentary film, *Hitler Lives*, which won an Academy Award in 1946. This led to a succession of B-pictures for the company, some of which turned out to be much better than many A-pictures.

When I met him again to talk about Eastwood he was in great form. Over some generous whiskies we reminisced about the ordeal of the last days of *The*

Shootist. He has a deadpan wit which didn't disappear when we went on the record. I asked him if he'd seen Clint in *Rawhide* and what opinion he had formed of him. He answered that this was without doubt the most destructive question he'd ever been asked because, although Clint didn't know it, he'd never seen him in *Rawhide.* He went on, however, to say that he'd seen the Spaghetti Westerns and thought they were marvellous, that Leone was excellent with the camera and that they contained a great deal of imagination. 'Of course, you can't take the stories seriously,' he added, 'they are what they are, they're Spaghetti Westerns. I enjoyed the fun.' Finally I asked him if he thought it was clever of Clint to create the role he did—the sparse man with no name—in the laconic style that he used. 'Well,' Siegel replied, 'from one standpoint, looking at his bank account, I would say he was brilliant.'

Eastwood invited Siegel up to Carmel for a weekend and the chemistry was instant. 'I don't know how Clint felt about me but I liked what I saw. He was a very pleasant chap and we had a drink or two, or a

Eastwood frequently does his own stunt work, as in this motorbike chase in Coogan's Bluff. *He is a perfectionist about detail and realises that his face should be identifiable in action scenes.*

"brew" as he said, and we went ahead and made the picture.' Jennings Lang was glad to approve the new pairing, telling Eastwood that whereas he was 'warm' in Italy, Siegel was 'warm' in France, where Siegel had a substantial following. However, neither Siegel nor Eastwood were happy with the script which, by then, was in its tenth draft. Dean Riesner from Clint's *Rawhide* days was brought in as a writer and he, Eastwood and Siegel found an earlier draft which was a much more acceptable basis on which to work. For the first time in his life, Eastwood was able to sit down and contribute to the dialogue at the time of writing, instead of being a 'script doctor' on the set.

His influence on *Coogan's Bluff* is discernible — not just because he doesn't utter a word until four and a half minutes after he appears and even then it is a cryptic 'put your pants on, chief' — but because, unlike the deputy in *Hang 'Em High*, Coogan has a pithy turn of phrase, the surface manifestation of a reservoir of laconic humour. When he takes his first taxi in New York, Coogan asks the driver: 'How many stores are there in this town named Blooming-

dales?' The driver replies, 'one'. 'We passed it twice.' When they get to their destination the taxi driver is adamant that 'it's still $2.95, including the luggage'. Coogan hands him the money. 'Here's $3.00, including the tip.'

Those who know Eastwood are familiar with this sparse, well-timed, dry style of delivery, often accompanied by a beautifully measured glance with his expressive eyes. The first time I met Eastwood, his press agent, Dick Guttman, was late. He rushed into Eastwood's office, grabbed a handful of peanuts from a bowl and while munching them apologised. 'I hope you started without me', he began. Clint paused. 'Yes, we've been doing some talking. Didn't want to start on the peanuts till you came, though.' On location in Mexico for *Two Mules For Sister Sara* someone observed how thin he had become. Eastwood came right back: 'Yes, lost about ten pounds waiting for my meals to arrive.'

On the back lot at Warners a girl rushed up to him in genuine anger. 'I've wanted to tell you this for a long time. You're a no good son of a bitch for always

making Mexicans the bad guys in your films and then killing them.' Eastwood looked at her. 'Don't be angry; I kill lots of other people too.'

Coogan's Bluff concerns the exploits of a policeman from Arizona, Walt Coogan, who is sent to New York to extradite a prisoner, Ringerman (Don Stroud), and bring him back to town. The film opens in Arizona with a character-establishing sequence: Coogan tracks down an Indian wordlessly, then on his way back into town, he ties up the Indian, horse-like to a railing outside a girlfriend's house while he pays a brief visit.

Coogan is then dispatched to New York, and arrives in cowboy hat and boots. The convict Ringerman is in hospital, and the New York police officer Lieutenant McElroy (Lee J. Cobb) refuses to turn him over to Coogan's custody. Coogan naturally resents this action and takes his prisoner anyway. Pride coming before a fall, he loses Ringerman, due to a plot hatched by the criminal's girlfriend (Trisha Sterling) who arranges for three villains to beat Coogan up.

McElroy comes to visit Coogan recovering in hospital from the attack, and tells him to drop the case, but Coogan refuses, gets out of hospital, tracks down the girlfriend and after an efficient seduction scene elicits directions from her to what he believes to be Ringerman's hideout. Once again he is deceived, only this time he gets beaten up by six men instead of three. Coogan doggedly finds his way back to the girl's apartment where he threatens to kill her. Eventually she leads him to Ringerman. By now Coogan

Coogan takes his prisoner, Ringerman (Don Stroud), back home.

is beginning to identify with his victim, so that when he finally captures Ringerman, he doesn't gun him down but follows McElroy's advice and adopts proper procedures.

His ruthless cool is softened by his struggles, and a flickering understanding of the convict's position begins to dawn. In the helicopter going back to Arizona, he hands Ringerman a cigarette. He also manages the suggestion of a relationship with a social worker, Julie (Susan Clark) for whom at first he felt nothing but antagonism. The film ends with her at the airport, waving him off.

The style of Coogan is Eastwood and so are some of Coogan's attitudes. When the Arizona deputy gets to the metropolis, the police are almost as much a hindrance to him as the prisoner, Ringerman, and his friends. Eastwood, however, knows where the audience sympathy lies. 'I think people who are frustrated with their work or their lives, want to go to a movie and be taken on a trip back to an era when the individual was supreme. They see the red tape and the bureaucracy in their own lives and they respect the individual who fights it.' He also had his own comment to make on urban living. Coogan takes a long look at the city of New York and reflects: 'I was just trying to picture the way it was before people fouled it up.'

The tautly-written script and the beneficial

presence of Don Siegel earned Eastwood his best reviews to date. *Time* magazine wrote: 'Eastwood, who has hitherto displayed nothing more than a capacity for iron-jawed belligerency in a series of Italian-made Westerns, performs with a measure of real feeling in the first role that fits him as comfortably as his tooled leather boots.'

While he was dashing around the streets of New York, plots were being hatched in Europe. The former agent-turned-producer, Elliott Kastner, wanted to make a big budget war movie with a top-line cast. One day while waiting for a train at a suburban English station he noticed that all the paperback books on sale seemed to be by one man—Alistair MacLean. He went to see MacLean and told him that Richard Burton was keen to play in a film written by him. Then he went to see Burton and told him Alistair MacLean was anxious to write a screenplay especially for him. Burton had seen MacLean's successful *Guns of Navarone* and was more than interested. The result was *Where Eagles Dare*.

When MGM embraced the project they knew they needed a substantial American action star to guarantee the box-office receipts in the States and their $800,000 offer to Eastwood was both timely and acceptable. (Burton was reputed to have received

Clint Eastwood's first visit to London in 1968 was to make Where Eagles Dare *with Richard Burton, his first international starring role.*

$1,200,000 as well as top billing.)

When Eastwood arrived at Heathrow Airport, London, in 1968, he was entirely on his own, with a bag in each hand. As he was about to go through customs there was a commotion ahead delaying his progress. He inquired of a policeman what the problem was and the officer pointed to the mêlée of people. 'It's Richard Burton and Elizabeth Taylor and their entourage. They've just flown in from Geneva in their private jet.'

At that time, the beginning of 1968, the Burtons must have been the most photographed and written-about couple in the world. When Richard declared his love for Elizabeth with a diamond worth half a million pounds it provided breakfast-time reading for everyone from Allahabad to Auckland. Wherever they went they were surrounded by a cloud of retainers and treated like surrogate royalty. As Eastwood stood in the customs hall he reflected that his new-found reputation wasn't in the same league as theirs when it came to acreage in the press. Nor did he want it to be. Since his ride to fame in *Rawhide* he had sedulously guarded the areas of his life that he deemed to have no relevance to his box-office success. He also wondered how he would get on with the turbulent couple.

As it turned out they got on excellently. Elizabeth came to the set for much of the shooting and chatted away amiably. Richard and Eastwood shared a schoolboyish sense of humour and a mutual respect

Above: Eastwood with Elizabeth Taylor and Richard Burton during the filming of Where Eagles Dare. *Below: handling the action as Shaeffer in this film.*

for each other's very different style of acting. It was Eastwood's first experience of working with a largely British cast: 'I enjoyed working with people who had been brought up in the more traditional theatre. I'd been brought up strictly in films. But basically it all comes down to the same thing. The picture was a bit of a satire, but no matter how much you're sending something up, you have to believe in it for the moment yourself.'

Burton told me that he was sympathetic to the potential clash of styles. 'I didn't know him at all, I had never seen him. Indeed he had a very difficult task on his hands because the other actors in the picture like Michael Hordern and Patrick Wymark and Bill Squire and Donald Houston were all classical actors, and Clint was, unquestionably, not a classical actor. However, within three minutes of shooting time we all realised we were in the presence of a very remarkable man. I was fascinated to watch his particular kind of behaviour and his movements. There is a certain line of American actors who are immensely different from British actors; Spencer Tracy, James Stewart, Bob Mitchum, they have a kind of dynamic lethargy, they appear to do nothing and they do everything.

'It was instructive to watch Clint move round those so-called classical actors because he reduced everything to an absolute minimum. If he had a four line speech, he would reduce it to four words and it was enormously effective. I'm afraid he used me a bit in those days; he allowed me to do all the talking.'

A point which Eastwood is only too happy to confirm. 'The character I played had tremendous amounts of exposition. We'd stop and we'd talk for hours about what's going to happen and the director and I felt that this was very impractical. So we let Richard's character handle the exposition—he has a beautiful speaking voice and he's very good at that sort of thing—and I would handle the shooting which they felt I was very good at.'

As he had demonstrated in an unmatchable succession of adventure stories, Alistair MacLean knew that the way to entertain an audience most grippingly was not to stay within the bounds of credibility but to take several paces outside them. This time Eastwood plays Shaeffer, a professional killer in the American army who joins an international commando team led by a British Major, John Smith (Richard Burton). The group is sent to the Bavarian Alps supposedly to rescue an American general who possesses highly valuable information. Actually the general is a fake, and the real purpose of the mission is to discover which one of their number is a Nazi spy who has succeeded in penetrating British intelligence. First one and then another commando is killed; the group succeeds in entering the impregnable fortress where the general is held, with the assistance of a woman agent, Mary Ellison (Mary Ure). However, three more of the unit are captured, forcing Smith and Shaeffer to surrender to the Nazis. The two men escape and gain entry to the castle again where Smith reveals the underlying mission and the three 'captured' commandoes are exposed as Nazi agents. The film concludes with a dramatic escape sequence as Smith and Shaeffer, the woman agent and the fake general hurtle through various explosions to escape from the castle by cable car. They eventually grab a special plane back to England. During the flight, in a final improbable twist to the plot, Smith forces one of the mission organisers to confess that he too is a double agent and allows him gracefully to commit suicide and avoid public scandal—the colonel jumps out of the plane.

The final escape sequence, as in *The Guns of Navarone,* fell firmly into the 'with one bound Jack was free' category, as Eastwood wrestled his way down the perpendicular mountain-side on top of the cable car. (Well, maybe not actually Eastwood. He does tend to call the film in private 'Where Doubles Dare'.)

It was a happy unit and Eastwood enjoyed himself in London. He gave the film's insurers cause for concern by renting a motorcycle and touring the local pubs; Jack Straw's Castle on Hampstead Heath was a particular favourite. Intrigued by the peculiar names the British traditionally give their hostelries, he later named his own restaurant in Carmel by an even more bizarre one: The Hog's Breath Inn.

His friendship with the Burtons blossomed. He and Elizabeth decided to appear in a film together sometime in the future and she suggested the property, *Two Mules For Sister Sara,* which he read and liked. A tentative deal was set up with Universal. When he

Burton observed that Eastwood's acting style had a kind of 'dynamic lethargy'.

went with Burton to the Austrian Alps for the location sequences of *Where Eagles Dare,* the beer and parties flowed. Even Raquel Welch was said to have been lured to the location by the knowledge that everyone was having such a good time.

Paradoxically when films are fun to make, they tend to turn out badly on the screen (although the reverse is not necessarily the case). But director Brian Hutton managed to combine the jollity of the filming with a crisp thrilling line of action which turned it into one of the biggest box-office hits of the sixties. Distributors were uncertain whether the name Burton, MacLean or Eastwood was the real reason people were flooding to see the film and used whichever was their preference; in truth it was a combination of all three.

The Oxford-educated Shakespearean actor and the former furnace stoker turned cowboy remained good friends although they never worked together again. When Burton was making *The Heretic* in Burbank Studios in 1976 he went along in his priest's costume to visit Clint's bungalow. The receptionist, not recognising him, told him the superstar was too busy to meet him. Her hand flew to her mouth and her heart to her shoes when the priest walked away with the words, 'Tell him Richard Burton called'. Later in the week Eastwood arrived, unannounced, where Burton was filming. 'How did you find me?' asked the

Shooting his way out of the Germans' castle in Where Eagles Dare.

Welshman. 'I just followed the pipes,' rejoined Clint, referring to Burton's mellifluous tones.

'I hope I'll work with him again,' Burton told me. 'Now he's so fantastically important maybe he'll give me a job.'

When Eastwood returned home from Europe in the summer of 1968 it was to meet for the first time Kyle Clinton Eastwood—his son. Maggie had been unable to protract her pregnancy any longer and Kyle arrived just four days before his father returned on 19th May. He had Clint's mouth and eyelashes, and Maggie's eyes and nose. Unfortunately Eastwood had only a month to admire him before his schedule took him to Baker, Oregon where he spent the next five months making his first, and last, musical, *Paint Your Wagon.*

If *Where Eagles Dare* had been his most enjoyable experience in movie making up till then, *Paint Your Wagon* certainly proved to be his least. Following the unstoppable worldwide success of *The Sound of Music* (a film that so mesmerised its audience into going to it again and again that one woman in Cardiff owned up to having sat through it more than three hundred times), Paramount decided to put all its eggs into the musical basket. Naturally they wanted the world's biggest female film star, Julie Andrews, to play the lead but she preferred to work with her husband, Blake Edwards, on *Darling Lili,* also for Paramount. So Jean Seberg was drafted-in instead. Paramount considered her a bit of a risk although she was popular in Europe. However, the company felt secure with a proven Broadway hit by Alan Jay

Lerner and Frederick Loewe (who hadn't done too badly with *My Fair Lady*), a trustworthy director in Joshua Logan who had made the film of *South Pacific* and two of America's top stars, Lee Marvin and Clint Eastwood.

The plot of *Paint Your Wagon* was based on a successful Broadway stage musical: Elizabeth (Jean Seberg) marries an aging prospector, Ben Rumson (Lee Marvin), but finds that she has to live not just with her husband but also his partner (known laconically as Pardner), played by Eastwood. The trio gets involved in several prospecting adventures, culminating in the collapse of a small town (incidentally called No Name City), which is caused by the tunnels the two men dig beneath it. Finally, Elizabeth remains with the younger man while her husband wanders off on his own. In a change of character for Eastwood, Pardner turns out to be the stayer, giving up prospecting in order to settle down and farm with his new-found love.

The triangular relationship between the arthritic and bewhiskered Marvin, his wife Miss Seberg and the charming 'Pardner' never jelled and the songs tended to interrupt rather than carry along the story-line. Moreover the Lear jets and helicopters used to take the cast to the location were better organised than the actual shooting, which ran out of time and over budget to the unharmonious tune of $17 million. In fact, Paramount's plans for their two big musicals

The stars of Paint Your Wagon *(1969), Clint's next
adventure in a new genre. For his musical début he
co-starred with Jean Seberg (right), and a bewhiskered Lee
Marvin (centre), who was her husband and Clint's
gold-hunting partner.*

sadly misfired. The expense of *Paint Your Wagon*
coupled with the unconvincing performance of Julie
Andrews, poorly directed in *Darling Lili,* brought the
company to the verge of collapse.

Eastwood's golf improved as he whiled away the
days when he wasn't on call, and so did his singing.
He took some lessons to reawaken the vocal chords
which had fallen into disuse since he played the piano
in the bars in Northern California and had suffered
the setback of muted public response to his single
'Unknown Girl'. The producers of *Paint Your Wagon*
didn't even know he could sing when they signed
him. 'I suppose I'd have been cast in the film
anyway,' Eastwood said later. 'They would have
looped me or something.'

He had two solos in the film: 'I Still See Eliza' and
'I Talk to the Trees', which were delivered as wistful

Attending the celebrity première of Paint Your Wagon *at the Pacific Cinerama Dome Theatre with his wife, Maggie, and Lee Marvin with his lady, Michele.*

soliloquies in a manner that ran totally counter to the tough and taciturn Eastwood character that the public really wanted to see. In America Harve Presnell's rendering of 'They Call the Wind Maria' emerged as the most popular song from the film but in England the unpredictable pop fans fell for Lee Marvin's basso profundo rumbling of 'I Was Born Under a Wandering Star' and it went to the top of the hit parade. (Eastwood's chances of emulating him may have been marred by his song: for many years earlier in England the comedian Spike Milligan had popularised the version, 'I talk to the trees, that's why they put me away'.)

Making a virtue of necessity, Eastwood analysed what was going wrong on and off the set of the film and determined he would never again get involved in such chaos. Being a major star he was privy to the behind-the-scenes disagreements and could observe that, even when they finished filming, there was little harmony on the committee.

'I saw that film in four different versions: the director's version, the producer's version and then the coalition of all the studio executives and their versions. The director's version, the first one, was actually the best one but that wasn't the one that got released. As an actor you're very, very vulnerable. They can make you look like an idiot if they want to.' With this lesson Eastwood resolved then and there to put his destiny firmly into his own hands. 'It wasn't the smoothest-running picture I've ever been on and, for that reason I started my own company and figured

I'd try some other approaches at production.'

He was as good as his word. With the exception of *Kelly's Heroes,* for which he had already signed a contract, Eastwood never again worked for anybody except himself. His company, Malpaso (named either after his manager's myopic advice about Almería or a creek of that name on the edge of Eastwood's ever-expanding Californian territory) was already in existence to alleviate his tax burden and hire out his services to other companies. Now it became a realistic movie-making enterprise.

Initially Malpaso had its offices in Universal Studios but later it moved to a discreet Spanish bungalow on the Warner Brothers lot at Burbank. Eastwood held the controlling stock but no office— the late Irving Leonard was the President. The company was run by Robert Daley, another man who has been a major influence in Eastwood's career. They had met in 1954 when they found themselves living in the same apartment block and were both working at Universal Studios—Eastwood as a contract actor and Daley as an accountant. At the weekends they would sit by the pool and discuss the film industry. Daley was from the first impressed by Clint's acumen. 'He's extremely knowledgeable about the business. One of the things I noticed when he and

I formed this company together, on the business aspects, he would ask me a question and he'd never ask that question again because once he'd heard the answer he'd never forget it.'

Daley expanded his knowledge of the film industry by becoming a first assistant and a unit manager. He and Eastwood shared a common business philosophy: put as much of the cost of the film on the screen rather than wasting it on limousines and etceteras. As a friend, Daley was also impressed by Clint's attitude to life. 'I remember the day he was signed to do *Rawhide*. I tried to find him to congratulate him but he was outside washing one of their two old cars—never more than one of them would run at any given moment. There he was in some very old clothes in the driveway washing the car and I tried to congratulate him but he just kind of shrugged it off. He thought it was just too good to be true and he wouldn't count on it. Almost like the Chinese philosophy, "Let's not talk about it because it will go away or something bad will happen".'

Very little bad happened after that. Daley, a sturdily built, powerful-looking man who radiates a confident authority now produces all of Eastwood's films. Around him he has formed a small but dedicated team. Fritz Manes, possibly Eastwood's best friend, left his job with television's Channel Two in San

Eastwood established: relaxing in the home of his dreams in Carmel, California.

Francisco to become an associate producer. Manes had been at school with Eastwood. Even then he had discerned the drive in the man. 'He was always a natural leader but a natural leader with a different type of approach. He never had to look behind him because he always knew that *they* were there. And that holds true right now within the film business. Clint never looks behind him because he knows that the troops are there and that they're always performing, and if they're not performing he knows about it.'

Manes takes a special interest in the publicity of Malpaso's films and often has a small part in them himself, usually on the safer end of a gun. He and Clint are devoted fishermen and have a succession of hilarious anecdotes about trips they have spent together. Sonia Chernus, who pointed Clint in the direction of *Rawhide*, left CBS to join the company as a script reader, and the office was masterfully run by the secretary-cum-receptionist Judy, 'Jude the Prude' as she was sometimes known, who could switch from an iron curtain of protection to the most courteous of welcomes, depending on who was bidding for the great man's time.

So by the end of 1968 Eastwood had put his life into a more than stable perspective. He was thirty-eight years old, he had a happy marriage, a son, his own company, a recently completed dream house in a location that exceeds anyone's dreams and a substantial accumulation of land. He was also the fifth most popular film star in the United States.

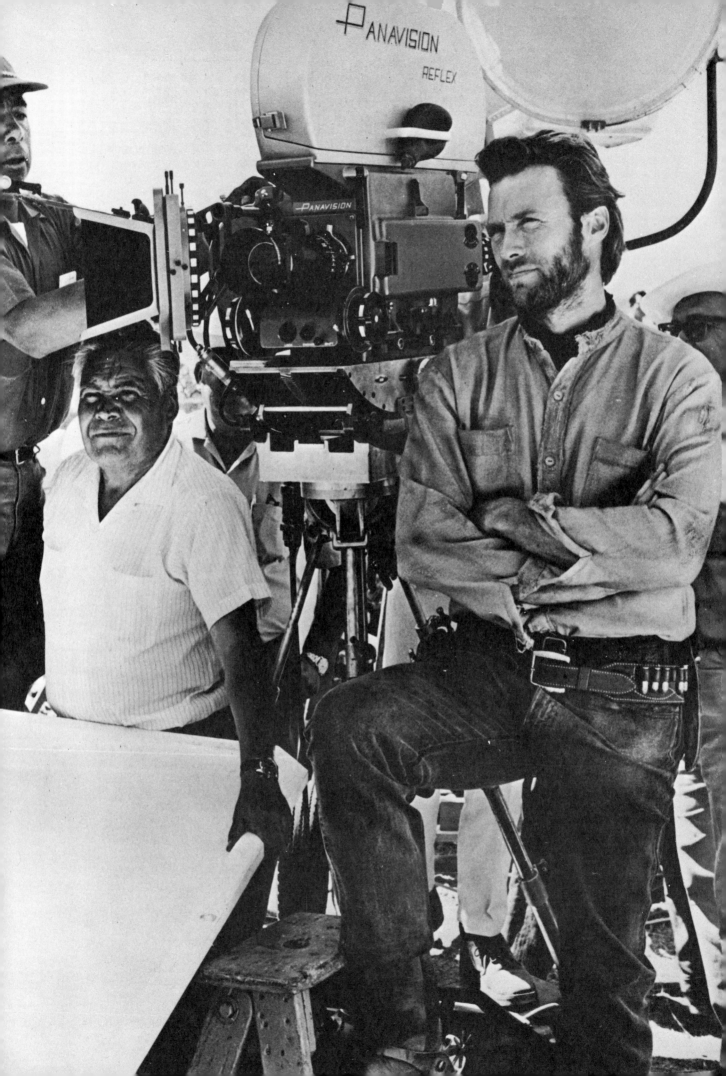

THE MYSTIQUE DEEPENS

Eastwood was flattered by Elizabeth Taylor's invitation to be her co-star. She was, at that time, the most written-about woman in the world, as famous for her private life as for her public performances but nevertheless a talented screen presence and a perfect foil for him. His only attempt at a romantic lead in *Paint Your Wagon* had been less than successful in his own estimation, and here was an opportunity to redress that error and break out of the 'Loner' image. So he lost little time in going ahead and setting up the movie *Two Mules For Sister Sara.* After their successful collaboration on *Coogan's Bluff,* Siegel was happy to direct and with a Taylor-Eastwood-Siegel property on offer Universal were only too pleased to join up with Malpaso. Since it was decided to shoot the picture in Mexico, the Government of that country had to approve the script which, to nobody's surprise they readily did, since it centred on the peasant struggle against the occupying French forces, and the statutory Mexican film partnership was formed. One of the country's favourite actors, Pedro Armendariz Junior, was cast, ironically, as a French officer and hundreds of locals were hired to work in front of and behind the camera.

In the spring of 1969, Eastwood flew to Mexico; everything was ready to go but suddenly Elizabeth Taylor wasn't. Whether she had gone cold on the idea of playing opposite Eastwood or had merely disliked the thought of three months of discomfort on a Mexican location is unrecorded, but preparations were so far advanced that it was impossible to cancel the project. A rapid search for a replacement ended with Shirley MacLaine, fresh from *Sweet Charity,* a film musical that had failed to excite the public. The script was hurriedly rewritten to accommodate her tomboy style and twinkling humour; no easy task since it's hard to think of two actresses more dissimilar than her and Elizabeth Taylor.

The story is set in the middle of the last century. Mexico, having suffered the Spanish invasion, now has a French occupation to contend with. To add insult to injury, the French have installed an Austrian emperor, Maximilian, on the throne. Juarista guerrillas —the possible equivalent of Sandanistas in Nicaragua this century—are fighting to restore power to the people. Sister Sara, supposedly a nun, has espoused their cause and is accordingly hiding from the French troops. When Eastwood, playing what else but a lone hired gun owing allegiance to neither party, comes across her, she is about to be raped by three men. Luckily for her he dispatches them in his own time-honoured fashion. But unlike the Man With No Name

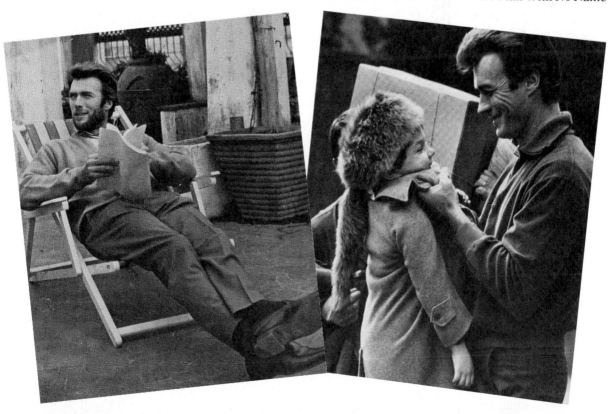

Above: Eastwood preparing for the filming of a sequence where he is wounded by an Indian arrow in Two Mules For Sister Sara. *Left: Less than nun-like behaviour from Sister Sara.*

(in this film he's called Hogan) he doesn't turn and ride away but accompanies her in her flight. Her behaviour intrigues him as it becomes increasingly less nun-like: she smokes cigars, she downs tequila and her language becomes more and more profane. She explains that she has a special dispensation for these excesses. Hogan's enchantment with her reaches its peak when she skilfully removes an Indian arrow from his body having even more skilfully anaesthetised him, by getting him drunk first. The scene works better than any of the knockabout humour that precedes it and is reputed to be Eastwood's favourite in the film. After helping her to blow up a French supply train he is persuaded to organise the Juaristas in an attack on an impregnable French fort. (Made of papier mâché, it took the unit construction workers six months to build and the director one night to destroy.) Having respectfully held his distance because of her holy status, Hogan learns on the eve of the attack that she is not a nun, but a prostitute. After the successful onslaught on the French he has sufficient energy left to satiate his long-suppressed desires, but by now he is under her spell and the film ends with him, Sancho Panza to her Quixote, riding into the desert behind her, minding her belongings on two mules. This end is in considerable contrast to the usual conclusion of Leone's films, in which the Stranger merely disappears into the mists of time. The change of image was certainly the reason why the audience didn't warm to the picture with anything like the enthusiasm they exhibited for Eastwood's previous characterisations.

The emphasis was wrong; Miss MacLaine had top billing. As Eastwood observed to De Witt Bodeen, the Hollywood writer: 'The film is really a two-character story, and the woman has the best part—something I'm sure Shirley noticed. It's a kind of *African Queen* gone West.' But their chemistry never reached the heights of Hepburn and Bogart—a challenge made harder by Miss MacLaine's ill-health. She was sick, the production was delayed and she just wanted to 'finish the picture and get the hell back to humanity and civilisation'. Nearly all the American cast and crew fell foul of Montezuma's Revenge—only Eastwood stayed healthy, fortified by a diet of pineapples and papayas. Even he lost a lot of weight and informed visiting journalists that on his return to America he would build himself up on grain-fed steaks.

Siegel's action sequences in blowing up the train and taking the fort were as powerful as ever and his eye for authenticity didn't let him down, but the long desert sequences between Eastwood and MacLaine seemed even longer because his pacing was awry and the script bare. Even the characterisation' of Hogan was unsure. Despite the memories conjured up by the tinkling strains of Ennio Morricone's score, Eastwood was portraying a man who was too verbal and too fallible for his public to accept.

Off the screen he was still the shy, gentle man that the public never saw. When required to kill a rattlesnake, at first he refused and then did so only with extreme reluctance—'It wasn't the happiest thing I ever did.' One evening the English journalist, Meriel McCooey, observed an assistant director trying to stamp to death a moth as big as a bat that was interrupting the scene. Eastwood shouted, 'Leave it, leave it, they need killers like you in Vietnam,' then cupped the insect in his hands and guided it to safety. 'I think violence like that is so unnecessary,' he told McCooey. 'It wasn't doing any harm. A little while back the word went round that we needed iguanas for the film so this guy turned up with a bundle of them strung on a string like a bunch of bananas. I bought the lot for five pesos each and let them all go.'

Another journalist reported that Eastwood got so angry with a horse on the set that he punched it in the mouth, an act that seems so out of character that I confronted him with it. He was happy to deny the story which had surprisingly become widespread. 'I don't know where that rumour came from. There's plenty of reason to get mad at horses but it isn't their fault. There's a lot of aspects of filming they don't like. They don't like microphones across the top of their heads and they don't like reflectors in their eyes. Besides I think I've matured to the point where I'm a lot less temperamental than I used to be.

He had to exercise further restraint before he could fulfil his intention to make all his future films under the Malpaso banner. He had already contracted to go to Yugoslavia for five months in 1970 to make *The Warriors*—a film subsequently retitled *Kelly's Heroes,* indicating the emphatic performance Eastwood gave in the title role. Restraint was made easier by an offer of a salary and a percentage that looked like topping the million-dollar mark for the first time in his career. The picture was also going to be in the competent hands of Brian Hutton, who had demonstrated a magician's sleight of hand in turning the less than credible exploits in *Where Eagles Dare* into a box-office hit.

The script, by another Englishman, Troy Kennedy Martin, was in the funny-macho style of *The Dirty Dozen,* with more emphasis on the fun. Telly Savalas, yet to be immortalised as Kojak, put on his fatigues once again, and Caroll O'Connor, yet to be immortalised as Archie Bunker, played a General. Eastwood's main foil was Donald Sutherland, fresh from *M.A.S.H.* and trailing the same iconoclastic attitude to the army; in fact Sutherland very nearly stole the film in his role of a spaced-out tank commander. Don Rickles, the American comedian, looked after the Ernest Borgnine role. Mr Rickles is wont to portray himself as an irascible and heartless man on American television, so much so that Johnny Carson once remarked that Rickles's idea of a good joke was to ring up all the prisoners awaiting execution on death row and tell them they had been reprieved and then ring back later to say 'only joking'. On the set of *Kelly's Heroes* Rickles found himself on the receiving end of some callous Eastwood humour. Having injured his leg, albeit only slightly, the sight of blood made him think he had been shot. As the others anxiously consoled him, Eastwood audibly remarked, 'Better get Shecky Greene into costume.' Rickles, it is reported, was not amused.

The plot of the movie was a simple one, guaranteeing the minimum of complexity and the maximum of action. The film was set during World War II in post-D-Day France. Private Kelly (Eastwood) learns that there is a cache of $16 million dollars' worth of Nazi gold bullion in a town still held by the Germans. Being less interested in winning the war than in a little self-enrichment he decides to liberate the hoard privately. Even he is unable to take on the Nazi war-machine single-handed so he is obliged to recruit some fellow conspirators, inevitably the motley band that has graced American movie army platoons since Sergeant Bilko shouted his first command. Eastwood is convinced that the retreating Germans will blow up the bridge leading into the town but tank commander Donald Sutherland chides him for his bleak outlook: 'Don't keep giving me the negative waves—come on with the positive waves.' In a memorable scene Sutherland and his men observe the bridge through their binoculars. With glee Sutherland points out that it is still standing. As the Germans blow it up before their very eyes, there is a pregnant pause and then the unnecessary observa-

The last film Eastwood made for someone else before he formed his own company, Malpaso: MGM's Kelly's Heroes *(1970), a war adventure story directed by Brian Hutton.*

tion, 'No it ain't'. Eventually he, Eastwood and Savalas advance on the German tank guarding the gold to the strains of a mock Morricone score. The mission is ultimately successful with the men happy to let their General take the glory of liberating the town while they divide the more tangible reward.

On the level at which the movie appeared to set its sights—loud action, broad comedy and larger-than-life characters—the film was very successful and its enduring popularity on television reruns is witness to this. But Eastwood divined a good deal more in the original screenplay and was very disappointed in the end product, as he told Arthur Knight, the American journalist and film studies professor, who interviewed him for *Playboy* magazine in 1974. 'That film could have been one of the best war movies ever. And it should have been; it had the best script, a good cast, a subtle anti-war message. But somehow everything got lost. The picture got bogged down shooting in Yugoslavia and it just ended up as the story of a bunch of American screw-offs in World War Two. Some of the key scenes got cut out. I even called up Jim Aubrey, who was then the head of MGM, and said, "For God's sake, don't

run that picture for the critics until Brian, the director, has had a chance to do some more work on it. You're going to cut off maybe millions of dollars in box-office receipts." Aubrey said he'd think it over, but I'm sure when he hung up the phone he said to himself, "What does this frigging actor know about millions of dollars. Forget it." It was released without further work and it did badly.'

Not surprisingly today the 'frigging actor', knowing quite a lot about millions of dollars, has final cut on all his films and no studio chief would dream of alienating him by turning down such a request.

To protect himself from the vagaries of the star-studded, big studio picture, in 1971 Eastwood returned to the safe and welcome arms of Don Siegel. He had loaned the director a copy of Thomas Cullinan's novel *The Beguiled* after reading it and enjoying it himself during the making of *Two Mules*. After *Kelly's Heroes* Eastwood was no longer sure that it was the correct next move for himself as an actor, but Siegel was, and he reconvinced Eastwood that the story had great potential and was a timely change of direction for him. To this day Siegel remains adamant that the decision was a good one. He told me: 'I can't speak for Clint but I know that when we did *Beguiled* he was very, very happy. He feels it's his best film. I feel it's my best film, even though it was an unsuccessful film.'

Eastwood (Private Kelly) co-starred with Donald Sutherland (Oddball), who nearly stole the film in his role as a spaced-out tank commander. Right: Private Kelly attempts to take on the Nazi war-machine single-handed.

The Beguiled is a period piece, set in the American Civil War. Eastwood plays Corporal John McBurney, a wounded Yankee who finds refuge in the unusual surroundings of the Farnsworth Seminary For Young Ladies, an oasis of gentle manners and repressed sexuality run by the despotic Martha Farnsworth (Geraldine Page). She is prevailed upon by her assistant Edwina Dabney (Elizabeth Hartman) and by the girls not to hand the soldier over to the Confederates—a blue rag tied to their gate would alert the passing troops to an enemy within—but to nurse him out of his delirium and heal his wounded leg. Mindful of the continuing risk of being betrayed and, as yet, not strong enough to run away, McBurney uses the only weapon within his depleted resources to assure a safe stay—sex. He beguiles each of the ladies in turn, both the young and old, so that each one thinks that he has conceived a passion for her and, being charming and handsome, he has very little difficulty in finding his attentions returned. Even Miss Martha, whose previous sexual encounters seem to have been restricted to a dalliance with her brother, falls: 'If this war goes on much longer I'll forget I was a woman.' The delicate balance McBurney must maintain to make each woman think that he has eyes only for her comes apart in the arms of the nubile Carol: 'I'm seventeen but I know a lot more than girls my age ... games for two are more fun.' Having promised both Miss Farnsworth and Miss Dabney that he will spend the night in their beds, he hobbles up the stairs to the room of the succulent pupil and is discovered there *in flagrante delicto* by Edwina. As he tries to get out she flings him down the stairs, letting her ladylike manners drop in her desolation: 'You lying son of a bitch, you bastard, you filthy lecher. I hope you're dead.'

He isn't but he is powerless to resist the bitter revenge that the ladies have in store for him. Miss Farnsworth, quite arbitrarily, declares his wound is gangrenous and with her pupils carries him to the dining room table. A tearful Miss Dabney drugs him with laudanum and wine while her boss, with the gruesome skill of a master-butcher, methodically amputates his leg. It is a symbolic castration, the price he must pay for devious philandering.

Fate temporarily intervenes on McBurney's side. During his recovery he finds a gun and this time with menace instead of charm becomes master of the household. Fired with wine and driven by anger he turns on the women. He dismisses Edwina as a 'virgin bitch', he reveals to the girls that Martha had an incestuous relationship with her brother and, worst of all, he smashes Randolph, the pet tortoise of little Amy who had originally found him when wounded and, up till then, unwaveringly adored him.

The next day, he announces his plans to leave and, surprisingly, to take Edwina with him to be his wife. A farewell supper is prepared. Miss Farnsworth instructs Amy to pick some mushrooms. The infant replies, schemingly, 'I know just where to find them.'

In the penultimate scene, worthy of a Victorian melodrama, the girls and staff sit down with McBurney for dinner. Gentle, polite conversation and polite table manners are the order of the day and the pupils hold back on the mushrooms until their guest has helped himself. The poison doesn't take long to work and the next morning they wrap him in a winding sheet and bury him in the garden.

It is a film that establishes Siegel as a master of his chosen profession. In less subtle hands the story could have assumed farcical overtones but his final blend of sensuality, mystery and sheer horror prevents the audience from ever thinking that aspects of the tale bound into the realms of the absurd. As ever, his sense of place is impeccable. He shot it far away from the sound stages of Burbank on location in an old house in Louisiana. Eastwood considered himself a sufficient draw in his own right, so he was freed from the necessity of casting the film with Hollywood female leads and in Geraldine Page and Elizabeth Hartman he had actresses of real quality who rewarded

Below: The opening scene from The Beguiled *(1971) which Don Siegel considers his best-directed work. Set against the backdrop of the Civil War, Eastwood plays Corporal John McBurney, who seeks refuge in a girls' Seminary.*

Above: McBurney exercises his charms on Carol (Jo Ann Harris). Right: As McBurney, Eastwood proved he was clearly an actor of the widest possible range and talent.

him with unswervingly plausible performances.

From the moment the film begins the audience is aware that a guiding hand is imprinting an original style and tone. Starting with an ancient still of Abraham Lincoln, a montage of photographs with a sound track of the sounds of war effectively gives the story its context in time and place. The picture begins to move and the colour literally bleeds in as the camera pans across to Eastwood's bloody leg. We know that we are about to follow one man's story against the background of war. Eastwood's reedy voice sings presciently 'Come all ye fair maids . . . death will come marching at the beat of a drum.' At the end of the film when he meets his own death in such an unexpected manner for a soldier, the ironic refrain is repeated.

There is an unreality about the house, and the echoing Southern voices of the inmates come as from a dream. Eastwood, who is delirious, takes time to comprehend the reality of his situation. With an editor's instinct, Siegel uses flashbacks and voice-overs to sketch the characters of the four leading ladies. The sooner we know them, the sooner the quadrille can begin. Although every woman is clothed from ankle to collar, a musty sensuality hangs over

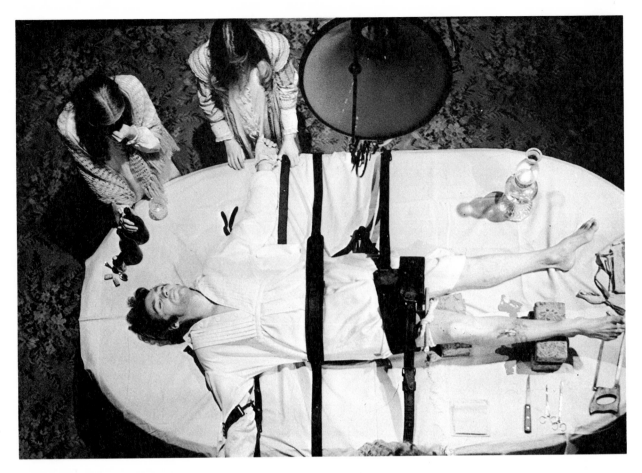

The amputation scene from The Beguiled: *symbolic castration for a philanderer.*

the house, more provocative than any atmosphere in a Playboy mansion. When Miss Edwina sighs 'the war is so close. If the Yankees win they'll rape every one of us', there is more than a hint of hope in her voice. Eastwood becomes rapidly aware that beneath the Southern primness there lurks an earthy lust and exploits his position as the only male, ultimately to his doom. Once Siegel has his audience in his grasp he plays on its feelings mercilessly, switching abruptly from Eastwood's unfulfilled ecstasy in the bed of the sensuous Carol to his unwatchable agony as the bloody Geraldine Page saws into his fibia.

As McBurney, Eastwood had an unaccustomedly wordy role. At times he was required to be the life and soul of the dinner table and his technique for winning the ladies over, especially Edwina, consisted of a considerable amount of questioning and persuasion. The audience is left with few clues as to how truly calculating McBurney is in his pursuit of the ladies; he could be merely lustful. Eastwood's performance, though suffused with charm, gives little away. When he switches to the gun-toting drunk at the end, there is still nothing in the character to indicate he would be ruthless with his captives. Eastwood gives a good performance but one that could perhaps have been bettered by several of his more experienced contemporaries. *The Beguiled* is a gem of a film, but the credit reposes firmly with the director.

Eastwood himself remarked later, 'It probably would have been a more successful film if I hadn't been in it' and he was right. Universal appeared to

have a corporate breakdown over its release. They cancelled the première in the week it was due to open and, instead of placing it in one or two suitably chosen art houses, they subjected it to a blanket release. Of course the traditional Eastwood fans were disappointed. 'They didn't like seeing me play a character who gets his leg cut off, gets emasculated. They wanted a character who could control everything around him.'

The film wasn't a success in America, a fact that still rankles with Siegel. 'It was the stupidity and bad handling by the studio, the way they promoted it. *The Beguiled* wasn't a picture where Clint wins the Civil War single-handedly, but from their publicity you'd have thought it was and that was one of the major reasons why the picture wasn't a success.' In London and Paris where the film opened more quietly the film and the director received due acclaim and it remains a copybook example of screen craft. It may not have won Eastwood any new fans but, as he noted himself, 'It was good for me in a career sense, because it did give the few people who saw it a different look at me as a performer.'

During the shooting of *The Beguiled* Eastwood made a short feature about Don Siegel which was later seen on television. He was flexing his own muscles as a director. One of the reasons he liked working in an intimate atmosphere with Siegel was that he had a chance to throw in some suggestions of his own, an opportunity which is less available on a big budget film. 'He gives off lots of ideas,' Siegel told me, 'and I call those "Clintus" shots and I welcome them. At the same time it gives me the incentive to come up with a "Siegelini" shot which occasionally is better than the one he suggested. So it's kind of fun working with him. He knows his craft—there's no question about that. He's had lots of experience and you have to be on your toes and alert.'

Even as Eastwood and Siegel were putting the finishing touches to their location scenes in Louisiana, Eastwood's business partner Robert Daley was setting up *Play Misty For Me,* which Eastwood intended to direct. While Malpaso put up all the funds for this, Universal were still to handle the distribution and had a say in the choice of actors for the film. Robert Daley had no doubts about his partner's capacity to handle Malpaso's first wholly-owned movie. 'He's extremely knowledgeable; he has never stopped learning in this business. Even after seven and a half years on *Rawhide* he was always on the set, always observing. They had different directors on nearly every show, he was watching everything that went on, constantly asking questions.'

Having made the decision to become a director,

Clint on set with Donna Mills, for Play Misty For Me *(1971), a claustrophobic thriller which Eastwood chose as his directorial debut.*

Eastwood had little difficulty in getting the necessary union credentials. As he remarked later, 'All you need to get into the Director's Guild is for someone to give you a job. So I gave myself a job. I said, "Kid, you got the job".'

Eastwood had optioned the sixty-five page outline of *Play Misty For Me* when he was making *Where Eagles Dare.* It was by a friend, Joe Heims, and he was intrigued by the story because it was largely true. When he signed a three-picture deal with Universal during *Two Mules For Sister Sara,* he suggested to Jennings Lang, the head of production that he would like to do *Misty.* The response was less than enthusiastic. Eastwood recalls: 'I hate to tell you the problems I had even getting that show started, because I had executives at Universal ask me, "Who wants to see Clint Eastwood play a disc jockey?" And I said, "Who wants to see him play anything?"'

He assured Lew Wasserman, the President of Universal, that he could 'make it cheap, all on natural sets'. Wasserman replied, 'Great, take it and run with it.' Not fooled for one moment by the studio chief's readiness to accede to the whim of the nation's Number Two box office star (Paul Newman was Number One) Eastwood later told an interviewer: 'I know exactly what they were saying behind my back, probably saying, "We'll let the kid fool around with it. He'll do that and then he'll probably do a couple of Westerns for us, or some other adventure-type film that will seem more commercial at the

outset."' The studio's lack of faith was made more evident when he told them he was going to direct. Instead of paying him his 'regular deal' under his contract, they forced him to act in it for nothing and take a percentage. To his subsequent satisfaction he made more from the film that way after a couple of re-releases and a profitable sale to television.

The 'Misty' of the title was the Errol Garner record. Dave Garland (Eastwood) is a late-night disc jockey. His girl friend is out of town and one night, in a bar, he is propositioned by an attractive girl, Evelyn Draper (Jessica Walter). He goes back to her apartment and when the prospect of a night together looms she anticipates his reluctance. 'You don't want to complicate your life?' He agrees. She provides the ready solution. 'That's no reason we shouldn't sleep together if we want to.' He acquiesces and she reveals that she has already formed a crush on him and it was she who had phoned nightly with a request for 'Misty'.

Thereafter she does everything possible to complicate his life. She pesters him, chases him, interrupts a business lunch with a lack of grace verging on the educationally sub-normal. When Dave's girl-friend returns from Europe, Evelyn spies on them and threatens to make their tenuous relationship even more fraught by moving in with him. When he refuses, she reveals, at last, her truly psychotic state by ripping his home to shreds with a knife and assaulting his cleaning woman. She is taken to a psychiatric hospital and is seemingly safely out of the

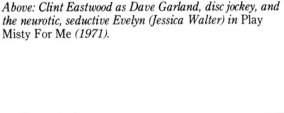

Above: Clint Eastwood as Dave Garland, disc jockey, and the neurotic, seductive Evelyn (Jessica Walter) in Play Misty For Me *(1971).*

way. Some six months later, Dave learns from his girl-friend, Tobie (Donna Mills) that she has a new room-mate called Annabelle. He thinks nothing of it at the time, because Tobie is always changing her sharing arrangements. He is surprised to hear Evelyn on the phone again requesting 'Misty' and even more surprised when he finds her at the foot of his bed, her knife poised to kill him. She disappears but, to his horror, a few nights later, while broadcasting his late-night show at the studio, he realises that Annabelle might be Evelyn. Unable to leave his programme, he urges a friend, Police Sergeant McCallum (John Larch) to go to the house. Later, Dave arrives there himself to find his friend dead, with a pair of scissors sticking in his chest. He rushes in to find Tobie trussed up and Evelyn about to kill her. In the nick of time he rescues her and in the ensuing struggle Evelyn falls to her death on the jagged Pacific rocks far below. As Tobie and Dave cling together the strains of 'Misty' come over the radio.

Jo Heims had known of a psychotic like Evelyn, a woman who would disguise herself to keep an eye on the man with whom she was obsessed, who attempted suicide and then tried to kill him. Eastwood himself had read of the case of a young man who had been released from an institution six months after attempting to knife a woman to death: to the woman's intense shock she bumped into her assailant in a supermarket after he had been set free. Moreover the general theme of the movie was personal to him. As Clint

recalled in his interview with *Playboy* magazine, 'The *Misty* sort of thing happened to me when I was very young, twenty-one years old, before I was married. Sick jealousy isn't confined to any particular age, but most people I know, male or female, who have gone through that *Misty* type of insane jealousy had it happen at a very young age. It appealed to me because I've had this situation happen to me in my own life, this thing of having somebody clinging and clutching at you, not allowing you to breathe.'

Eastwood had judiciously surrounded himself with men whose work he had come to respect when working with Siegel. Bruce Surtees, whose masterful lighting had done much to establish the Gothic claustrophobia of *The Beguiled,* was cameraman— as he was to be on nearly every other Eastwood movie when he was free. Carl Pingitore who cut *The Beguiled* was editor. Eastwood also brought in Dean Riesner, one of the writers on *Coogan's Bluff,* to change his own part slightly. While greatly respecting the balance Jo Heims had achieved between the male and female leads, he felt that Dave Garland was possibly too passive and needed to be more sexually assertive. In the cleverest stroke of all he gave his old mentor, Don Siegel, a part in the movie as Murphy, the barman. 'A lot of people thought that I was using him in the picture as a buffer. Subconsciously maybe that was the idea; "I know I've got a really good director on the set if anything goes wrong." But he was so nervous about his first acting part that he'd

Below: In Play Misty For Me, *Eastwood created a very effective atmosphere of suspense, mystery and violence, a considerable achievement when both acting and directing.*

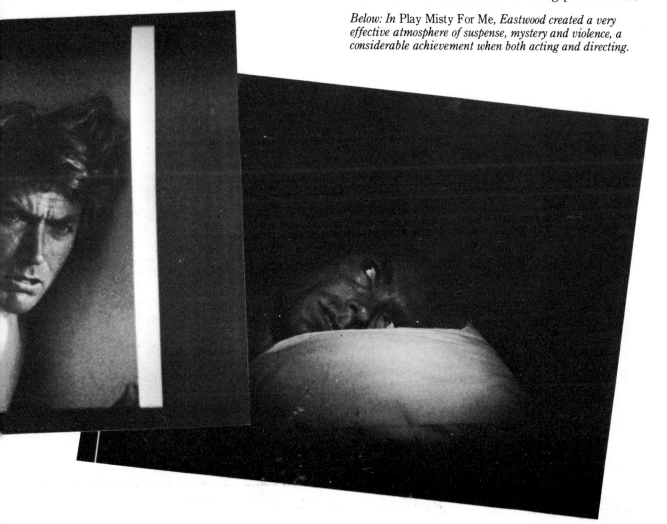

*Dave Garland grapples with Evelyn when her true psychotic nature is revealed. (*Play Misty For Me.*)*

have been absolutely no value to me.'

Siegel is equally jocular about the experience: 'He was very stupid indeed because in the very first sequence he ever shot in his life, I was a bar-tender with the impossible name of Murph. It was very dangerous because I'm not an actor and I was very nervous about it because I didn't want to let him down. But because of his excellent direction, because of his giving me confidence, even with my own crew, I was able to give a reasonable performance—not a good performance, but a reasonable one.'

Against the wishes of the studio, Eastwood cast Jessica Walter as Evelyn. He had seen her some years earlier in *The Group* and although her career had not taken off from there, he surmised, correctly, that she could provide the terrifying mix of sexual attraction and psychotic abandon that the part required. She so impressed him to begin with that he found, as Siegel had warned him, that he was neglecting his own part in favour of hers. Although he used video equipment to obtain an instant replay of the takes, at the end of the first week he had to shoot additional close-ups and reaction shots of himself to balance their scenes.

Much of the film was literally a home movie, for Eastwood shot many of the exteriors on the two hundred acres of coastland he owned on the Monterey Peninsula. It was wise to use territory he knew well but some of the critics felt he over-used it, that the lingering helicopter shots of the surf-battered coastline intruded too much on the pace of the film.

Eastwood was complimentary about the team that surrounded him, not least about his producer, Bob Daley. 'A creative producer can relieve a director of an enormous load of details and follow-through, as well as making important decisions on casting, locations and other production problems. Of course once the camera starts rolling, the director is on his own. When I stress the importance of an organization, I do not mean to imply that the old concept of dozens of people standing around assists the director. On the contrary, when I went into directing I brought to it the philosophy that a director needs a lean, creative, hand-picked crew—large enough to do the job but small enough so that everyone has a sense of participation and constant involvement.'

Two hundred hours of *Rawhide* and endless wasted months on the locations of over-budgeted star-studded pictures had taught Eastwood the best method of leadership. 'One lesson I learned very quickly during the shooting of *Misty* was that by keeping everyone involved in what you, the director, are doing, crews will work twice as hard and develop a tremendous *esprit de corps*. If you explain what effect you are striving for instead of saying merely "Put that case over there", or "Set that lamp down there", your crew will become totally involved.

'All of them were extremely professional. I had the distinct impression at first that they were all waiting for me to prove myself as a director. But that lasted exactly one day. By the second morning we were all working together as a totally involved, compatible unit. My second lesson was to be carefully prepared and well-organised, but yet remain flexible, so that we could move from set to set easily and without strain.'

As a feat of budgeting and organisation, *Misty* went flawlessly. Eastwood brought the film in $50,000 under its $950,000 budget and four days under its

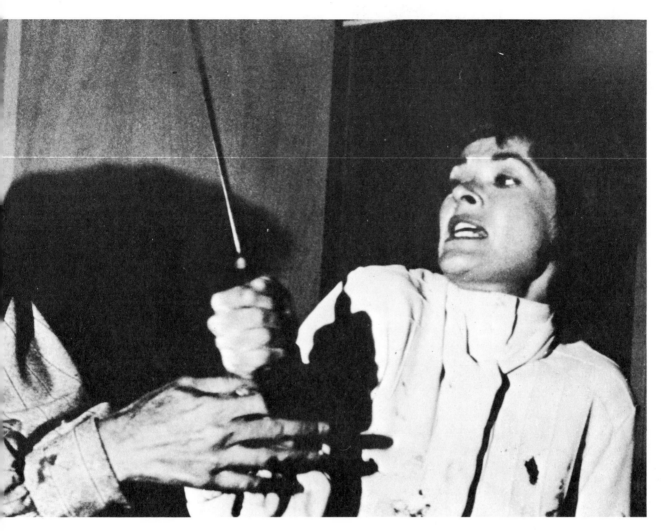

planned five-week schedule. Accustomed to many top directors who are plagued by indecision and cover themselves with thousands of extra feet of film, his crew were delighted to work for a man who was so sure and purposeful in his final aim. His cast were pretty impressed too. Jessica Walter observed, 'He's not insecure like some directors who impose things on you because they are nervous. He made me feel I could do it, whatever it was, and he left the role up to me. He has faith in people.'

While his technique on location left little to be desired, his innocence in the cutting room occasionally showed. Possibly he lost faith in Donna Mills's slightly flat performance as Tobie—admittedly she had only lean amounts of script to build on—and failed to imprint her sufficiently on the story. The soft and tender woodland scene where Dave makes love to her to the strains of 'The First Time Ever I Saw Your Face' was tasteful in its execution, but a weak substitute for a more realistic exposition of their relationship. But the mood of the story was superb, especially the low-key music and style of the disc jockey's life juxtaposed against the rough, lonely wildness of his natural surroundings. Eastwood constructed the stomach-knotting climax with as fine a hand as Hitchcock and then had the good sense to end the film at the moment of high drama, giving no

explanatory coda to send the audience out of the cinema with some further psychological assurance. When you turn the key in your front door after coming home from *Misty,* a fear is in your soul that wasn't there before.

Being as yet unheralded as an actor in his own country he had every reason to believe that the critics were hardly waiting to applaud him as a director, but they had the intelligence to welcome obvious talent when they saw it. Andrew Sarris in *The Village Voice* was the most fulsome: '*Play Misty For Me* marks a surprisingly auspicious directorial debut for Clint Eastwood as a director ... it is one of the most effectively scary movies of this or any year.' He expressed a few reservations, as did Jay Cocks in *Time* who nonetheless noted, 'Eastwood displays a vigorous talent for sequences of violence and tension.' Roger Greenspun in the *New York Times* was less respectful: 'It is sad that this film with its locale and some of its moods out of *Vertigo,* and its central obsessional action almost an inversion of Preminger's wonderful *Laura,* should echo so briefly in the imagination.'

It may have echoed briefly for him but it echoed throughout the world continuously for the next decade as it was run and rerun in art houses and on television. Eastwood the director had arrived—with a vengeance.

DO I FEEL LUCKY?

In 1970, with *Misty* completed and a satisfactory avalanche of offers for new movies pending, Clint took his wife Maggie to Italy. Film fans in that country had a certain proprietorial love for the star, since he had risen to eminence in Italian movies—although they had been entirely shot in Spain—largely owing to the talents of one of their top directors. Never having courted the limelight in America, Eastwood had rarely been subjected to public adulation and so was little prepared for the hysteria that greeted him in Milan. He was by far the most popular film star in Italy and in most of Europe, but he was more than that; he was a legend, a mythic hero emerging from a fantasy fable. The fan worship was coupled with respect. They gave him an award for his artistic merit, he was invited to speak to admiring and interested students and cinema intellectuals on his work, and he was fêted at receptions by the highest in the land. He enjoyed it, but it wasn't his style. He later told me that he doubted if he could ever pluck up enough courage to return to Italy and risk facing it all again.

Left: The archetypal 'Dirty Harry' pose; the professional killer just this side of the law. Below: Magnum Force *(1973), and right:* Dirty Harry *(1971).*

The Beguiled had a première in Milan where it was received with the credit it deserved. The audience teased him with calls of *niente funghi*—'no mushrooms' —referring to his poisonous demise in the film. But when he returned to California he embarked on a project that was to prove more dangerous and controversial than anything Miss Farnsworth could dish up—*Dirty Harry*.

The story, *Dead Right* by Harry Julian Fink and his wife, R. M. Fink, had been doing the rounds. It was a good one and provided a strong male lead. Various screenplays had been written to suit various stars. At one stage Frank Sinatra was going to do it but had to pull out as he had a badly injured hand. Paul Newman had been interested but the central character in the version he read was too scruffy—a bit like television's *Colombo*—and he is reputed to have suggested Eastwood for the part.

When Warner Brothers offered it to him, he insisted that they bring in Don Siegel to direct. Dean Riesner was once again put on the script to bring the story back to the Finks' original concept, and to polish up the Eastwood character to an even greater super-human level of action. After all, in the public mind Clint Eastwood could perform feats that Paul Newman and Frank Sinatra would not attempt.

Don Siegel was delighted with the project. 'I was fed up with the scripts that constantly came across my desk where the cops were sadists and perverts, etc, etc. It seems to me that when we're in a time of need who do we call on for help? We call for a cop to

help us. I'm not a cop lover. It doesn't mean that if a hard-nosed cop does the wrong thing I condone it, any more than I condone a psychopathic killer. But I thought it was about time that we called a spade a spade.'

Lest the audience be in any doubt where the film's sympathy lay, it began with a close-up of the memorial plaque in the San Francisco Hall of Justice: 'In Tribute to the Police Officers of San Francisco Who Gave Their Lives in the Line of Duty.' We move quickly to a cheerful gathering where lissom Californian beauties frolic in a swimming pool. Not for long. A rooftop sniper squeezes his trigger and a cruel scarlet stain spreads across the water as a young girl dies. The seemingly senseless killing is soon given a motive. The killer Scorpio (a character having affinity with the Zodiac killer who had in real life prowled the streets of San Francisco) demands $100,000 from the police or else his next victim will be a 'nigger or a priest'.

Enter Inspector Harry Callaghan alias Dirty Harry alias Clint Eastwood. Before he has time to act on the ransom note, he demonstrates his lethal credentials by foiling a bank raid. He upends the getaway car with a shower of deftly-placed bullets from his .44 Magnum, scarcely bothering to put down the hamburger he is munching. He further impresses his green and unwanted partner, Chico (Reni Santoni), with his steely nerves in bringing down a would-be suicide from a perilous ledge.

The police chiefs drag their feet on Scorpio's

Director Don Siegel: 'I loathe gratuitous violence . . . I infer violence, it's lying there waiting for you but I don't really have that much violence in my pictures and certainly in Dirty Harry there wasn't.'

demands. A black youth is found, murdered by him. Harry and Chico track down Scorpio (Andy Robinson) but they let him slip away in a rooftop shootout. Another note tells the police that the killer has kidnapped a fourteen-year-old girl, buried her alive with a little oxygen and now wants $200,000 if she is to be returned alive. Harry is dispatched with the ransom but Scorpio leads him a merry dance around the city until he ambushes the lone detective in Mount Davidson Park. Harry is badly beaten and about to be killed when Chico demonstrates his worth by emerging from the bushes to save him, only to be seriously wounded himself.

Harry has managed to wound Scorpio in the leg and after questioning the doctor who treated him, tracks down the killer to Keazar Stadium where the psychopath works as a groundsman. There he brutally questions him to find out where the girl is, and when the man resists he shoots him in the leg. Scorpio is taken into police custody and the girl is found dead but because of Harry's illegal cross-examination, the killer is released.

Against orders Harry continues his pursuit. Scorpio pays some $200 to have himself beaten up in order to try to frame the cop. While Harry is contending with these charges, Scorpio hijacks a school bus and heads for the airport demanding money and a getaway plane from the police. In the original script he was to be killed on the plane by a police sharpshooter. In the Eastwood-Siegel-Riesner film, Harry leaps from a bridge onto the bus. It crashes. He chases Scorpio to a wooden landing-stage, where the killer, ruthless to the last, seizes a young boy who has been fishing, to cover himself. Harry puts a bullet into the killer's shoulder. The child gets away and Scorpio loses his gun.

Harry now has him at his mercy. Instead of arresting him he levels his gun at him and utters the menacing words, 'I know what you're thinking, punk. You're thinking did he fire six shots or only five. Now to tell you the truth I've forgotten myself in this excitement. But seeing as this is a .44 Magnum—the most powerful handgun in the world, that will blow your head clean off—you've got to ask yourself a question. Do I feel lucky?' The killer's hand nervously hovers over his dropped gun. Harry challenges him once more: 'Well, do you punk?' With a maniacal laugh, Scorpio goes for his gun but is blown into the water. As the police siren approaches, Harry pulls off his badge of office and chucks it into the pond after the body.

The film might easily have passed for a popular tale of cops and robbers or, more particularly, cop and psychopath had it not been for the ruthlessness of Harry's methods. In this character, Eastwood brought the rude justice of the lawless West to the regular laws of the modern city and to many this was morally unacceptable. Perhaps Harry's behaviour would have been less controversial had he merely been a renegade cop who broke the rules when roused by anger, but in the cool neon light of his superior's office, he is unrepentant about his behaviour. The District Attorney says, 'You're lucky I'm not indicting you for assault with intent to commit murder. Where the hell does it say that you have the right to kick down doors, torture subjects, deny medical attention and legal counsel? Where have you been? What I'm saying is that man had rights.' Harry replies, 'Well I'm all broken up about that man's rights.' When the District Attorney tells Harry that it will be a waste of time to spend taxpayers' money on a trial, even the rifle is inadmissable evidence, Harry states what to him is obvious: 'Then the law's crazy.'

By that stage in the film the viewer is so much in sympathy with Harry's dilemma, and he has been fashioned as such an attractive, basically upright, well-intentioned hero, that there is little doubt that a mass audience is on his side and against the protection given to suspected criminals in rulings such as *Miranda*. This established that an alleged criminal has to be informed of his rights; all policemen must carry a card informing the arrested party of his right to remain silent and not thereby to incriminate himself. I saw *Dirty Harry* with a primarily black audience in Washington and they, to a man, were on the side of the law-dispensing cop. When Pauline Kael saw it, 'Puerto Ricans in the audience jeered—as they were meant to—when the maniac whined and pleaded for

his legal rights.'

As ever, Miss Kael gave the most articulate expression of concern about the film's motives. She noted that Scorpio not only embodied all evil, but was subtly endowed with the left-wing connotations of long hippy hair and a peace badge. Sniffing an anti-liberal conspiracy she instances that it is a Berkeley law professor who advises the murderer should be released—another jab at the radical element. For her, 'the dirtiness of Harry is the moral stain of recognition that evil must be dealt with; he is our martyr, stained on our behalf.'

In her *New Yorker* review she wrote: 'On the way out a pink-cheeked little girl was saying, "That was a good picture" to her father. Of course the dragon had been slain. *Dirty Harry* is obviously just a genre movie but this particular genre has always had a fascist potential and it has finally surfaced. If crime were caused by super-evil dragons, there would be no *Miranda,* no *Escobedo;* we could all be licensed to kill like *Dirty Harry.* But since crime is caused by deprivation, misery, psychopathology and social injustice, *Dirty Harry* is a deeply immoral movie.'

I suggested to Miss Kael that maybe she took the whole thing too seriously, that such issues were incidental to what was a fast, fantasy action picture. She didn't think so.

'You must realise that political attitudes are

*Thwarting a potential suicide: Eastwood directed this sequence himself. (*Dirty Harry, *1971.)*

carried and very intentionally carried in some of these films. The John Wayne and Clint Eastwood films made in the heyday of the Nixon era were carrying the line for a political position in this country and such pictures were very definitely shaped in those directions. It is not merely that these people express certain attitudes off-screen; their scripts are shaped in terms of what these stars believe and the movies swing a certain kind of sentiment. We all know that movies are not really taken so lightly by the audience and when a reactionary set of values in a vigilante spirit is built right into the structure of the films I think it's incumbent on a critic to analyse exactly what's being said in the movie.'

I carried Miss Kael's words across the continent to the rocky headland near Carmel where I was talking to Eastwood. Of course he'd heard them before.

'I'd say she's crazy. It's not about a man who stands for violence, it's about a man who can't understand society tolerating violence. When *Dirty Harry* came out it was at a time when an awful lot of films had been done concerning the rights of the accused, and all of a sudden this film came along where somebody was concerned with the rights and the comfort of the victim. So somebody called that fascist. Well I don't think it's fascist. He was just a man who didn't understand. . . He says to the District Attorney, "Well if that's the law, if a man

The cold and ruthless detective Harry Callaghan sets out to capture a madman.

can be sent out on the streets on a technicality like that, then the law's wrong," and that's the way he believed. Now whether that's right or wrong that just happened to be one character I play. I've played other characters which are purely opposite.'

While finding Miss Kael's conspiracy theory a little too extreme, I nevertheless felt that Eastwood was discarding his responsibility possibly too lightly, so I pointed out to him that he had played Dirty Harry three times (the character appeared in the sequels *Magnum Force* and *The Enforcer*): 'Do you approve of him? I mean he does seem to go around slaughtering people, being his own judge and jury very often too.'

'Well, he doesn't really. He's always in a situation where he has to get somebody who's very lethal, the killer or whoever he's after is not somebody who's picking a pocket somewhere. In the case of *Dirty Harry* it was a psychopathic killer. Now how do you take him out? He wants to get him off the streets so that nobody else becomes a victim, that's the feeling of the character. You can attach names to things like that such as fascism or whatever you want to call it but that's not the point. We, ourselves, Great Britain and the United States, have imposed our feelings on other people. After World War II we went to Nuremburg and we tried members of the party in Germany at that time. We tried them and convicted them for not adhering to a higher morality. Well, that's the way Dirty Harry is. He listens to a higher morality above the law and he feels that the law is wrong and he should fight that or try to solve it. It has no bearing on

This famous stunt, jumping onto a moving bus from a bridge, was performed by Eastwood himself. (Dirty Harry, 1971.)

Rightist or Leftist or anything like that. It was just one incident in a man's life at a certain period.'

Siegel pointed out that he wore a peace symbol himself and the reason the killer had one on his buckle was that 'it may remind us that no matter how vicious a person is, when he looks at himself in the mirror, he's not capable of seeing the truth about himself.'

I asked Siegel whether he felt any responsibility about the amount of violence in the film, whether he believed that it could bring out latent violence in some people who saw it.

'I dimly remember that at the end of Hamlet there are five bodies lying around, so that's balderdash. This constantly plainted ditty against violence, if people didn't want it they wouldn't go to the movies. I loathe gratuitous violence. I fight very hard against it. My violence is very sharp and abrupt. I infer violence, it's lying there, waiting for you but I don't really have that much violence in my pictures and certainly in *Dirty Harry* there wasn't. I thought *Dirty Harry* had something to say and I felt we said it, even though Pauline Kael couldn't understand it.'

Eastwood was equally certain that *Dirty Harry*'s violence would have no effect on the susceptible. 'If a weak or unhinged person mirrored Dirty Harry, he'd be on the side of the right because he's on the side of good as opposed to evil. *Dirty Harry* is not a story about a sicky. If you do a story like *Taxi Driver*, it's a story about a sick man who's ready to go out and shoot people. Now if you mirrored that character then that would be something, but the *Dirty Harry* character is man on the side of the public, and on the side of tranquillity for the public.'

More disquieting than any prospect of *Dirty Harry*'s influencing members of the public was the request from a police department in the Philippines to have a 16-millimetre print of the movie to use as a training film. It is frightening to consider what sort of results that might have. In fact, Eastwood is traditionally popular with the police but turns down invitations to address them since he makes no claims at all to being an expert on law enforcement.

The controversy aside, the film was enjoyable to make, the fourth collaboration and the most winning product so far of the Eastwood-Siegel duo. When Siegel fell ill, Eastwood took over the direction for a few days, most notably during the scene where Harry stops the high-dive suicide. 'The studio allowed six nights for this shot', Eastwood told a visiting *Life* reporter. 'I told them I could shoot it in two. So I'll finish it in one—really stick it in and give it a twist.'

He was comfortable in shooting it in the city he knew best—San Francisco—and with the people he knew best: Bruce Surtees on camera, Carl Pingitore on editing, and himself doubling as associate producer to the redoubtable Bob Daley. Using this experienced team and with a discreet score from Lalo Schifrin who

85

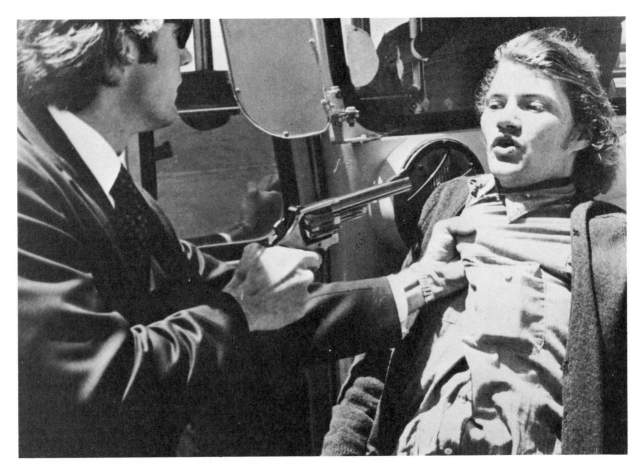

The kind of rough treatment for criminals that made audiences cheer for Dirty Harry *(1971): threatening the villain, played by Andy Robinson.*

had composed the music for *The Beguiled,* Don Siegel imposed a resonant sense of place on the city and the locations within it. The football field where Harry interrogates Scorpio has a melodramatic feel about it as the two men act out their conflict in the bare acreage of green sward.

Eastwood threw caution to the winds and did a risky stunt jumping from the bridge onto the moving bus. 'We had the camera on the bus and it was the only way to do it. . . . You leap right into the camera they're going to know who it is.' (Later the speeding bus pushes a slow Volkswagen out of its way and off the road, a moment, Eastwood told me, he always relished since it usually got a cheer from Californian audiences, familiar with the irritating presence of old VW bangers clogging the highway.)

The film was a runaway success, going instantly into profit and multiplying those profits to this day. Dirty Harry, the character, was equally instantly established, so much so that after the 1974 Zebra killings, the graffitti 'Dirty Harry, where are you when we need you' appeared on a wall in San Francisco.

While Miss Kael's criticisms did not exist in isolation it would be wrong to suggest that all critics were equally outraged. As is often the case with such a controversy, the ultimate benefit was to the producers of the film, since people who normally would avoid a Clint Eastwood picture went to see it to find out what all the fuss was about. Not only were some critics not offended, but often they weren't all that impressed by the picture. Roger Greenspun began his review in the *New York Times,* 'The honourable and slightly anachronistic enterprise of the cops-and-crooks action movies over the last few years (*Madigan, Coogan's Bluff*) takes a sad and perhaps inevitable step downward in *Dirty Harry.*' He put his finger on his own disappointment with the film. 'It is not the hard-hat sentiment that I find disturbing in all this, so much as the dull-eyed insensitivity. *Dirty Harry* fails in simple credibility so often and on so many levels that it cannot even succeed (as I think it wants to succeed) in perversely complementary psychoses.'

Murf, in *Variety* was equally dismissive for much the same reasons: 'You could drive a truck through the plotholes in *Dirty Harry,* which wouldn't be so serious were the film not a specious, phoney glorification of police and criminal brutality. Clint Eastwood in the title role is a superhero whose antics become almost satire. Strip away the philosophical garbage and all that's left is a well-made but shallow running and jumping meller.'

Eastwood himself was obviously stung by the adverse reaction but affected not to be. Talking of critics he said, 'Those folks take themselves and movies too seriously. When I go to the movies, it's to have a few laughs and a couple of beers afterward. I don't worry about social injustice.'

Why should the critics dismiss a film to which the public is still so magnetically attracted? It isn't really for Eastwood to analyse, but in making a film he has an accurate sixth sense which lets him know how far he can go in terms of superhuman feats, implausible, sharpshooting and miraculous escapes. In *Dirty Harry* he read it to perfection. That is what the mass public wants from an Eastwood hero; someone with the cool but not the class of James Bond, who is reassuringly indestructible and in real situations can adopt the fantasy mastery of a traditional Western loner. He may be beaten up, but never beaten—by the criminals or by authority.

By the time *Dirty Harry* reached Europe in 1972 Eastwood once again found he had more friends among the press. I talked to Dilys Powell, doyenne of the British film critics and an unabashed Eastwood fan, and she tried to explain why.

'We're all appalled by violence and all critics say how perfectly awful it is. But when violence is turned against violence we all become extremely moral about it and say, "Oh no, we can't have people taking the law into their own hands." Well when Dirty Harry finds the law doesn't back him up and says, "Okay, I'll manage the law on my own", I think that is a reflection of a feeling in society that sometimes the law doesn't act firmly enough. . . just as any kind of violence reflects the society we live in. Therefore I think it is quite interesting, though morally one can't but disapprove of it.'

At the end of *Dirty Harry* Eastwood chucks his cop's badge into the pond. It was a scene he was reluctant to do but Siegel, perhaps mindful of the greater implications of the film, insisted on it. It seemed to prevent any possible sequels without a good deal of explanation but when the character grew in popularity and Malpaso saw good economic sense in following it up, Harry rejoined the San Francisco Police again in 1972 for *Magnum Force,* with minimum explanation. Over a beer in his studio room I taxed Eastwood with this omission. He grinned mischievously. 'Maybe there was a bit of elastic attached to the badge. It sprang right back into his hand after the movie finished.'

Although three films were to intervene before he made the sequel, *Magnum Force,* released in 1973 and a further three before he made the third in the series, *The Enforcer,* in 1976, it seems logical to follow through this analysis of the Dirty Harry character at this point. (Eastwood assured me that he didn't intend to make any more Dirty Harry films after this trio, but I suspect he will always remain open to persuasion.)

Although the critics didn't let him know that they wanted more of Dirty Harry, the public did. He was sitting, disguised, in a public movie theatre one evening trying to gauge the public reaction to the first picture. At the end the black man who was sitting next to him and who hadn't recognised him, turned and said, 'Man, San Francisco just lost one damn good cop.' The part very much established him in America. 'Kids come up to me and say "You feel lucky punk?" Just the other night I met Muhammad Ali and he said, "Give me that look you give the bad guy when you tell him he's got ten minutes to get out of town." I told him I didn't have a gun so I couldn't do it.'

He was able to do it in *Magnum Force.* The film begins with a close-up of a .44 Magnum which turns to threaten the audience with the unmistakable voice of its owner echoing his challenge from a previous incarnation: 'This is a .44 Magnum, the world's most powerful hand-gun, and it will blow your head into little pieces. What you've got to do is ask yourself, are you feeling lucky.' Pause. Bang. It triggers off Eastwood's most violent urban film to that date.

Magnum Force *(1973).*

87

Magnum Force. *Above: 'What does a girl have to do to go to bed with you?' 'Try knocking at the door.' Adele Yoshioka played opposite Clint, photographed here standing on a box to bring her up to Clint's height. Below: Filming with director Ted Post. Right: The chase; after escaping from the car, Harry eludes the vigilante cops on an aircraft carrier.*

A racketeer, Carmine Ricca, has been cleared of murder, due to the usual and frustrating court technicality. He leaves, a happy and free man. Not for long. A motor cycle cop pulls his car over, seemingly for a traffic violation and ruthlessly slaughters him and the other three occupants. Harry is soon on the scene, this time with a new black partner, Early Smith (Felton Perry), an appropriate source of appeal for Eastwood's substantial black following. It transpires that Harry is no longer in the homicide squad, he's been demoted to a stake-out squad by Detective Lieutenant Neil Briggs (Hal Holbrook) because of his previous unconventional methods.

Nevertheless he soon demonstrates that he has lost none of his considerable skills. Enjoying a hamburger at San Francisco Airport he becomes embroiled in a hijack. To the sublime satisfaction of the cinema audience, frustrated by watching long drawn-out hijackings on television news, he boards the plane, claiming to be a pilot, and shoots all the hijackers.

Harry meets an old colleague Charlie McCoy (Mitch Ryan) who seems unnaturally upset about the ineffectiveness of the courts and Harry fears that he may be the killer cop. Later, in the police firing range, he meets four young traffic cops who are more than impressed by his erstwhile lethal methods. With a wave of underworld killings on the increase, Harry is eventually told to work with Detective Lieutenant Briggs to solve them. He still suspects the murderer is McCoy until the latter is killed and, by setting a clever trap to check the bullets in the guns of the four young motorcycle cops, Harry finds that they are the culprits.

He confronts them. They admit their guilt, naively expecting him to join them. The leader, and killer of McCoy, Davis (played by David Soul, an actor later to be yoked with Starsky as a much more liberal cop, Hutch, in the highly successful television series), incants his muddled interpretation of what he thought was once Harry's philosophy: 'We're simply ridding society of killers that would be caught and sentenced anyway if our courts worked properly ... it's not just a question of whether or not to use violence. There simply is no other way, Inspector. You, of all people, should know that.' When challenged by another of the young men, 'Either you're for us or against us,' Harry doesn't seek to change their attitudes. He merely informs them, 'I'm afraid you've misjudged me.'

He tells Briggs that he has found the killers but Briggs reveals that it is he who has organised the vigilante squad and, since Harry has found them out, he too must be eliminated. In the car ride to his intended execution, Briggs tells him why they are doing it. 'Anyone who threatens the security of the people will be executed. Evil for evil, Harry. Retribution.' Harry replies, 'That's just fine. How does murder fit in? You know, when the police start becoming their own executioners, where's it going to end, eh, Briggs? Pretty soon you start executing people for jaywalking, and executing people for

traffic violations. Then you end up executing your neighbour because his dog pisses on your lawn.' Briggs argues, 'There isn't a man we've killed who didn't deserve what was coming to him.'

'Yes there is. Charlie McCoy.'

'What would you have done?'

'I'd have upheld the law.'

'What the hell do you know about the law? You're a great cop, Harry, got a chance to join the team but you'd rather stick with the system.'

'Briggs, I hate the Goddamn system. But until someone comes along with some changes that make sense, I'll stick with it.'

'You're about to become extinct.'

He isn't. Briggs is. Harry escapes from the car, fends off an attack from the vigilante cops in a tangled motorcycle chase on a disused aircraft carrier, and dispatches them all to their graves.

As Briggs goes to his—detonated by the car bomb meant for his victim—Harry lets drop the ironic refrain that has accompanied him throughout the picture: 'A man's gotta know his limitations.'

Of course, the film was structured as a rebuttal to the criticism of the first *Dirty Harry,* but Eastwood-style, not in words, in action—and was much bloodier than its predecessor. He got John Milius—well known from *Dillinger* and *The Life and Times of Judge Roy Bean*—to write the original story, based on the Fink character. With his usual eye for emerging talent, he hired Michael Cimino, later to get an Oscar for *The Deerhunter,* and gave him his first major

The end of the motorcycle chase for Harry, but only a temporary setback. (Magnum Force, 1973.)

break as co-scriptwriter. They got on well together. When I asked Eastwood who devised the memorable line 'A man's got to know his limitations', he acknowledged shyly, 'I think it was from me. I think I made it up,' and later expanded: 'Mike Cimino came up with it when we were dealing with the first scene in New York. I always liked a recurring kind of theme. We decided the Hal Holbrook character was to become the antagonist in the film and Harry feels the other guy should know his own limitations.' (Whether or not he himself does remains to be seen.)

Eastwood also explained the origin of the young cops. 'Harry was fighting the ultra-right wing organisation that was brewing within the police force. It was a danger that was based on a real life incident—the Brazilian Death Squad—where a sub-group within the police was knocking off criminals indiscriminately, acting as their own judge and jury. They were doing it much more than the Dirty Harry character was, so he fights that.'

He hired Ted Post (once of *Rawhide,* later of *Hang 'Em High*) to direct and while the film lacked Siegel's indelible sense of place, Harry emerges as a more powerful and dominating figure. Post often shoots him from below to imprint his stature on the piece. Harry is also a more rounded character. He even has sex. Inevitably, as is usual with the Eastwood persona, the initiative has to come from the female, unsuccessfuly from McCoy's widow and extremely directly from the Chinese girl who lives downstairs. 'What does a girl have to do to go to bed with you?' Pause. Brilliant double take. Then, 'Try knocking at the door.' She succeeds.

He is also very funny, in a dry sub-zero fashion, no mean feat in a movie knee-deep in blood. Enough to make Alan R. Howard in the *Hollywood Reporter* proclaim, 'Eastwood has never had such a winning way with a funny line.'

If the object of the film was to sell tickets, which it was, then it succeeded. The film grossed $6,871,011 in its first week of release in the USA. If its object had been to appease Pauline Kael, which it wasn't, then it failed.

The writers, she suggested, twisted the criticism of the earlier film to their own purposes, taking their plot gimmick 'from those of us who attacked *Dirty Harry* for its fascist mediaevalism. The villains now are a Nazi-style élite cadre of clean-cut, dedicated cops who have taken the law into their own hands and are cleaning out the scum of the city—assassinating the labour racketeers, the drug dealers, the gangsters and their groupies. They are explicit versions of what we accused Harry of being; they might be the earlier Harry's disciples, and the new Harry wipes them all out. . . *Magnum Force* disarms political criticism and still delivers the thrills of brutality. Harry doesn't bring anyone to court; the audience understands that Harry is the court.'

What further worried Miss Kael was the hero's lack of emotion. 'Eastwood couldn't express grief any more than he could express tenderness. With Clint Eastwood, the action film can—indeed must—drop the pretence that human life has any value. At the same time Eastwood's lack of reaction makes the whole show of killing seem so unreal that the viewer takes it on a different level from a movie in which the hero responds to suffering. In *Magnum Force* killing is dissociated from pain; it's even dissociated from life . . . since it's without emotion, it has no impact on us. We feel nothing toward the victims.'

Her indignation is undoubtedly justified, but since the invention of cinema—especially in the cowboy and the war film—people die and nobody cares. It is because of the popularity and potency of Eastwood movies and the way the audiences identify with their hero, that Miss Kael attacks his seeming nihilism. There's no middle way in the debate. On paper her logic seems water-tight; in the cinema Harry's assertion that, 'There's nothing wrong with shooting as long as the right people get shot,' is the very reason the audience is there. He even manages to get across his reactionary prejudices with a libertarian laugh. When it is suggested the young vigilantes may be 'gay', Harry opines: 'If the rest of you could shoot like them, I wouldn't care if the whole damn

The Enforcer (1975). Kate, Callaghan's partner, played by Tyne Daly.

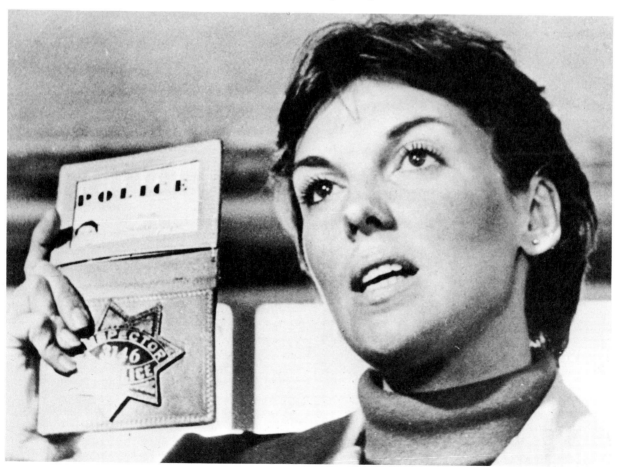

department was queer.'

Eastwood's decision to make the Dirty Harry films in San Francisco was inspired in part by his knowledge and affection for the place. He would meet childhood friends and old neighbours while filming. Its proximity to his peaceful retreat at Carmel also mattered, as well as the extensive help and welcome given to his company by the local police department. But in real life it was the city where young people made their mark in a manner that perplexed and raised considerable fears in the sober citizens of America's Eastern seaboard. In the late sixties the hippies and flower children made their spiritual home in Haight Ashbury. During the seventies the Gay Movement came out of the closet and demanded its rights *en masse,* centred round the Castro Street area. And in the mid-seventies a story that rivalled Watergate for column inches had its beginnings in the Bay Area—Patty Hearst and the Symbionese Liberation Front.

The scriptwriters lost no opportunity to include these elements in the underworld fabric of their stories and in the third film, *The Enforcer,* made in late 1975, Harry's main foe is the self-styled People's Revolutionary Strike Force, committed, it transpires, to nothing more than lining their own pockets.

Stirling Silliphant and the inevitable Dean Riesner, who together wrote the screenplay, followed the safe precedent of the first two movies. Harry quickly establishes his action-not-words *modus operandi* by driving his car through a liquor store window to free the owners, who are being held as

The Enforcer (1975). Top: Working with James Fargo, the director. Right: Harry Callaghan, the lone avenger.

hostages. Demoted to the personnel department, he scorns bureaucracy in general and in particular the Mayor's policy of attracting women into the force, but he is saddled with one, Kate (Tyne Daly) as his by now obligatory 'minority' partner. He finds black militants are not his enemies but his allies: when Mustapha, the black leader, is arrested to boost the Mayor's prestige, Harry actually resigns this time and continues his pursuit of the revolutionaries as a loner. His female aide risks her own job to help him and eventually sacrifices her life in the cause. They chase a prime suspect through the seamy 'massage parlour' underworld of the city and kill a leading gang member, Wando, who has disguised herself as a nun. Discovering that the Mayor is being held captive on Alcatraz Island, they make for the abandoned fortress for the final shootout. Kate, Harry's assistant, is killed and Harry shows unaccustomed emotion as he finally puts a bullet through the gang leader, Bobby Maxwell (DeVeren Brookwalter) with the bitter cry 'You fucking faggot'.

The film is a step backwards in style and content from the previous two. Harry seems to have reverted to his first incarnation: 'What kind of a department are we running when we're more concerned with the rights of the criminals than of the people we're supposed to be protecting?' and displays unusual brutality in roughing up a man who feigns heart attacks instead of paying his restaurant bills. Advertised as 'The dirtiest Harry of them all', it is also the weakest. Without the experience of Siegel or Milius to help him, Eastwood took a gamble on Jim Fargo, his assistant director on some of his previous films and the result was competent action but a noticeable lack of depth and subtlety. On location Eastwood was very much in charge, happy to omit pages of script in order to get on with the action, as in the liquor store sequence. 'What does he want?' he said to Fargo. 'He wants a car. So he should just take one and get on with it—like a mini-Entebbe raid.' Equally with the action sequences Eastwood insisted on further takes until they were done to his own satisfaction. He would discuss with the crew and advisers the exact risk involved in doing a stunt, like jumping through a skylight, before he was certain that it would look good and also keep him in one piece for the next take. When I suggested to him that the final rooftop scene was possibly too long to hold the audience's tension, he half agreed, pointing out that they had to extend it a little more than they wanted to make up the film's length. Back in Ferris Webster's editing room in Burbank studios, it was Eastwood and not Fargo who went through the final refinements before the film went to neg-cutting. I watched them at work one afternoon and it was impressive to see an almost Kubrick-like attention to detail, as Eastwood agonised over one extra close-up in a car chase, which he knew would give the scene an added sense of danger.

For the millions around the world who believed the words of the poster: 'Clint Eastwood *is* Dirty Harry' the film provided ninety-six minutes of delight and escape. For the critics, as ever, it provided its own sticks to be beaten with. But in reviewing it and in summing up the Dirty Harry character as a whole, Andrew Sarris in the *Village Voice* lucidly put his finger on Eastwood's position in the modern cinema. At the time when the Dirty Harry films were making their mark around the world, so was a television cop series—in the mid-seventies the world's most popular television programme—*Kojak.* Sarris drew an accurate distinction between the two men. He pointed out that Kojak, unlike Harry, was a man of the city and also unlike Harry, believed as much in rehabilitation as in redemption. 'Whereas Kojak celebrates the steady grind of law enforcement and enjoys living in the city, Harry glorifies the victories of the lone avenger who seems to ride off into the sunset even when he is driving a squad car.'

And further comparing the Eastwood Harry with Hoffman's *Marathon Man,* De Niro's *Taxi Driver* and Redford in *Three Days of the Condor,* he suggested that the last three characters appealed to Manhattanites because they evoked psychology, whereas Eastwood evoked mythology. 'There is something intransigently irreducible in Eastwood,' wrote Sarris, 'some corner of his soul no shrink can ever penetrate. Eastwood is not the first instance—nor will he be the last—of dynamic imagery in the service of dubious ideology, which is to say you may wind up liking his movies even when you disapprove of their message.'

I couldn't have put it better myself.

WHAT DID YOU SAY YOUR NAME WAS?

On 23 July 1971 the cover of *Life* magazine consisted of the full, smiling face of Clint Eastwood with the legend, 'the world's favorite movie star is—no kidding—Clint Eastwood'. The significant words were 'no kidding', for they anticipated the surprise that they would cause their readers. The conclusion had been reached in a poll conducted for the Hollywood Foreign Press Association; and even in America Eastwood was the second leading box-office draw, behind Paul Newman and in front of Steve McQueen and the perennial John Wayne. At the time Eastwood hadn't even completed *Dirty Harry* (it was released in December 1971), and his most popular film to date in America was *Hang 'Em High*. But the accompanying article pointed to the snowballing popularity of the Spaghetti Westerns—they had been re-released fifteen times up to that date and all-night screenings when all three were shown consecutively were becoming something of a cult. The writer informed her American readers that the 'unspectacular television actor from the long-running *Rawhide* series' had in the space of seven years become a star who commanded a million dollars plus a percentage for every film he made.

The 'no kidding' might have been taken as a prophetic warning for Clint's next movie. When he finished *Dirty Harry* he returned to the West to work for the first time—and the last—with John Sturges in *Joe Kidd*. Malpaso had acquired the story, originally called *Sinola*, and they had every reason to expect that Sturges, with quality Westerns like *Bad Day at Black Rock, Gunfight at the OK Corral* and, especially, *The Magnificent Seven* under his belt, would be the right man to further Eastwood's cowboy career. In the event he wasn't. The excellent sketching of characters and the poignancy of the dilemma of the Mexicans which made *The Magnificent Seven* (courtesy, once again, of Akira Kurosawa) such a classic movie were sadly lacking in *Joe Kidd* and the film never escaped from the entanglement of its own screenplay.

Eastwood, as the eponymous hero, imported some of the qualities of the Leone Stranger but lacked his style, his wit and his class. The film was set in the small town of Sinola, New Mexico, at the turn of the century. Mexican peasants were losing their birthright to powerful American cattle barons, and American justice was doing little to uphold their claims.

Kidd, a rough, dishevelled and hung-over cowboy, finds himself in jail with some aggrieved Mexicans. Despite bearing witness to the justice of their claims, he is swayed by an offer of $500, which he manages to increase to $1,000, into joining the big-time landowner Frank Harlan (Robert Duvall) and his posse,

Left: High Plains Drifter *(1972) was directed by Eastwood and has become a classic Western. Above: Clint Eastwood in the title role of* Joe Kidd *(1972).*

Above: Eastwood and Barbra Streisand with their Golden Globe awards presented by the Hollywood Foreign Press Association, as World Film Favourites, 1971. Below: A rude awakening for Joe Kidd.

to track down the Mexican leader, Luis Chama (John Saxon) and his fugitive band. He is given further impetus in this task when he discovers that the escaped Mexican leader's men have stolen some of his horses.

However, his commitment to Harlan's cause grows weaker the more he observes the landowner's methods. At one stage Harlan takes over a small Mexican town and threatens to kill all the inhabitants if Chama does not give himself up by a specified deadline. Kidd defuses the situation by getting hold of a Mauser and spraying the village with automatic

fire. He then rides away and captures Chama. He brings him back to justice, but discovers that Harlan has perverted even the law and ordered the Sheriff's men to kill both Chama and himself. He also discovers that Chama is no moral figure either. But with dogged persistence he kills Harlan, and hands Chama over to the Sheriff. As Arthur Knight wrote in *Saturday Review* (1972), 'Joe Kidd, in his single-minded purpose of turning the corrupt Mexican over to a corrupt justice, is demonstrably mad.'

What could have been an intriguing morality tale of mixed motives was reduced to a competent action picture, the best moment of which is when a train with Kidd on board leaves its tracks and ploughs through the town—bursting through walls as if they were made of cardboard.

The distinctive touches of the Eastwood travelling company were there: Bruce Surtees' photography, Lalo Schifrin's score and Ferris Webster's editing. In fact Webster had been under contract to Sturges for twelve years and had cut his best pictures but confessed that the director then went through a 'period of awful pictures—what I call dogs'. He told me that he considered Eastwood a better director, because he was more down to earth, and that he has been the senior editor on most of Clint's movies since then. Jim Fargo, too, who was Sturges' assistant on *Joe Kidd* went on to assist Eastwood and eventually directed *The Enforcer*.

Because they were happy to see Eastwood back

Joe Kidd was a murky story set in Mexico, where both sides of the village feud were equally corrupt. Eastwood with his co-star, Stella Garcia.

in the saddle, the faithful fans made *Joe Kidd* a box-office success. The critics were less kind. One called it a 'rest after *Dirty Harry*', and Michael McKegney in the *Village Voice* deemed it 'dull and heavy'. He did perceive the quality of Eastwood's own performance, however: 'Eastwood manages to hold our attention with the same brand of humorously low-keyed, bottled-up violence that Sturges evoked with Steve McQueen in *The Great Escape* almost a decade ago. The casual authority with which Eastwood wields a shotgun while chucking down sandwiches and beer convinces us that John Wayne's mantle as Avenging Conscience of the Right will not go unclaimed after the Duke's passing.'

Eastwood must have realised that he could have directed the film better himself. His next project which he did direct proved that he was right.

If you ask almost any successful producer for the most important piece of advice that he has learned through bitter experience, there's a good chance he'll say—as many have said to me—'Make sure the script's right before you start shooting.' It sounds so simple, but it rarely happens. Quite apart from the revisions made to bring it to the satisfaction of the producer himself, the director will inevitably want to make changes and so will any star actors and, even worse, their agents. Often the final shooting script

bears little resemblance to the one that initially caused the backers to put up their money or the studio to espouse the cause. There are exceptions that have worked, of course. I watched Dustin Hoffman busily rewriting and having rewritten for him his part in Kathleen Tynan's script of *Agatha*. It caused anxiety and delays, but Hoffman pointed out to me that *Casablanca* had been rewritten pretty much from day to day. *Agatha* proved to be no *Casablanca*, sadly.

For *High Plains Drifter* Malpaso hired one of the best scriptwriters in the business—Ernest Tidyman. He had just received an Oscar for his screenplay for *The French Connection*. It was money well spent. Tidyman perceptively extracted all that had appealed to audiences throughout the world in the 'No Name' character from the Leone Westerns, and then brilliantly wove a tale around this figure that embodied the righteous law-giving brutality of a turn-of-the-century Dirty Harry. Finally he took the greatest risk of all. He made the film a myth—and it worked.

Malpaso then made its second sensible decision. They got the man who is undoubtedly the best director of Westerns in the world today to direct the film—Clint Eastwood. With *Misty* Eastwood had laid the foundations of a strong individual style. He told me, 'I never really fashioned myself on any particular director. I liked Wellman for *Ox Bow* and I liked Ford for *The Quiet Man*. It was a terrific experience working with Sergio in Spain, working

97

High Plains Drifter (1972). Eastwood starred as an avenging Stranger once more, riding into town in a beautifully shot opening sequence.

with people with a slightly different outlook. Then I worked with Vittorio de Sica—he was terrific, an ex-actor, directing, very interesting to watch and an extremely ordered man. Then I came to Siegel, an extremely well-organised guy. I came to him after several films with less organised directors—they were good, aspects of their personality worked well but they weren't positive. Siegel's a guy who, for better or worse, puts down what he sees and if the shot's good he prints it and walks away from it. He doesn't fudge around on it. So he's not afraid to make a mistake. That was an interesting concept, because if you take over the responsibility of directing a film, it's very easy not to want to finish.'

Many top actors, despite their aspiration to become directors, cannot make the quantum leap from the cosseted status of the leading player to the tough and solitary position of the man who has to worry about everything on the production all the time. Eastwood never accepted the flattery or appendages of being a major star on the set and, having always been his own man, found it easier to adapt to the loneliness of the leader.

'It's lonely in the sense that you have to make the final decisions, but I'm fairly good at that, because I'm fairly decisive. Whether I agree with the end result or not, I'm not afraid to put down what I have in my mind at the moment. But I surround myself with very good

A close shave for Clint in High Plains Drifter: *unknown to the three town heavies he conceals a gun beneath the towel.*

people and so it isn't lonely in that respect. I mean, I try not only to cast the actors that I use but also to cast everybody who works with me so that you have very good input. I like to solicit input from everybody. Siegel does the same thing.'

The three main props of the production team were the men he most wanted to work with: as producer, the tough and slightly intimidating Bob Daley; as cameraman, the cheerful and casually excellent Bruce Surtees and the gruff and experienced Ferris Webster as editor, a man who could probably piece together an action scene better than anyone in Hollywood.

Many of the most important decisions in film making are taken before the negative runs through the camera, and when planning his film, Eastwood wisely avoided the traditional Western street on the back lot at Burbank or any of the permanent ones in the desert just outside Los Angeles. Instead, he settled on an exotic location in the Sierras: Mono Lake, east of Yosemite National Park, an area made familiar throughout the world by the breathtaking photographs of Ansel Adams. The story dictated that most of the town be destroyed at the end of the film so it was expedient to build one. It certainly gave the film a fresh and rarefied look among Westerns, something very much in keeping with the story. Eastwood was pleased with the photography: 'The brilliant colours of the backgrounds and the changing cloud formations gave us the opportunity to get some very effective shots.'

The weather held, enabling them to come in two days under their six-week schedule, something to be proud of in a large action picture running two and a half hours. It is more than a superstition in movies that when the luck runs with you, everything goes right. John Wayne told me that on *True Grit* their luck held until the final day when they couldn't get enough snow-making machines to give the necessary winter aspect to Matty's graveyard farewell to Rooster. The director, Henry Hathaway, decided to film it without snow, but when the unit awoke the next morning two inches of fresh natural snow coated the location, far into the horizon. As in all things, luck

seems to come more readily after careful preparation and hard work.

High Plains Drifter has surely the most dramatic opening sequence of any Western. Through the shimmering desert, Bruce Surtees's 500 millimetre lens discovers a lone horseman. The high-pitched dissonant music, by Dee Barton who scored *Misty*, has more than distant strains of Morricone, the composer for the Spaghetti Westerns. The camera pans with the horseman to reveal a small town by a lake—Lago. The horseman rides in, the camera tracking behind him, intercut with faces of suspicious locals—even a coffin maker with his wares—and instantly one is reminded of Leone and his faithful reproduction of Kurosawa. A coach driver cracks his whip. The horseman turns, flinches. He enters a bar and the quality of the dialogue immediately sets the film apart from the lacklustre scripts of the Spaghetti Westerns.

'A beer and a bottle.'

'Do you want anything else?'

'Just a peaceful hour to drink it in.'

A town heavy intervenes: 'Flea-bitten range-bums don't usually stop in Lago. Life here's a little too quick for them. But maybe you think you're fast enough to keep up with us.' The horseman replies, 'I'm faster than you'll ever live to be.'

High Plains Drifter. *Eastwood's first encounter with his female co-star, Mariana Hill: he rapes her after killing three men within minutes of arriving in town.*

True to his boast he kills the heavy and his two friends within minutes, and also rapes the town belle who responds, as any Eastwood feminine victim is obliged to, with resistance turning to relish. The town midget, Mordecai (Billy Curtis) offers him a cigar as a placebo. 'What did you say your name was again?' he inquires. The Stranger takes a puff. 'I didn't.'

The Man with No Name has returned, this time, quite literally, with a vengeance. The townsfolk, it transpires, need protection from three gunmen, shortly to be released from gaol, and they permit the Stranger to galvanise them into action. His less than benevolent dictatorship is spiced with cool humour. The name Billy Borders is mentioned to the Stranger. 'Don't know the man,' he confesses. 'You didn't have much time to,' comes the reply, 'because you shot him yesterday.' When his rape victim, Callie Travers (Mariana Hill) inaccurately empties a pistol at him during his bathtime, he casually resurfaces like a U-boat, cigar still in his mouth, and in an aside to his side-kick Mordecai, ruminates, 'I wonder what took her so long to get mad?' His fellow chauvinist suggests, 'Maybe because you didn't come back for more.'

The locals accede to his every request and he pushes them to the limit, even forcing them to paint the entire town blood red. 'When we get done,' says one of them, 'this place is going to look like hell.' This is the Stranger's intention; he takes a brush and strokes out the name 'Lago' on the town sign and writes 'Hell' instead.

In a series of flashbacks, primarily from the Stranger's point of view and later from Mordecai's, it is revealed that the townsfolk stood by and let the three men now emerging from gaol bull-whip their Marshal to death. The Marshal had discovered that the basis of the town's prosperity, a mine, was actually on government land and not on the towns-people's own. He was going to report this, so no-one felt obliged to intervene when he met his vicious end. His body now was lying outside the town in an unmarked grave: 'They say the dead don't rest without a marker of some kind . . . he's the reason this town's afraid of strangers.'

Now they have reason to be afraid of the three men who paid the price for the crime in which they all acquiesced. The Stranger analyses this fear: 'It's what people know about themselves inside that makes them afraid.' The town's reaction to him is schizoid. A group of vigilantes try to kill him, supposedly clubbing him to death in bed, but the corpse is merely a dummy. The Stranger repays them with a stick of dynamite. Despite their training, the remaining locals are horrified when they realise that he does not intend to remain for the final showdown. They argue, 'The rest of us have an agreement with you.' He replies, 'Right now I don't feel too agreeable.' 'We'll pay you $500 a head.' '$500 an ear.'

Eastwood directs a sequence from High Plains Drifter, *energetically absorbed as always.*

As with his Spaghetti counterpart, money appears to speak louder than morals with this hero. Nevertheless he leaves town before the deadly three arrive, and the pusillanimous locals permit them to kill, pillage and set fire to their houses at will. When all seems lost a whip comes speeding out of the darkness, lashing one of the gunmen to death. The second is hanged by the whip and the third confronts the Stranger face-to-face against the backdrop of the burning town. His gun is useless against his lethal adversary and as he, too, meets his death he screams in agony, 'Who are you?'

It is a question that is repeated at dawn when the Stranger rides out of the smouldering hulk of the town and through the graveyard. 'I never did know your name,' remarks Mordecai. 'Yes, you do,' affirms the Stranger and the camera pans round to reveal that the former Marshal's grave is unmarked no longer. 'Marshal Jim Duncan—Rest in Peace.'

Quite simply the Stranger *is* Marshal Jim Duncan. He has come back from the grave, an avenging angel of death. Now he can return to his grave in peace. Hints that the Stranger is the Marshal have been placed throughout the movie, as firmly as clues in a Hitchcock thriller, but the audience is not accustomed to the metaphysical in a Western and many people, who could accept that Leone's Stranger came from nowhere and returned to nowhere, found it hard to believe that Eastwood was now offering a more profoundly mythical view of the Western. *Variety* was happy to dismiss the film as 'a nervously humorous, self-conscious near-satire on the prototype Eastwood formula', and many others were equally lukewarm: 'ritualised violence and plodding symbolism make for heavy going,' wrote an English critic. But these opinions are completely misguided. *High Plains Drifter* is one of the half-dozen most important Westerns ever made and when Eastwood takes his rightful place in film history alongside Cooper and Stewart and Wayne, this is the film that will be seen as the quintessential example of his art. Already, serious writers are beginning to realise this. Bruce Jay Friedman, in a high-flown philosophical piece for *Esquire,* peppered with arcane references to Heidegger and Kierkegaard, believes 'Clint Eastwood's remote, alienated style is a goddamned metaphor for our time,' and, perceptively observing the transformation of the man into his roles, he emphasises, 'He doesn't just play those mythic fellows who suddenly loom out of nowhere with a scanty past. He *is* one. . . Let Eastwood just keep on refining mythic, although how he's going to refine what he did in *High Plains Drifter* is a question I'd rather not have to answer.'

Unlike Cooper and Stewart and Wayne, Eastwood didn't just star in the movie: he directed it and helped to devise it. He had read about the Kitty Genovese case when thirty-eight people witnessed a girl being murdered and no one even called the police. He also agreed readily when I suggested the similarity between *High Plains Drifter* and *High Noon*.

'There is a parallel in the message, in the morality of the thing. In *High Noon* the man is

A flashback in High Plains Drifter—*the Marshal meets a brutal end at the hands of the townsfolk. Buddy Van Horn stood in as Eastwood's 'double', maintaining the doubt about the Marshal's identity until the end. (Later Van Horn directed* Any Which Way You Can, *1980.)*

struggling to get this town to come to his assistance in his time of need but he can't seem to get anybody to come to his assistance except the woman he loves. In *High Plains Drifter,* it's a man coming back to a town that has deserted the Marshal in his time of need and taking vengeance on that town—making them suffer a little.'

But he was happy to parry my other suggestion that maybe he acted just a little bit like Gary Cooper: 'Not consciously. I think he's done some marvellous roles. The other day I saw *Sergeant York* and the first half of that was one of the best performances given by anybody, but the second half got kind of messagey so he didn't have as much to do. In *High Noon* he was marvellous. But I don't think I act like him. No.'

Eastwood again used his video-playback system to check the takes on *High Plains Drifter,* and since the town had to be destroyed at the end, he shot the film in the correct continuity. He said it helped to speed up the editing and he and Ferris Webster set up a small log cabin on the location, 'with a great view of pine trees, snow-covered mountains and bright skies. . . ' He continued: 'Most cutting rooms are abysmally depressing for no reason I can figure out. Few of them have windows or any relief from grey walls and racks of film cans. I have since discovered that if we set up cutting rooms with a little atmosphere, even if it consists of only one window, then everyone's creativity—the editor's, the director's, everyone's involved—is heightened and therefore work is speeded up. Why be depressed if you don't have to be?'

There was no reason to be depressed about *High Plains Drifter,* Eastwood took an inventive and cleverly written script and, with a sure sense of pace and purpose, directed a classic Western. It was the apotheosis of the Stranger who had set him on the road to success and satisfaction. Although he has never said so, I doubt if Eastwood will ever feel the need to play that part again. When he rode out of Lago it was forever. His achievement can rest secure: it is well and truly realised.

Eastwood needed a rest after the arduous location

101

at Mono Lake, and he had always maintained that he wanted to spend more time with his family. This was increased by one on 23rd May 1972 when Maggie gave birth to a long-awaited daughter. They called her Allison. Her father was more than forty years older than her but when I met them four years later they had formed a bond that was understanding and loving. Eastwood had found two deer that had been deserted by their parents in a storm, and Allison and he had reared them by feeding them milk from a baby's bottle. Followed by their faithful basset-hound, Sidney, Allison could hardly bear to let her father out of her sight and, indeed, climbed all over him as he attempted to answer some questions in front of the television cameras.

After *High Plains Drifter,* Eastwood went from the sublime to the slight, professionally, when he chose his third picture as director, *Breezy.* His loyalty to his close colleagues is undentable but occasionally accounts for slight misjudgements. Jim Fargo was not an experienced enough director to make *The Enforcer* as powerful a film as it should have been; equally, although Jo Heims came up with a gem of a script for *Misty,* her story for *Breezy* belonged more in the realms of the made-for-television movie than in the cinema. Clint's own reservations can be gleaned from the fact that he didn't act in the film, claiming that as he had never directed a love story before, he needed to put all his attention behind the camera, but patently the leading part was originally meant for him.

In the end, the role went to William Holden—an Oscar winner for his performance as the sergeant suspected of being a spy in Billy Wilder's *Stalag 17* and a stalwart of Peckinpah's *Wild Bunch.* (He was later to distinguish himself even further in Lumet's *Network.*) Holden enjoyed the experience of working with Eastwood: 'I'd forgotten what it's like to make pictures this agreeably. I'll work with Clint any time he asks. Besides, he can't pull any crap on me, because he's an actor, too.' They tested various unknowns for the female lead (including Sondra Locke who was later to play an important part in Eastwood's life) and eventually cast Kay Lenz whom Robert Daley had seen in a television movie with the improbable title of *The Weekend Nun.*

The story was modern. Eastwood said, 'I thought it was a very common story these days. It was the rejuvenation of a cynic, a man who was totally engulfed by cynicism. He had been the divorce route, he'd had some monetary success but as a person, emotionally, he'd had no success and he learned this through a teenage girl.' Where perhaps they misjudged the audience appeal was in the fact that the menopausal men to whom the film might be a salutary lesson, were more likely to be at home watching television than queuing for the cinema, and the Kay Lenz character was insufficiently well-drawn to appeal to her own generation.

Holden plays a divorced real estate dealer, Frank Harmon, who rattles around his comfortable Laurel Canyon home like a pea in a pod. Breezy (Kay Lenz) offers herself to him, for no very clear reason save for the fact that he is kind enough to give her a lift. He rejects her but they are brought together over a common concern for a wounded dog. He beds her but cannot accept a relationship until the husband of a

Below: With his two children, Kyle, and Allison as a baby. Right: With his daughter, Allison, a few years later.

Above: Eastwood, director of Breezy *(1973), with his star, William Holden. The story tells of an older man's reluctant love affair with a young girl. Below: In* Thunderbolt and Lightfoot *(1974), the old gang again; Jeff Bridges, George Kennedy, Eastwood and Geoffrey Lewis.*

close friend is killed; this event brings Harmon face to face with his own loneliness. He realises that you must seize life's opportunities when they are presented to you and the film ends on the optimistic note that perhaps the two will stay together.

It was made with Eastwood's by now customary polish and timing but that wasn't enough to please the critics. However he didn't blame them for the film's lack of success. 'You can't blame it on reviewers because if the film's good and the reviewer doesn't see that it's good, that doesn't mean that the public will stay away from it. The public stayed away from it because it wasn't promoted enough and it was sold in an uninteresting fashion.'

As with *The Beguiled*, Universal's promotion and distribution campaign found disfavour with Eastwood, and so did the censor. 'I don't think Breezy deserves to be R-rated at all. But it is, because some twenty states in the Union have statutes that say showing the nipple on a woman's breast to children is obscene. That's the first thing we come into contact with when we arrive on this planet: a woman's breast.

Why should that be considered obscene?'

When I read this slight outburst in *Playboy,* I was intrigued to find out how permissive Eastwood was regarding sex in the cinema. So I asked him about this and he replied, 'I don't know. If you're talking about straight pornos or something, to me those are just boring. They're usually done with Rexall Drugstore lighting and not terribly interesting people. I prefer films where people just kiss. No, within the confines of a love story I suppose somebody could eventually some day make an interesting film. *Last Tango in Paris* had a lot of sensational things in it. It had some very good individual scenes but as an overall film I didn't think it was a terribly even picture. Whether it says anything or tells anything that is interesting or even entertaining remains to be seen.'

When I pressed him further to consider whether he thought the cinema had become too permissive, and whether some form of censorship was desirable, Eastwood had definite views. 'I feel the public will find its level. The public should be able to see what it wants. I'm not for censorship. There are too many people in the world who are always trying to impose their views on somebody else. I think that was a big problem in the past, and it's a big problem right now today. I think if the public is interested in a film they should see it. I think eventually pornography will wane. After a while people will say "Ah, we've had that" and look for something else. I don't like certain things, but that doesn't mean because I don't like them the guy across the street or the guy down the way has to adhere to my thoughts.'

In fact, in *Thunderbolt and Lightfoot,* the film that followed *Magnum Force,* there were some unusually explicit sex scenes for an Eastwood movie —they included a motel bedroom encounter with a hooker, and later a scene where a naked copulating couple is tied up during a bank raid. The young writer, Michael Cimino, who had struck a mutual chord with Eastwood during script sessions on

Thunderbolt and Lightfoot (1974). A little light romance for Thunderbolt: Jeff Bridges in drag as Gloria.

Magnum Force, came up with an idea for a 'buddy' movie, a genre that had gained momentum since the pairing of Jon Voight and Dustin Hoffman in *Midnight Cowboy* and Robert Redford and Paul Newman in *Butch Cassidy and the Sundance Kid.* Eastwood was partnered with Jeff Bridges—son of Lloyd, a family friend and a stalwart of Clint's and Maggie's annual charity tennis tournament at Pebble Beach. Cimino was given his first chance as director.

It was a gamble to use a young, untried hand but he was safely squeezed between Bob Daley as producer, Frank Stanley (who had shot *Magnum Force* and *Breezy*) as cameraman and Clint himself as *éminence gris.* Orson Welles once observed that you could learn everything technical about film making in half a day, and while the remark owed more to hyperbole than to truth, a good cameraman, a good first assistant and a sympathetic editor can protect the novice from finding that his shots won't cut together. The very first shot of *Thunderbolt and Lightfoot*—a faultless composition, fifty per cent wispy Idaho sky, fifty per cent cornfield—establishes an elegant style which Cimino maintains throughout the film. The second scene—Clint Eastwood as we have never seen him before, wearing spectacles, his hair slicked back and dressed as a vicar delivering a sermon in a crowded country church—immediately makes one realise that the film may be quite different from any of Eastwood's previous ones. But the third scene, in which the vicar is chased across a seemingly endless cornfield by an irate gun-firing George Kennedy establishes that all is not as it seems to be.

Eastwood is rescued by Lightfoot (Jeff Bridges), who has just relieved a car salesman of $3000 dollars' worth of automobile, and a partnership is quickly created, with the veteran Thunderbolt asserting his experience and virility over the raw Lightfoot. Casting off his vicar's clothes Thunderbolt then takes his belt and endures agonising pain as he uses it to pull his dislocated shoulder into place.

Thunderbolt is being pursued by Red Leary (George Kennedy) and Eddie Goody (Geoffrey Lewis) who are former partners of his in crime and who believe he has the half million dollar takings from their last bank raid. They mean business. While Thunderbolt and Lightfoot enjoy themselves with two young ladies named Gloria and Melody, Leary and Goody wait outside. 'Are you sure that's their car?' wonders Goody. 'That's their hearse,' says Leary.

After an inventive car chase up hill and down dale through Montana's stunning scenery, Thunderbolt outwits his former partners and finally convinces them that he hasn't got the money. All four then join forces to raid a government vault, using a 20-millimetre cannon to blast their way in. Lightfoot—whose conversation Cimino has effectively constructed as a chain of clichés—dresses up as a woman to distract the night watchman and this adds some ribaldry to the joking relationship he has struck up with Thunderbolt. The raid is successful, but the film rapidly switches from sweet to sour. Goody is killed in the

getaway and Leary viciously kicks Lightfoot's head in, before being caught by the police. Although the two buddies find the original cache of half a million dollars and Thunderbolt treats Lightfoot to the Cadillac he yearns for, it is too late. In a scene reminiscent of Dustin Hoffman dying on the way to Miami in *Midnight Cowboy*—just when the promised land is in sight—Lightfoot dies in the car. Perhaps for the first time in his life, Thunderbolt realises that the takings aren't everything. As he drives into the horizon it is with a sense of loss rather than gain.

It was a triumphant début for Cimino. His script combined wit and the naïve philosophy of the motorised cowboys. 'Leary, I had a dream about you last night.' 'About what?' 'I dreamt you said hello to me.' At the beginning of the film when Eastwood recites his sermon for the benefit of his felonious friend, 'and the lion shall lie down with the leopard' (Cimino used it purposely to portend the liaison between Lightfoot the lion and Thunderbolt the leopard), the younger man asks 'What's that—a poem?' 'No,' replies Thunderbolt, 'a prayer'. At the end of the film the younger man is still seeking answers from his senior partner. 'Where you heading?' 'See what's over the next mountain.' 'We won, didn't we?' 'I guess we did—for the time being.'

The theme was to be reflected to advantage in Cimino's later and greater work; *The Deer Hunter* was more about comradeship than violence. Cimino said, 'I don't think that contemporary work necessarily celebrates violence but it has to deal with it. It has become such a catchword in modern film criticism that I think when the word is used, it blanks out many other qualities in the film which are then ignored. It's often a smokescreen for wanting to avoid dealing with what is there. It's fashionable to talk about violence. It doesn't make good copy to write about the nature of friendship.'

He created the part for Eastwood and in doing so drew greatly on his actual personality. For those people who know the real Clint Eastwood, no film part better conveys the style, the warmth and the dry delivery of the man himself. It was also typical of his generosity, when his status was higher than ever in America that he should split the lead in a Western so generously with such a lesser-known actor.

When one compares Eastwood's career with the progress of other equally highly-rated stars, a difference is discernible. Redford and Newman rarely succeeded individually to the extent they did jointly in *Butch Cassidy* and later *The Sting.* McQueen reached the apogee of his fame, his asking price and his success and then retreated into quasi-retirement. At this stage in his career, what set Eastwood apart was that he became almost a movie workaholic. Money no longer had any persuasive part to play in his decisions. Whether running Malpaso or reading scripts as an actor or preparing them as a director, his professional life had acquired such a momentum that he just had to keep on making films.

Right: Box office greats: Paul Newman and Clint Eastwood.

ANYTIME YOU'RE READY CLINT, ROLL

It remains something of a mystery why Clint Eastwood made *The Eiger Sanction*. Admittedly it had been a successful novel (by Trevanian), but the main character, Jonathan Hemlock, a mild art teacher, had to be severely amended by three writers, Hal Dresner, Warren B. Murphy and Rod Whitaker, before the part reflected the qualities necessary for an Eastwood hero. Clint hinted at what he wanted to achieve when he said, 'It bordered on a Bondish sort of thing in certain areas,' but Hemlock rarely exhibited the laconic acuity and ruthlessness of 007.

Eastwood hoped that Don Siegel would direct but the latter was too conscious of the drawbacks. 'I said to him "What good am I going to be to you when you're 10,000 feet up and I'm 3,000 feet up and there's 7,000 feet separating us and I say "Anytime you're ready, Clint, roll?"' It was a movie that had a dramatic ascent of the dreaded North Face of the Eiger as its climax and, naturally, Eastwood the actor was intending to essay it in person. He took Siegel's advice and decided to direct the picture himself. 'We just couldn't find anybody who was interested in climbing so I went back to directing. I just liked the story. There wasn't anybody I really knew who was available at the time that I thought

Left: Eastwood directed and starred in The Outlaw Josey Wales *(1976). Below: Two very different locations for* The Eiger Sanction *(1975). Left: Eastwood relaxing between arduous sessions of mountaineering training. Right: In the Swiss Alps with old friend George Kennedy.*

would comprehend this one—at least the way I did. I mean, it's just a question of opinion; they may have executed it better. No-one really knows until they do it. You just read certain projects that you think you can do, and other projects you think you can't.'

Having burdened himself with the daunting chore of directing, Eastwood remained steadfast in his intention to make the picture as authentic as possible. 'The Eiger is a mean mountain. The challenge of it for me is to actually shoot a mountain-type film on a mountain, not on sets. The only ones made in the past were all filmed on sets, and the mountains were all papier-mâché mountains.' True to form he went off to Yosemite National Park for three weeks' training with the climber Mike Hoover. While his courage was as ever to be admired he would have spent his time more productively on the script. It turned out to be a pretty thin screenplay.

Jonathan Hemlock is living a quiet life as an art teacher when, one day, an emissary from 'C11' offers him a 'sanction'—jargon for an assassination contract. He agrees, not only for the usual Eastwood bounty—in this case $20,000—but also for the unusual addition of a Pissarro painting. He flies to Zurich, duly sanctions the intended victim, Kruger, but finds that an air hostess with whom he has become friendly is another C11 agent—she disappears with the money. He is forced into agreeing to perform a second sanction, this time on a fellow climber while they are both on an ascent of the Eiger. In passing, he disposes of a couple of unsavoury characters while

The Eiger Sanction (1975). Left: Fleeting romantic interest with another agent, played by Vonetta McGee. Below left: Clint takes aim at one of his victims. Below right: Eastwood made this film himself after Don Siegel turned it down—he felt Clint would be too far up the mountain for anyone else to direct him well.

he is training in Arizona, and then returns to Switzerland for the final showdown, this time not in a Western street, but on the North Face.

Siegel didn't like it—'I didn't think the story was any good'—but was impressed by the way Clint handled it. 'He did a very good job of directing a difficult, dangerous film.' One of the main faults was the length; at over two hours Eastwood failed to make it gripping enough to hold the audience. 'The landscapes tend to obliterate the actors,' wrote the usually pro-Eastwood Dilys Powell in the *Sunday Times.* 'Long and ponderously predictable ... the film takes an unconscionably long time to reach its climax,' said the *Financial Times,* a criticism generally echoed by other papers. But unlike *Breezy,* in which he did not appear but only directed, it had Eastwood in front of the camera as well as behind it, and so it soon went into a healthy profit. To date, according to *Variety,* it has taken a solid $7,155,000 in the United States alone.

Although Frank Stanley was, once again, the main lighting cameraman on the film, he was aided by four men with better heads for heights who did the mountain work: John Cleare, Peter Pilafian, Jeff

Schoolfield and Peter White. A number of professional mountaineers took part in the film and one of them, a young British climber, David Knowles, was killed by a rockslide on the second day of filming. Eastwood, who was nearby, saw it happen. He was stunned and deeply moved by the man's death. 'I like to think that this film may, in its way, be a tribute to David and his fellow climbers—they're a breed apart,' he said afterwards. In its way, it was.

The process of directing, acting and climbing was an arduous one for Eastwood. 'Usually, in about the last quarter of the film, you start having doubts: I wonder if this is any good, I wonder if this story point is really right. But you've been thinking about it so long you just have to shut your mind off and say, wait a second, three months ago this was fine and that's the way it's going to go. You have to stay with the blueprint at that point. It's a terribly mind-fatiguing job to be both actor and director. Just being a director is a very time-consuming job, the pre-production and the post-production work especially. It really isn't the eight or nine weeks that it takes to shoot the film that is the problem—it's all the time it takes afterwards. If you direct films, you can't really act in too many.'

So when he embarked on his next project, *The Outlaw Josey Wales,* Eastwood was at first very happy that someone else—Phil Kaufman, co-writer of the screenplay—should direct. But the pressure

The Outlaw Josey Wales (1976) was considered by critics a personal tour de force for Eastwood.

111

wasn't off for long. Kaufman dropped out early in the location and Eastwood once more was forced reluctantly to pick up the director's reins. Fate, as ever, was on his side for it turned out to be a personal *tour de force*. At the same time it became his favourite film although he was shrewd enough to add, 'It might just be because it was my last film as director.'

A degree of confusion attends the parentage of the story *The Rebel Outlaw: Josey Wales.* Eastwood told Patrick McGilligan during his interview with him for *Focus on Film* in 1976, 'It was written by a guy who had never written a book before, a half-Cherokee Indian with no formal education, not even grammar school. He is very much a self-taught person who became famous as an Indian poet and teller of stories. Somebody talked him into writing one down.'

He went on to relate how Forrest Carter, the forty-six year old writer, had sent him a copy from the limited edition of seventy-five. Robert Daley read the story, and enthused to Eastwood about the 'soul' in it. When Eastwood had finished it he agreed with his partner, and they immediately called Carter in Arkansas and bought the screen rights.

Two years later, after the film was finished, on 26 August 1976, the *New York Times* ran a story revealing that several people in Montgomery,

Alabama, had seen Forrest Carter on NBC's *Today* show telling Barbara Walters that he was a cowboy who had turned to writing, and identified him as Asa Carter, a speechwriter for Governor Wallace. Other local people made the same identification from the author's picture on the back of the book jacket. Evidently, Carter had helped to shape the Governor's 1963 inaugural address which included the less than liberal sentiments, 'I say segregation now, segregation tomorrow, segregation forever'. Later, in 1970, Carter actually ran against the Governor when he considered Wallace had become too soft. Inevitably, he lost. Whatever were the true details of Carter's existence will never be known as he has since died and his mystery has died with him. However, he certainly provided Eastwood with the Western he was looking for. 'I'd done satiric Westerns in the Italian-made films and there was an element of heroism in those, but I'd always wanted to do a more traditional classic Western saga, with time lapses and episodes. I never found a story until I found the one by Forrest Carter.'

It had the necessary elements to make a classic. Josey Wales has no desire to become an outlaw. Few men do. Circumstances force it on them. At the beginning of the film he is a peaceable Missouri farmer whose wife and child are murdered by Unionist vigilantes, the 'Kansas Red Legs'. The film

opens in 1858 when the semi-discipline of the Civil War has been reduced to the chaos of marauding private armies. Wales joins a Confederate gang and for the next seven years exacts a multiple revenge on the Unionists, killing them without political cause or pity.

At the end of formal hostilities a price is placed on his head so he makes a picaresque journey south to Texas. On the way he picks up various companions: Jamie (Sam Bottoms), whose life he saves and who repays the favour only to die from his wounds; Lone Watie (Chief Dan George) who instructs him in the ways and thoughts of the Cherokees; Little Moonlight (Geraldine Keams), who like Josey is an outcast; Grandma Sarah (Paula Trueman) and Laura Lee (Sondra Locke), whom he rescues from the Commancheros.

After surviving the dangers of their journey under the protective wing of Josey, the group sets up a commune of sorts on a Texas farm. Wales tries to pass his self-sufficient qualities onto them so that they can if necessary survive without him. He shows them how to use guns and protect the farm against invaders. He negotiates a peace with the local Commanche Chief, Ten Bears (Will Sampson). Having satiated his reserves of bitterness and revenge, he is charmed by the whimsical Laura Lee and falls in love with her. After years of trail and tribulation, there is real hope that he can resume his previously placid life by the hearth and on the soil.

The film has the magical combination of well-researched fact and cowboy fantasy. Eastwood discovered that the 'Kansas Red Legs' were guerrillas, actually sanctioned by the State of Missouri. 'They were a State militia; they were like a vigilante group who, under the guise of protection, did a lot of bad deeds.' Moreover, he was determined to put across the sad shambles that the Civil War left in its wake. 'There are in this film a lot of thoughts about war and the victims of war.'

The fantasy, as ever, was Eastwood. Josey Wales switches from peasant farmer to lethal killer with the minimum of target practice. His shooting becomes as accurate as his tobacco spitting (an art that took Eastwood months to perfect). Whether he is merely taking a split second to reverse the guns he is pretending to hand over to some captors and hand over some bullets instead, or whether he is decimating a meadow-full of soldiers with a captured machine gun, or appearing out of the sun to terrify a band of Indians into thinking he is an entire army in himself, he remains superhuman and inviolable. It is the essential Eastwood persona that is a magnet to the public and a mystery to the critics.

The plethora of killings aside, *The Outlaw Josey Wales* is undoubtedly the most tender film Eastwood has made to date. Josey's firelit love affair with Laura is triggered off by such wistful sentiments as 'Clouds are dreams floating across the sky of your mind', but it rings true that a man blinkered by revenge and hardened by the sheer need to survive could be drawn to an innocent girl, able to escape from the

The Outlaw Josey Wales (1976). Top: Chief Dan George played Lone Watie. Centre: Sondra Locke appeared with Eastwood for the first time, as Laura Lee. Bottom: Josey Wales takes his revenge on Terrill, played by Bill McKinney.

terrors of her environment into the poetry of her reveries.

Sondra Locke had already won an Oscar nomination for her role in *The Heart is a Lonely Hunter* but after that her cinema career had dipped. 'I tried to run before I could walk,' she said. Both Jo Heims and Jessica Walter had recommended her for *Breezy* but Eastwood 'didn't see her in that role'. Her career got a

Many critics agreed that the character of Josey Wales revealed a new mellowness and depth of characterisation in Eastwood's interpretation as actor and director.

much-needed fillip from *Josey* and she was duly grateful. 'With this movie, Clint has been very generous to me. It was a script I loved. It had heart, it had power and visually it was quite beautiful. I had admired Clint for quite some time, and I felt his screen presence as something unique, direct and strong. I'd admired his work as a director. I particularly liked *Play Misty For Me* and *Breezy* and, happily, working with him fulfilled my expectations.'

A masterstroke of casting was Chief Dan George as Lone Watie. He, too, had received an Oscar nomination, for playing Old Lodge Skins in Arthur Penn's *Little Big Man*. A real Indian—he was former chief of British Columbia's Tse-lal-watt tribe—this seventy-six year old grandfather struck up a perfect partnership with Eastwood, sensitively timing the soft humour in their relationship. When Josey casually outdraws and kills four men, the old Indian asks with genuine interest, 'How did you know which one to kill first?' Editor Ferris Webster recalls that the Chief had some difficulty remembering his lines. 'One of the funniest things I've seen was in a two-shot where Clint is with Dan George and he's trying so hard for Dan George to remember his lines that he's actually mouthing them with him.'

Eastwood enjoyed directing the Chief. 'He's terrific. He had no real acting training but he thinks

naturally, he listens naturally, he does a lot of things that actors train for years to do well.' He also enjoyed directing himself. 'When I'm directing Eastwood, I listen to myself a lot.' The results showed. 'People know more about this character than about any of the others I've played where the stories worked around just an incident in their lives. This is a saga. Josey Wales is an enigmatic hero who drifts across the plains, going from farmer to killer and back to farmer. It's also the first Western I've made that women seem to like.'

Certainly Dilys Powell warmed to it. 'I think he has very sensibly begun to mellow his attitude towards society in his films. In *The Outlaw Josey Wales* he still plays a solitary figure but it isn't quite the same kind of solitary figure. He's not simply the avenger, not simply a man with a rifle. He is a man who at the same time defends women and children and the weak. It's a different image and very promising. I think it's a very, very good Western.' And even Pauline Kael, while deeming Eastwood 'an extremely mediocre director,' acknowledged: 'I think *The Outlaw Josey Wales* is perhaps an improvement.'

Unlike Miss Kael, I think *Josey Wales* demonstrated that Eastwood is a director of considerable stature and innovation. The film runs for two and a quarter hours but it has a masterly rhythm to suggest the days and years going by. As in the Leone films, violence erupts in the action only intermittently and is all the more effective for being unexpected. Eastwood's versatility in handling the humour with

Chief Dan George, the tender scenes with Sondra Locke and also his ability to handle one hundred and fifty uncontrollable Navajo braves are qualities that few directors possess. Moreover, he is able to make small scenes memorable just by injecting an understated piece of levity into them, as with the boatman for instance who whistles the appropriate theme depending on whether his passengers are Unionist or Confederate. 'Humour,' comments Eastwood, 'makes the characters more human.'

Not everyone appreciated his talents. Richard Eder in the *New York Times* found fault with every aspect of the film, deeming it 'a soggy attempt at a post-Civil War Western epic'. Richard Schickel in *Time* magazine found that Josey's Trail had 'a fair amount of dull slogging along the way' but noted, 'The film has its pleasures as well'. He ended his review by acknowledging the place Eastwood had now carved for himself in the American cinema. 'In a Western where spacious landscapes and historical distances seem to soften the impact of his brutal methods of problem-solving, Eastwood is not simply a symbol of the modern taste for random and gratuitous bloodletting in films. Rather, he reminds us of a traditional American style of screen heroism — a moral man, slow to rile but wonderfully skilled when he must finally enforce his concepts of right and wrong. In these moments he links us pleasingly, satisfyingly with our movie pasts, rekindles briefly a dying glow.'

Josey Wales was a gamble. As they were making it Eastwood remembers, 'Some executive from some studio came out and said, "Westerns aren't doing anything" and the general Hollywood studio wisdom was to avoid completely the previously cast-iron genre. Even big names like Newman, Nicholson, Brando and, unthinkably, Wayne weren't drawing audiences to the box-office for Westerns.' Nevertheless, Malpaso and Warners invested $3,700,000 in *Josey Wales* — Eastwood's twenty-sixth film and his fifth as director. To date it has taken $13,500,000 in America and probably as much as that again in the rest of the world. By the end of 1976 the grosses of Eastwood's films worldwide exceeded $250,000,000.

For his next venture, however, he was persuaded, reluctantly, to return to the character of Dirty Harry. 'Warners wanted me to do it very much', he revealed mockingly, 'and I hate to see grown men cry.' By now Malpaso had moved their premises from the Universal lot to Warners Burbank Studios, headed by Eastwood's former lawyer, Frank Wells. The company was prepared to do anything to keep their golden goose happy, permitting him to deliver the final cut of his films without studio interference — a rare deal in the cinema. After his tireless work as assistant director

Sondra Locke co-starred again in The Gauntlet *(1976). Eastwood directed and acted in this violent saga of a loser cop, Ben Shockley, trying to bring a key witness to trial.*

The Gauntlet *(1976). Sondra Locke plays Augusta Mally, a hooker and star witness in a murder case. Shockley and Mally endure several violent encounters with the mob on their journey back to Phoenix.*

on *Josey Wales,* Eastwood promoted Jim Fargo to director on *The Enforcer.* The public appeal of the third *Dirty Harry* proved stronger than ever, netting $24,000,000 in the United States.

I think I may have been present at the birth of his next film, *The Gauntlet.* I was sipping my coffee with Eastwood and Joe Hyams in Eastwood's darkly furnished room in the Malpaso hacienda—more of a study than an office, with only a snarling poster of Josey Wales to indicate its occupant was a film maker rather than a psychiatrist. Hyams, a short, economically built man with a silver crew cut and a penchant for being at the controls of fast planes and even faster cars, is vice-president of publicity at Warners. His main value to the studio is that, unlike almost anyone else in the place, he doesn't run scared of major stars and, accordingly, people like Hoffman, Redford, Streisand and Eastwood like him and confide in him. That afternoon he was subtly trying to feel the water on what would be a winning combination for Warners: Eastwood and Streisand.

'Barbra's got this great script, Clint,' enthused Hyams. 'It's about a cop who brings a hooker back from Vegas to Phoenix to stand trial. Just think of the box-office combination if you did it—fantastic scenes between them.' There was a short pause. 'Really,' said Eastwood. At the time the Hollywood trade papers were rich with stories of Miss Streisand's overbearing dominance on *A Star Is Born.* Her director, Frank Pierson, even wrote a long article complaining about his pincered position between Miss Streisand and her producer, Jon Peters. 'Joe, I like Barbra a lot; she's a talented girl.' Hyams's eyes

lit up. Eastwood took another handful of cashew nuts from the bowl in front of him and continued, 'But I'm nearly fifty years old and I don't think I could afford to spend six months of my life working with that woman.'

In the event he made *The Gauntlet* himself with Sondra Locke as the hooker. The major appeal of the script by Michael Butler and Dennis Shryack was that it combined a fast-moving violent action picture with an unusual love story and a much-desired role reversal for him. Knowing that he could always command success as the lone Western hero or as Dirty Harry, Eastwood's problem was to find scripts that were different; not an easy task. 'We see a ton of scripts that are just copies of what I've done before. That's not really adequate over the years. But if I read something that entertains me and it fits in, if I feel it at an instinctive level, then I'll buy it. But I don't go out and say, "Well, this will change my image". If I think the overall piece will make an interesting movie, a movie that I think I'd like to see if I was a member of the audience, then I accept the film on that level. I'm not just interested in playing a role; I'm interested in doing a whole film.'

By this stage in his career, 1976, Eastwood's personal power in Hollywood was without precedent. No other star, past or present, has had to rely to such an extent on his own instincts to guide his career. Eastwood says modestly—and truthfully—'I've made some good decisions, I've made some bad ones too. But I've made enough good ones along the way to keep people's confidence in my selection.'

The challenge of playing the cop, Ben Shockley, in *The Gauntlet* was that the character was virtually the opposite of Harry Callaghan: he's a loser, a man resigned to doing twenty years in the force and then looking forward to collecting his pension. His car is full of empty whiskey bottles, his life is a shambles, he's never even been given a big case let alone solved one. He is sent from Phoenix to Las Vegas to 'bring back a nothing witness for a nothing trial'.

The 'nothing' witness, Gus Mally, is not the man he expects; in the first place she's a woman, Augusta Mally, secondly she's a hooker, thirdly, despite her non-stop profanities, she's a graduate of Finch College and lastly—and hereby hangs the tale —she's not a 'nothing witness'. The mob who are to be tried will do anything to prevent her testifying and so will Shockley's own boss, the Phoenix police commissioner, who is in league with them.

The dangers inherent in their journey together only slowly become apparent to Shockley despite the fact that the Vegas police literally raze to the ground the couple's initial hideaway, while they remain inside almost to the last moment. (It is one of several spectacular scenes in which 35 special effects men spent $1,000,000 alone in attack and destruction sequences. 2,800 man-hours were spent rigging the building with 7,000 explosive squibs to produce the effect of the house falling down from an incessant torrent of bullets.)

Now joined against mutual adversity, the hooker

and the cop survive successive onslaughts beginning with an attack from drug-crazed Hell's Angels. Augusta Mally uses the gun, while Ben Shockley, stepping out of character to provide a moment of delight for Eastwood fans, punches a female Angel in the face. Next there's a predatory helicopter sent by the Commissioner to mow them down, which explodes after flying into some high-tension wires (costing $250,000 in special effects). Ben is beaten up, Augusta is raped and, as a climax, they face the Gauntlet itself—the massed ranks of the Phoenix police force who let off 8,000 shots at Shockley's 13-ton steel-fortified bus.

Finally, Shockley makes it. He defies them all and delivers his charge to the magistrate. 'He's like a professional fighter who's trained every day in the gym but never had to fight until now,' explained Eastwood. 'All of a sudden he finds himself in a situation that he has to fight himself out of—he may be thicker than the girl but his determination is the same and hopefully that will be the appeal of the film.'

Within the maelstrom of these assailants, Shockley and Mally manage to transform their original dislike for each other and each other's way of life into a love of sorts, 'in the African Queen type tradition,' hoped Eastwood. As the couple begin to understand each other, they realise how their relationship could serve each other. She would no longer need to be a whore. He could regain his self-esteem as a policeman. Shortly before the final showdown Mally telephones her mother to say she has found Mr Right; from then on there is an added imperative that they survive in order to give their love and their relationship a chance to work out.

Sondra Locke achieved the improbably-written transformation from hooker to sociologist convincingly: 'The most natural, unaffected performance of the year by any young actress', wrote Tom Allen in the *Village Voice*. 'She blossoms forth as a young Susan Hayward or Barbara Stanwyck.'

But in this film, more than ever, Eastwood wasn't trying for any plaudits from the critics; probably the reverse. 'The overkill is part of the entertainment,' he claimed. 'You just have to accept it on an outrageous level.' There were those who didn't. '*The Gauntlet* is the pits' (Judith Crist); 'No more than a pretext for an extravagant display of gunplay, a steady stream of verbal obscenity and a bit of nudity and sex', (*The Catholic Conference*). But these comments only served to inform Eastwood that at least he had been excessive enough to upset some people. It would be awful to think you're being outrageous and to outrage nobody. Andrew Sarris in the *Village Voice,* who is generally the most perceptive analyst of Eastwood's work, was able to read between the lines to see Eastwood's intent. 'Gradually it begins to dawn on the audience that the Eastwood character is not nearly as bright as he thinks he is and that Eastwood, the director, is poking fun at Eastwood the macho legend.'

With a touch as deft as Nastase in his prime,

Shockley and Mally emerge from the bullet-torn 13-ton steel fortified bus at the climax of The Gauntlet; *the Gauntlet itself being the massed ranks of the Phoenix police force.*

Eastwood knows just how far he can take an audience with him. By surviving the unsurvivable, the Phoenix Ned Kelly proved to himself once more that the mass audience will suspend all sensible disbelief—as they do in the best of the Bond films—providing the action carries them and their fantasies along.

In the context of many of his other films, *The Gauntlet* is hardly one of Eastwood's most substantial works. The appeal of an unlikely love affair between opposites, fertilised by an unceasing barrage of gunfire was undoubtedly considerable. But as a whole the film tended to operate rather as an exercise in special effects than as any more considered piece of social statement of the kind that gave such strength to *Dirty Harry.*

Undoubtedly Eastwood likes to toy with his image and his audience to find out just how far he can go. The first flurries of dismay usually come from the executives at Warner Brothers when Clint announces a new project and I must confess that I was equally apprehensive when one vice-president showed me the script outline for Clint's next film. It read quite normally—Eastwood was to play Philo Beddoe, a barroom brawler in love with a country singer, Lynn Halsey-Taylor (Sondra Locke). He has a couple of close mates, Orville, who promotes his fights, and Clyde, an orangutan. An orangutan? What would the Universal executive who asked 'Who wants to see Clint Eastwood play a disc jockey?', have said if he'd learnt he was going to make a movie with an orangutan? Who *did* want to see Clint and Clyde? The American public. They paid a record $48,000,000 —double the receipts of his next most popular film

Eastwood's next film was a new departure: in Every Which Way But Loose *(1979) he goes for comedy, and co-stars with Clyde, an orangutan.*

The Enforcer—to see *Every Which Way But Loose.* As Eastwood said, 'If I feel it on an instinctive level, then I'll buy it.' After *Variety* reported the film's tremendous success in America in January 1979, Eastwood revealed that his manager, his attorney, his agent and his producer had all advised him against the comedy. He stood by his own counsel. 'I had done a lot of hard R-films geared primarily to an adult audience. When I read this script, I saw it as an opportunity to reach down into the next generation. This story had a hip twist that would keep the adults satisfied and the animal works well with the kids.'

In hindsight it is possible to divine Eastwood's reasoning for such a dramatic change. He was nearing fifty; his personal fortune was so shrewdly spread in property, companies and in his films themselves that I doubt if even he knew what he was worth but it wouldn't be a bad guess to begin at $50,000,000 and start counting upwards. He was beyond a doubt the biggest box-office draw in the world. Nobody, neither the major studios nor the critics, could cause him the slightest concern—he had a direct line to the public. He had succeeded in sharing the lead with a woman, Sondra Locke, in an unusual love story, *The Gauntlet*, and that same woman was at the time having a potent effect on his own thoughts about life. He was less cautious and vulnerable, more able to let his hair down and have a little fun, revealing to the public his genuine appetite for absurd humour that was known only to his close friends. For the first time in his life he was able to

comprehend and enjoy the magnitude of his success. Besides, his friendly rival Burt Reynolds (with whom he shared a *Time* cover in January 1978 under the banner 'Hollywood's Honchos') had shown him the way with *Smokey and the Bandit.* Both men were now in the position where money was not the prime concern in their choices. Burt Reynolds had decided to make *Smokey* as a personal favour for his friend Hal Needham, taking a risk with a style of film very different from his macho image. The film, which cost $4,000,000 to make, grossed about $100,000,000 in 1977 alone. Clint now found himself faced with a similar choice, and determined to risk it.

The first requirement imposed on them by Jeremy Joe Kronsberg's screenplay was to find an orangutan. The usual places to go for this are the coastal forests of Borneo and Sumatra where orangutans dwell in trees. Clint wanted one that could walk so he and Bob Daley went to the MGM Grand Hotel in Las Vegas. There Bobby and Joan Berosini introduced them to Clyde, 165 pounds of orangutan, who appeared in their revue at the hotel. He was eleven years old and had been in training for nine years but had never worked with anyone other than the Berosinis. They were very doubtful about loaning him for the film. 'We wouldn't have done it except for Clint,' said Berosini and his trust proved well founded.

'The man could easily be a professional animal trainer if he wanted. He's very calm and very secure which puts an animal, particularly an intelligent, spontaneous animal like Clyde, at ease straightaway.'

Clyde was already trained but the next move was to find someone to train Clint, since he had to do a considerable amount of professional boxing in the film. Al Silvani had worked with him on *Paint Your Wagon* and, as well as training such eminent professional boxers as Rocky Graziano and Floyd Patterson, had obtained a reputation as the best boxing consultant in Hollywood, his most notable coup being his work with Sylvester Stallone on *Rocky*. Eastwood was already in good shape and Silvani was impressed by his aptitude. 'Clint is a natural upright boxer. He's a big guy with a great reach which makes the jab an easy thing to teach. What I had to show him was balance and movement, to get the power up from the legs and into the punch. When he puts together some of those combinations, well, he's not fooling anybody. It's something beautiful to see.'

Since he had enough to contend with, acting, boxing and playing with an ape, Eastwood got Jim Fargo to direct and also brought in other old mates like Geoffrey Lewis, who plays Orville, and who had been with Clint in *High Plains Drifter* and *Thunderbolt and Lightfoot*; Bill McKinney (who plays Dallas) from *Josey Wales*, Fritz Manes as associate producer and the faithful Ferris Webster as editor. All these ensured that the film remained tightly within the

Above: Philo Beddoe, the prize-fighter. Below: Eastwood rehearsing 'a very natural method actor', as Clyde's trainer, Berosini, described him.

Every Which Way But Loose *(1979). Sondra Locke played a country singer, Lynn Halsey-Taylor, and had to sing in front of a live audience. 'It was a scary experience, believe me. . . .'*

Malpaso family. Sondra Locke, now firmly part of it, had to learn some basic guitar chords and steel herself to sing in front of a live audience. Eventually she enjoyed it: 'It was a scary experience, believe me, but it was also very reassuring. I had a good time and it helped my confidence.'

The plot of the film was a lean frame on which to hang plenty of brawling, singing, car-chasing and general monkey-business. Eastwood as Philo Beddoe is a truck driver who earns some extra cash from bar room brawls underhandedly promoted by Orville. He is attracted to a delicate country singer, Lynn, and accompanied by Orville and Clyde (whom he wins in a bet and who acts as a sparring partner and simian confidant) plus Orville's girl friend, Echo (Beverly D'Angelo), pursues Lynn across the Southwest in a Chevvy pickup truck. They in turn are pursued by a motorcycle gang and two cops who have a score to settle with Philo. In a somewhat arbitrary sub-plot Orville's dotty mother (Ruth Gordon) looks after the homestead, blasting the motorcycle villains with her shotgun and making a mess of her driving test. The four eventually track down Lynn to Taos, New Mexico where Philo takes a fall and loses the fight to the legendary Tank Murdock and his heart to the waif-like country singer.

Clyde is excellent. He drinks beers, plays dead when Clint pretends to shoot him, has a masterful touch with obscene gestures and lends a genuinely sympathetic ear when Clint confides, 'When it comes to sharing my feelings with a woman my stomach turns to Royal gelatin.' Clyde's achievement is seen to be all the greater when his trainer revealed, 'We can control Clyde's actions seventy per cent of the time with off-camera cues, but thirty per cent of the time he is on his own. You may say he is a natural method actor.'

Clint is at his best when he is aping Clyde. He leaps from the trees to ambush the pursuing cops and, having beaten them up, pounds his chest and lets out a Tarzan-like roar. The film is hardly a great work of cinematic art, but very funny in patches, sloppily put together.

Sondra Locke sang sweetly and acted to Clint's satisfaction. 'Sondra is an outstanding actress,' he said, 'she has a great intuitive sense, she picks up suggestions immediately and she contributes her own ideas calmly without pretension. She's secure enough as a performer to follow her instincts and she's open to changes which allow a role to take shape as she works.' Sondra said of her role, 'She's a foil for Clint's part, exposing him to a different side of his own personality, helping him grow and understand a little more about himself. He's the toughest guy around when it comes to fighting, but this girl has him buffaloed. It's a nice idea with a clever application, which isn't really too different from lots of conventional relationships.'

Big country music names like Eddie Rabbitt, Mel Tillis and Charlie Rich provided the soundtrack and this undoubtedly appealed to the numerous white hill-billy fans who have always made up the majority of Eastwood's supporters. Clint was anxious to expand that audience. 'People think of me as appealing to the straight, hardhat crowd, but I've had a lot of feedback on this picture from professionals saying how much they enjoyed it.' But the critics hardly fell in love with the movie, one of the cruellest cuts coming from *Newsweek*: 'James Fargo directed every which way but well. One can forgive the orangutan's participation—he couldn't read the script—but where is Eastwood's excuse?'

It turned out to be the second most popular film in 1979, beaten only by the insuperable *Superman*. As it happened, both pictures were released by Warner Brothers for Christmas 1978 and when the company was made aware that Clint was uneasy in case he got second-best treatment, they orchestrated the biggest opening ever for an Eastwood picture in 1,246 cinemas across America. Five weeks later it was still in 1,170 of them.

Well in advance of this release, as is traditional, the film was shown to the critics. The man from *Variety,* the Bible of the entertainment industry with its finger on public taste, wrote: 'This film is way off the mark. If people line up for this one . . . they'll line up for any Clint Eastwood picture.'

Yes.

LIVE AS YOU WANT TO LIVE

In 1978 Eastwood made his fifth movie with Don Siegel: *Escape From Alcatraz.* It was nearly ten years since they had worked together on *Dirty Harry* and it looked as though the relationship had lapsed. The reasons remain unspoken but in many ways, as with Leone, the apprentice had outstripped the sorcerer. The films Eastwood directed himself had certainly proved more commercially successful than the first three Siegel films and, in the case of *The Outlaw Josey Wales* at least, he had demonstrated himself to be a more accomplished director. When he decided not to be director himself he had chosen younger men like Michael Cimino or Jim Fargo who would certainly permit him to retain considerable control, a requirement he now valued as much as anything else. With the sixty-seven year old Siegel there was always the danger he might lose that command and slip back to

Left and below: Eastwood gave a brilliant performance as Frank Morris in Don Siegel's Escape From Alcatraz *(1978). Right: Discussing a scene with Siegel on set.*

the status of a mere actor. Moreover Siegel's work in the seventies lacked the stamp of his earlier classics. Films like *Telefon* and *The Black Windmill* got a poor reception from public and critics alike, and although he enjoyed a moderate success with John Wayne's last film, *The Shootist,* this was probably more due to public sentiment than to directorial skill. The film lacked the clear exposition and taut action of Siegel's earlier work, perhaps due to his overriding concern for the health of his ailing star.

But Clint and Don had remained great friends and when Eastwood told me, 'I'd like to work with him again; I think he's terrific', I had no doubt he meant it—providing the right project came along.

It was Siegel who provided the offer, a clever bait, since it was a story that would have fascinated Eastwood because it took place virtually on his doorstep. On 11 June 1962 three bank robbers, Frank Morris and two brothers, John and Clarence Anglin, did the impossible: they broke out of Alcatraz. The gloomy prison fortress, sitting forbiddingly on Devil's Island, just a mile away from the taunting lights of San Francisco, was allegedly escape-proof. Of the thirty-nine men who tried to get away in its twenty-eight-year history, twenty-six were recaptured, seven were shot and three were drowned. But Morris and the Anglins were never found and to this day nobody knows whether they made it to Angel Island or if they drowned in the attempt. J. Bruce Campbell wrote a book about the escape and Don Siegel bought

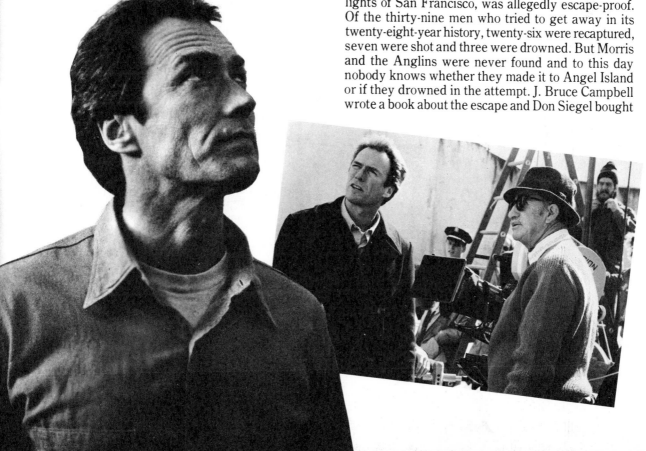

Morris on the boat going over to Alcatraz.

They had access to sewing materials in their prison jobs, and Morris told them how to fashion life-jackets and a home-made raft of sorts from old raincoats.

There were extreme security precautions at Alcatraz: a warder for every three prisoners as opposed to every nine as at a regular prison; twelve head-counts of prisoners every day and sporadic searches of cells without any warning. Miraculously, none of the men's escape preparations were discovered.

On the night of 11 June 1962 the three men dimmed the lights in their cells, put the dummy heads on the pillows, removed the false grills from the ventilation shafts and scaled up the pipes and cables behind the cell block to the roof. A fourth man had been included in the plan but his nerve failed him at the last minute and he stayed behind. The twenty-foot high steel mesh fence that surrounded the exercise yard evidently proved no obstacle to the other three and they launched their raft in to the chill waters and lethal currents of San Francisco Bay. Nothing was ever heard of them again. Two of the life-jackets were later recovered and so was a sealed pouch containing some letters and a picture of the Anglins' mother.

It has always been assumed officially that they drowned—hardened criminals rarely lie low for long after a jail break. Also, it was known that they were aiming for Angel Island—twice as far away as the mainland, a near impossible target with their makeshift equipment. Even Eastwood doubts whether they made it. 'I think they took the wrong direction in making for Angel Island. They gave themselves nearly twice the distance to cover. They would have been better off taking their chance of landing in the San Francisco area.'

The film follows the known facts of the escape assiduously, permitting itself only one act of poetic licence at the very end. Throughout the film Siegel uses a yellow chrysanthemum as a symbol of 'heart', to indicate that although the brutal system may have removed everything from the inmates save the questionable privilege of remaining alive, in some men at least their spirit survives. 'Doc', an elderly inmate who has spent twenty years there but who is permitted to paint and cultivate chrysanthemums, introduces the concept. One day the warden (Patrick McGoohan) brutally puts a stop to his permit to paint. In a jarring scene Doc chops off his own fingers in the prison workshop—Eastwood bitterly picks them up and thrusts them at the negligent warder whom he had asked to keep an eye on Doc. Later in the film a vase of chrysanthemums appears on the breakfast table. The warden angrily grabs them from the vase, claiming they are prohibited. Litmus, a loveable Italian inmate with a pet mouse, jumps to his feet to protest and promptly dies of a heart attack. The warden crushes the flowers. But when the men have escaped, the warden lands by helicopter on Angel Island to supervise the search for any traces of them. Just as he assures his deputy that they have definitely

the rights to it, knowing that only one man could convincingly attract the public to watch a two-hour movie about the taciturn Frank Morris.

Morris was a loner, a rebel against society, the quintessential anarchic hero that Siegel loved—Lee Marvin in *The Killers,* Steve McQueen in *Hell is for Heroes,* and Richard Widmark in *Madigan* were all similar types in films which he had directed. In *Alcatraz,* Morris's past is economically summed up when a fellow prisoner asks him 'When's your birthday? 'I don't know.' 'What kind of childhood did you have?' 'Short.'

In fact the real Morris was the son of an unmarried chorus-girl who abandoned him when he was three. Despite a life of crime he had a near-genius IQ of 133 and it was this intelligence that enabled him to mastermind the break-out. It took him and the brothers Anglin more than a year to prepare the ground. Morris discovered that the ventilation shaft that was connected to each of their cells was just large enough to permit a lithe human body to wriggle his way out along it. With home-made tools he slowly picked at the concrete surrounding the grill in front of his shaft and over the months replaced it with a papier-mâché version constructed from prison magazines. Using the same material he made a model of his head, painted it flesh colour and glued on human hair removed from the prison's barber shop. The Anglins followed his instructions and did the same.

drowned, he finds a single yellow chrysanthemum on the rocks. No chrysanthemums grow on Angel Island.

Stereotype characters, such as Doc and Litmus, make the film a less inventive work than it should have been. A further example is the inevitable psychopath homosexual, Wolf, who indicates that Eastwood is a potential victim but realises he has met his match when he approaches him in the showers one day and gets a knee in the groin and a bar of soap in the mouth for his troubles. His two subsequent knife attacks on Eastwood in the exercise yard are also deftly repulsed. Another familiar type of character is English, the leader of the Black mafia, who sits in the yard in self-imposed segregation from the white inmates. On acquaintance English proves to be a nice guy. Wrongfully incarcerated for killing two white rednecks who attacked him in Alabama, he is serving two sentences of ninety-nine years back-to-back. 'Are you through killing white guys?' Eastwood inquires. 'Why?' asks English. Eastwood moves away. 'Figured next time I wouldn't turn my back on you.'

The biggest stereotype of all is the warden, although Patrick McGoohan tries as hard as he can to endow him with some individual personality. Apart from the flower-crushing and constant attention to his nails, he is permitted by the scriptwriter merely to mouth phrases that might have come from the prison handbook: 'No-one has ever escaped from Alcatraz alive.' 'We don't make good citizens, we make good prisoners.' 'If you disobey society they send you to prison; if you disobey the rules of prison, they send you to us.' 'Alcatraz was built to keep all the rotten eggs in one basket. I was specially chosen to make sure the stink from that basket doesn't escape.'

But two elements in the film are starkly real and more than make up for the shaky scriptwriting: one is the central character, which will be considered in a moment, and the other is Alcatraz itself. Siegel's overwhelming achievement is to send the audience to prison for two hours. I cannot recollect another film that has so chillingly effective a sense of place. The claustrophobia, the lack of colour, the timelessness, the implicit suppression of any joy, the barbarity of being caged like an animal, all these qualities come across with such reality that one experiences a total sense of relief when the camera moves into the yard for even a brief spell of daylight. In this Siegel is faultlessly aided by the subtle camerawork of Bruce Surtees—always Eastwood's favourite cameraman. Siegel's technique in this respect is unmatchable. As Vincent Canby wrote in the *New York Times:* 'Film students have a way of leaping into the art while still ignorant of the craft. Craft is something that a Siegel film demonstrates without half trying.'

With six movies under his belt as director, Eastwood was still mindful of the talents of his old mentor. 'Some of these new directors will shoot thirty

Morris encounters the psychopath homosexual, Wolf, played by Bruce M. Fischer, in the exercise yard.

AZ 1441

takes of a scene just because they don't know what they want. They wind up with thousands of feet of film, then they cry for some editor to come in and save their butts. If you can't see it yourself, you shouldn't be a director. Siegel can think on his feet and work fast. He has the guts to call "print" after the first take—he can see when it's good.'

They were also helped by the decision to shoot most of the film on Alcatraz itself, spending half a million dollars to reinstall electricity and restore the island fortress to its former shameful glory. The look of perpetual discomfort in the eyes of the inmates had a basis in reality—nearly all the actors fell ill working in the dank surroundings. Eastwood claimed, 'I've never known anything like it. It was like working inside a meat locker. It got right into your bones.'

Where Siegel's craft deserted him, in part, was in the actual escape. The details of stealing the materials, adapting them and then painstakingly chipping away at the concrete surrounding the grill have scant fascination. And by being faithful to the real event, the director failed to inject much tension into the final break-out. They got away with nobody noticing. There is a heart-stopping moment when Morris makes a trial run and a warder tries to wake up what we the audience fear to be the dummy head but which turns out to our relief to be a dormant Eastwood. But apart from that, the final hour of the film when the break-out takes place passes with minimal tension. It is a deficiency that should have been corrected at the time of final scripting. The fact

that we know Morris and the Anglins will get away need not necessarily blunt the excitement—Zimmerman, in *The Day of the Jackal*, masterfully built up the suspense right to the point when the killer finally has De Gaulle within his sights, although everyone in the audience knows that the President will not be killed. Siegel lacks Zimmerman's touch in this respect.

With this failure to thrill and a thin directorial statement behind it, the film might be relegated to the status of a proficient B-feature, were it not for one toweringly significant element: Clint Eastwood. For those who have followed his career from his portrayal of the lion-headed Rowdy Yates to his flirtation with Clyde the orangutan, Eastwood may have delivered more enjoyable .performances, but in *Escape From Alcatraz* he gives his best screen acting to date. It is a performance that is so idiosyncratic, persuasive and powerful that it is hard to think of any other major actor who could have given the film such a rock-like core. Even Gary Cooper, whom many people, including the director Vittorio de Sica and the critic Dilys Powell, have compared with Eastwood, couldn't have given Morris the rough, criminal aspect that is immediately recognisable. For one thing Cooper would have been too patrician and too elegant.

I am not alone in my admiration for Eastwood's finest movie performance. Charles Michener in *Newsweek* noted that Siegel was 'beautifully served by Eastwood's self-containment'. Frank Rich in *Time* magazine concluded: '*Alcatraz's* cool, cinematic grace meshes ideally with the strengths of its star. Not a man to sell himself to the audience, Eastwood relies on a small assortment of steely glances and sardonic smiles. Thanks to his ever craggier face, the gestures pay off better than usual and so do the occasional throwaway laugh lines. At a time when Hollywood entertainments are more overblown than ever, Eastwood proves that less really can be more.' And Vincent Canby commits himself to a definitive statement about Eastwood that no-one would have expected to read in such a critically prestigious newspaper as in the *New York Times* five years ago, still less when they were cancelling Eastwood's contract at Universal: 'Mr Eastwood fulfills the demands of the role and of the film as probably no other actor could. Is it acting? I don't know, but he's the towering figure in its landscape.'

Is it acting? No, not in the sense a full-blown performance on the stage by Olivier is acting, nor in the sense that an understated but mannered performance by Brando or de Niro is acting. In the style that he has made his own and with the undoubted additional acuity he has brought to his performance by having a keen and experienced director's eye, Eastwood has refined his art to such a rudimentary form that it almost begs definition.

The first fifteen minutes of the film consist of Morris being brought by boat to Alcatraz, inspected by a doctor and thrown into a cell. Throughout this Eastwood does not speak. But already the audience feels it knows the character. He has been through this before, he tries to control his mind, neither ruminating on his conviction nor agonising on his prospective sentence. He builds a barrier between himself and his environment, he suppresses his fear but he's not so foolish as to appear bold. Behind his impassivity his mind is calculating, he is summing everyone up, exuding what pride he can in a humiliating situation. Everyone knows, warders and fellow prisoners alike, that this is not a man to be tampered with lightly.

The rest of the film provides us with little more information about Morris, merely that he is there and he doesn't intend to remain there for long. Usually an Eastwood character is rounded with an animal sex appeal and more than a scintilla of dry humour. Here he has neither of those added qualities but he manages to make the man likeable without being warm, driven without releasing the control on his emotion and a natural leader without ever committing any act to assert his leadership. Yes, it is acting—not the kind of acting that a drama school can teach, but the intuitive performance of a man who is acutely sensitive to the various elements that combine to make up a scene in a film, and who can finely tune his own performance to make an apparently minimal characterisation have maximum effect.

Eastwood knew that the heavy subject matter of *Alcatraz* would inevitably prevent it from being a runaway success on the scale of *Every Which Way But Loose*. Nevertheless by the end of 1979 it had taken $21,000,000 in America, according to *Variety*, making it the fifteenth most popular film of that year and certainly the most financially successful of the Siegel-Eastwood partnership. But he had tasted the heady wine of mass audience appeal with his previous film and, with so few real challenges left to him in the cinema, he was determined to repeat that success in 1980.

Bronco Billy was a heaven-sent opportunity to do this, or rather a Dennis Hackin-sent opportunity, since he wrote the script. It enabled Clint once more to don his Western gear but this time as a contemporary cowboy who performs in a travelling Wild West Show. It can surely only be a case of spontaneous combustion that permitted Robert Redford to play a somewhat similar character in *The Electric Horseman* which was released six months previously.

Having decided to direct this, his seventh film, Eastwood assembled his by now familiar repertory company: Geoffrey Lewis (*High Plains Drifter, Thunderbolt and Lightfoot, Every Which Way But Loose*) as John Arlington, an inept con-man; Bill McKinney (*The Outlaw Josey Wales, The Gauntlet, Every Which Way But Loose*) as Two Gun Lefty LeBow, a one-handed cowboy; Dan Vadis (*High Plains Drifter, The Gauntlet, Every Which Way But Loose*) as Chief Big Eagle, a snake dancer; Sam Bottoms (*The Outlaw Josey Wales*) as Lasso Leonard James, a wizard with the lasso, and Sondra Locke (*The Outlaw Josey Wales, The Gauntlet, Every Which Way But Loose*) as Antoinette Lily, an exotic heiress from the East Coast. Clearly Eastwood felt security in the familiar team and was aware that their varying characteristics

Escape From Alcatraz *(1978). Frank Morris chips his way out of his cell with home-made tools, and fills the gap with papier mache.*

provided a suitably outgoing counterpoint to his own more reserved performance. 'Each film is a different play,' he said, 'so why not use strong characters who work well together? These people are the best—talented, flexible—and they like to work hard with no bellyaching.' He was able to rely on the goodwill and respect that he had built up among the players. 'Clint's the captain of the ship round here,' observed Bill McKinney. 'You don't see any shouting or hassling round here, do you?' And probably the team felt security in playing in the big league. Crowds would gather round the locations and an audible gasp would go up when people caught sight of the now legendary actor. Moreover working with people who understood him enabled him to be more relaxed. Directing himself in one take, Eastwood stood back smiling at the end and commented, 'I've got a feeling that was terrific. Let's print it.' To the uninitiated observer that might have seemed like an arrogant statement; to the team it was a joke, and within it the confidence that he *had* got it right. Of all the regular actors, Sondra Locke knows him best. 'I always saw something underneath those tough-guy roles that made him interesting—a hint of vulnerability, a certain boyishness and humour within the superman image. And when we got to know each other, the boyishness became even more apparent. I've always been surprised that people didn't pick on it right away. That, and Clint's great sense of humour.'

Behind the camera the old Malpaso team did the work, only this time it was no longer Malpaso—a new company was formed called Robert Daley Productions, to enable Clint's old friend and producer to branch out into non-Eastwood projects in the future. Betty Endo had taken over the role of 'Jude the Prude' in looking after the office but Fritz Manes, whose friendship with Eastwood extended for nearly forty years, remained steadfast as associate producer, with a primary responsibility for locations, stunts and keeping an eye on the purse-strings. Manes' admiration for his lifelong colleague knows no bounds: 'When Clint's shooting a page of script, he's not shooting the page, he's shooting the entire script. He has a way of looking beyond the scene as if he has already edited it in his mind. He knows exactly how it's going to go together and fit with the rest of the film. This is a true gift because so many directors can pull tremendous performances out of an actor and get beautiful camera angles but when it comes to putting it together, they can sit there for weeks and look at all the film they've shot but they can't figure out how it is going to work.'

As can be gathered from the names of the characters in the film, *Bronco Billy* is a comedy. Billy himself, a surprisingly talkative fellow for an Eastwood character, travels with his sadly run-down Wild West Show through the western states on the carnival circuit. Scatman Crothers plays the Master of Ceremonies, while Eastwood portrays a wily sharp-shooter and masterful horseman (Alan Cartwright devised some quite remarkable trick riding stunts for Eastwood). The high point of Bronco Billy's act comes when he ties his female assistant to a revolving board, surrounded with balloons, which he then guns down as the board spins round. Blindfolded, he bursts the last balloon with a throw of a dagger. Recruits for the job of assistant are needless to say hard to come by. Through chance, Bronco comes across a beautiful girl abandoned by her newly-wed husband at a gas station in Montana. Unknown to Billy, she is in reality a wealthy heiress of a mean disposition, whose even meaner husband has dis-appeared in desperation at her treatment of him. Bronco Billy and the heiress, Antoinette Lily (Sondra Locke) embark on a relationship based on their mutual difficulties—his to find an assistant, hers to get transport out of the wilderness—but as expected of a comic romance, they find themselves falling in love.

The relationship survives the burning down of their show tent, a failed attempt to hold up a train, and an unexpected encounter with the fugitive husband in a mental hospital where the Wild West Show goes to give a free performance in return for a new tent which the inmates sew. The husband has agreed to plead guilty to Antoinette's murder in return for a fat fee—she of course is alive and well and grudgingly beginning to enjoy her existence in hiding as Bronco's assistant. The hospital administrator is forced to alert Antoinette's family and the press to the fact that the missing heiress is not dead and she is returned to her family. But true love wins through in the end—Antionette flies back to her love-sick

Bronco Billy, and the film ends on a high note with a rapturously received performance in the new tent (made entirely of stars-and-stripes flags). There is little message beyond 'live as you want to live, be what you want to be, and have fun while you can'.

Sondra Locke loved the part. 'I don't like repetition and I know I would have a difficult time doing the same character over and over again because my attention would become a little less focussed with each performance. The role of Antoinette Lily is a good example of a real change because she is a character who has a different set of values and a different kind of motivation based on a completely separate background from Lynn Halsey-Taylor, the country singer in *Every Which Way But Loose*. She is a headstrong lady, accustomed to wealth and the convenience that money can bring. It makes her self-centred and arrogant, but she's really an intelligent, decent person at heart. It takes Bronco Billy McCoy to bring her down to earth and to show her alternatives about people which she never would have otherwise considered.' Miss Locke continued to be impressed by her director. 'Clint is very defined in his approach to individual character development and his ability as a director is revealed in terms of clarity, coverage and organization. He doesn't waste time because he understands the acting and film making process.'

The style and mood of the film were very much according to the appealing formula of *Every Which Way But Loose* and the locations, Oregon and Idaho, were the less sophisticated areas of America where Eastwood could find the earthy reality that he calculated would appeal to his new, wider audience. So would his own character: 'The story has a special quality that attracted me right away, particularly the idea of a character rejecting all the modern cynicism around him with a positive attitude about his purpose, his life, his self-image as a traditional hero, and his sense of what is important and what isn't.'

He relished the idea of exploring the talents of the actors he knew and getting even more from them than they realised they had to offer. 'I liked working on a collaborative basis. I think this is especially true when the film in question is lighthearted in nature. It makes actors a little more at ease and less insecure, which helps spontaneity.' His judgement in hiring actors new to him, like Dan Vadis from the Italian Hercules epics and Sierra Pecheur from the New York Playhouse of the Ridiculous (who played Chief Big Eagle and Squaw, respectively) underlines his completeness as a director. The joint task of directing and acting was almost second nature to him now. 'Although it seems difficult, it really isn't in a way because I've gotten used to it and I'm comfortable with both jobs. I don't believe, in my case, that either position interferes with the other, and I feel I've done some of my best work while both acting and directing,

Bronco Billy's new partner is the runaway heiress Antoinette Lily, played by Sondra Locke, now also having a marked influence on Eastwood's private life.

like in *The Outlaw Josey Wales.'*

Having the ability to finance and initiate any project he chooses to do, Eastwood has developed his instinct for selecting material to a fine art. 'I look for entertainment value in a script, which might sound simple, but it really isn't. The idea should create a visual image, like in a good book, that is either fun or interesting or different or some combination of all those factors. I also like things that have excitement, visual movement and conflict or drama. Lately, I've found myself drawn to things that have a lot of humour in them as well. I've always enjoyed movies that have a sense of fun about them and I thought that this was the right script to take me into that area. I don't feel that simply because you've done a few Westerns that you should always play cowboys, or that because you did a good job portraying a police officer that you should always play cops, regardless of how successful those films might have been.'

The synopsis of *Bronco Billy* does little to reveal its most telling virtue: it is wonderfully funny. Eastwood managed to spread his own understated, dry, subtle almost cynical humour throughout the story. The hick leader or, as he refers to himself with echoes of *Rawhide,* 'ramrod' of a fairly shambolic bunch of circus performers, he addresses the children in the audience as 'little pardners' or 'buckaroos'. The ineptness of his fellow performers is cleverly portrayed in some telling exchanges. One of the circus artists,

Bronco Billy *(1980). Eastwood directed and took the title role as leader of a run-down Wild West Show.*

Lefty, tells Bronco, 'The Chief got bit again by the rattlesnake.' Billy replies, 'I don't know why he can't just do the "Great Apache Flaming Arrow Act".' 'I thought you told him to use the gopher snake,' says Lefty; 'I did,' says Billy, 'but he's a proud Indian'. And later Lefty's own misfortune is sadly revealed when he asks for some back pay: 'You promised I'd have enough money to buy a wooden hand this year.' Billy replies, 'You should never have blown it off in the first place. I told you that shotgun act wouldn't work!'

Unlike the blunderbuss humour practised by Mel Brooks and imitated by many directors who should know better, like Steven Spielberg in *1941* where every joke is signalled and every character labelled, Eastwood leaves the audience in real doubt whether Bronco Billy is nothing more than a comic figure. True, he speaks in the long-forgotten runic of the old West: 'Get out of my truck, you yellow-bellied sidewinder', he demands through suitably clenched teeth, and further insults, 'You dirty varmint!' He also tends to call food 'chow' and ruminate in unrepeatable clichés: 'Don't you just love these wide open spaces where the deer and the antelope roam?' It is always just possible that Bronco Billy is nothing more than very simple, bordering on the simpleton. But then there are moments when his openness has a subtlety that suggests a depth of personality behind the cowpoke front. When he first meets the sophisticated Antoinette Lily, he introduces himself as Bronco Billy McCoy. 'Bronco' she repeats, with withering interest, 'What an amusing name.' 'My friends call

me Billy' he replies, without the slightest trace of humour. Is he too stupid to see her irony, or smart enough not to play her game?

He drives an antiquated red convertible with a moose head on the bonnet and pistols for door handles. One day he catches some children playing with them. The camera shows the threatening, shadowy figure of a cowboy stalking up behind them. A low, firm voice demands, 'Now turn around nice and easy'. They do. 'Are you really the fastest gun in the West?' asks a child, staring up at this mythical shape. He twirls his guns. 'Ain't nobody faster than Bronco Billy. Now look, I don't take kindly to kids playing hookey from school. I think every kid in America ought to go to school, at least up to the eighth grade.' The children look at one another and then at him. They are a little embarrassed. Eventually a little boy tells him, 'But we don't go to school today, Bronco Billy. It's Saturday.' Flummoxed and a little off balance, he splutters out 'Well, I've been riding late last night. A man and his brain get kind of fuzzy when he's been on the range.'

The scene is amusing enough in itself but another element is added when you realise that the image of the sinewy cowboy, a gun in either hand and a trace of menace in his face, backlit against the Idaho landscape is also that of the screen's most lethal killer during the past two decades. Despite Eastwood's claim, 'I don't try to be a parody of myself', he is doing precisely that and judging the limits very nicely. The old Eastwood only truly manifests itself once, during

Publicity shots on the set of Bronco Billy; *Eastwood's characterisation was a gentle self-parody.*

a bank raid when Billy loses his cool less because of the robbery but because the bandits cause a child to drop his piggy bank and break it—then the formidable features resume their bitter twist of revenge and the ever-accurate bullets fly.

Billy loves little children; he is constantly urging them not to get 'tangled up with hard liquor and cigarettes', and his last message in the film is delivered to them and to us, into camera: 'I've got a special message for you "little pardners" out there. I want you to finish your oatmeal at breakfast and do as your Ma and Pa tell you because they know best. Don't ever tell a lie and say your prayers at night before you go to bed. And so, as our friends south of the border say, adios amigos.'

He seems too good to be true, and, of course, he isn't true. Slowly Miss Lily reveals the man he was. He found his wife in bed with his best friend. 'What did you do to him?' she asks. 'I shot her,' Billy replies. He spent seven years in jail (although the woman didn't die) and it was there that he accumulated most of his band of outcasts—Doc was in for practising medicine without a licence, Lefty was a bankteller caught with his hand in the till, Leonard proves to be a Vietnam draft dodger, Chief Big Eagle a down-and-out writer and his squaw not even an Indian. And Billy himself? 'I was raised in a one room tenement in New Jersey. I was a shoe salesman until I was 31

years old. Deep down in my heart I always wanted to be a cowboy. One day I laid down my shoe horn and swore I'd never live in the city again. You only live once. You've got to give it your best shot.'

'Are you for real?' asks Miss Lily.

'I'm who I want to be.'

It is this last piece of philosophy, coupled with Running Water's later remark to Miss Lily: 'Don't you understand what Bronco Billy and the Wild West Show are all about? You can be anything you want', that caused some reviewers to be dismissive about the film. 'The mock sentimentality is only a cover for the movie's genuine sentimentality about becoming the person you want to be,' wrote David Ansen in *Newsweek*. But without the sentimentality the movie would lose much of its richness and especially the warmth that makes Billy and his gang so innocent and beguiling. Eastwood himself saw that cold humour could alienate an audience, but believed, 'It's the kind of film Frank Capra might have made', he said, 'romantic, funny, about a dreamy bunch of losers getting their act together.'

Newsweek apart, the critical acclaim, especially from the more intellectual papers, was considerable. 'It's time to take Eastwood seriously as one of the most honest, influential filmmakers in the world today,' wrote Tom Allen in the *Village Voice*. Janet Maslin in the *New York Times* found Billy one of Eastwood's 'warmest and most memorable characters... Mr Eastwood, who can be as formidable behind the camera as he is in front of it, is an entertainer too.' The advertisements in the American daily papers carried her quote, 'the best and funniest Clint Eastwood movie' and a host of other raves, quite unlike the critical response to *Every Which Way But Loose*.

But in complete contrast to the latter film, *Bronco Billy* was a comparative failure at the box office. Ironically, Eastwood who had long had a hotline to the public, bypassing the critics, now appeared to have found favour with the critics but not with the public. Warner Brothers scratched their corporate heads— maybe it was the poster, maybe people didn't want to see rodeo films, possibly it was the fact that it was a Western—*The Long Riders* died swiftly in the summer of 1980—possibly it was the general recession in cinemagoing. Kubrick's *The Shining*, Redford's *Brubaker* and Travolta's *Urban Cowboy* opened to nothing like the business anticipated from them in the USA—but people were willing to spend millions of dollars going to see the *Star Wars* sequel, *The Empire Strikes Back*.

There were two main reasons for the film's lack of appeal. Despite his success with *Every Which Way But Loose*, Eastwood's main image is still that of the resolute, self-sufficient tough guy and this is what the public wanted to see. Billy was, on the surface at least, too weak—Clint Eastwood is not a former shoe salesman and fantasist. Also, as a comedy, it was simply too gentle a parody for the mass American audience. American humour is traditionally loud, obvious and knockabout. Mel Brooks is food for the masses, so is the *National Lampoon's Animal House*, so is Burt Reynolds when his world collapses about him, so was Clint in *Every Which Way But Loose*—no humour could be broader than a man with a pet orangutan who has a punch-up in every reel. In Europe there is a tradition of drier, less proclaimed comedy whether it is *Monty Python* at its best or Jacques Tati's *Monsieur Hulot*. Many London critics responded with joy to Eastwood's new film. I was happy to give it its first rave review on BBC Radio Four's arts magazine, *Kaleidoscope*. (The slightly incredulous presenter, Michael Oliver, hadn't managed to see the film and had only read the synopsis so he accepted my enthusiasm guardedly.) But I was followed in quick succession by Alexander Walker in the *Evening Standard*—'*Bronco Billy* is the kind of surprise this summer needs. A really likeable movie. . . Eastwood has wrapped the film in a nicely diluted patriotism, a nostalgic feel for Old Glory. His own lined and taut face now looks like some bedrock document of the Constitution preserved in a hall of Congress. He takes himself seriously but keeps giving us the merest twinkle of a wink.' David Robinson in *The Times* declared, 'Only the autocracy and independence conferred by such supreme stardom and command of the box office as his could permit him to make such an odd, unfashionable, self-deprecating and wholly attractive film as *Bronco Billy*. . . The question of identity is the intriguing aspect of the gentle, genial

Eastwood followed up on the success of Every Which Way But Loose *with* Any Which Way You Can *(1980).*

character Eastwood creates in Billy. Even if he is not too great as a knife thrower (as his lady assistants painfully discover) and a total failure in his anachronistic effort to revive the art of train robbery; even if his show is insolvent . . . he is still—in the eyes of his infant audience, his show and himself—the hero and the Westerner he has dreamed himself to be. That, Eastwood seems to be hinting, is what being a star is all about.' Philip French in *The Observer* summed up, 'Clint Eastwood is one of the most vital forces in contemporary American cinema and only the foolish continue to ignore, patronise or dismiss him. As actor, producer and director he rarely fails to astonish . . . In his 1976 Western, *The Outlaw Josey Wales*, Eastwood played the leader of a party of emotionally crippled Civil War veterans on a healing journey to Texas. It was clearly about the rebuilding of America after the painful experience of Vietnam. This new film is a fable about the troubled America of Carter's Presidency, the need for community, the restoration of self-confidence and affirmative values . . . *Bronco Billy* is splendid family entertainment.'

The aim of family entertainment may have been more at the top of Eastwood's mind than the political motivation that French ascribes to him perhaps, but undoubtedly that was also in his consciousness in a less obvious way. But the insight with which the British critics were able to perceive Eastwood's attitude to his country and to his own status in the cinema, underlined yet again the greater respect and appreciation he has always obtained abroad.

Billy is who he wants to be—an opportunity open to most of us but taken by few. He is not a sham: his good manners, his concern for children and his own flock as well as his talent in the ring are all for real. On the outside he may seem like an outdated dreamer, but within himself he is a true Eastwood hero, his own man, unstung by ridicule or criticism, untrammelled by the petty irritants of the world and steadfast in abiding by his own moral code.

When I spoke to Clint some years later he was still clearly very fond of the film. 'It was a favourite project of mine. There was a certain purity, a certain fighting against the cynicism of the day. Maybe it was old fashioned, maybe it was too old fashioned. But it was a good film for me. It received a lot of attention from a lot of people that maybe didn't like the other films. It didn't do as well as *Every Which Way But Loose* but it still did very well considering that it was made for a very low price and wasn't intended to be a wide spectrum thing. You can't just do the same thing all the time otherwise I'd still be in Spain doing Westerns like I started out in the sixties. There's a time to move on and try something else.'

It also happened to be the favourite film of Sondra Locke, now firmly established as Eastwood's consort. 'I never thought I had the ability to be funny, to have comic timing, or even a basic understanding of comedy,' she confessed. 'My favourite film and role was *Bronco Billy*. That's the type of script I would love to find today. It's a fairy tale with a lot of off-beat characters in the little troupe. My part was all the more

Eastwood in middle age has become more confident and relaxed in his attitude to his life and career.

challenging because of the comedy aspect.'

Eastwood delighted in playing against type. There is a scene where Billy permits himself to be humiliated by the sheriff in order to stop his friend being arrested. Now, humiliation without subsequent revenge is hardly in the traditional Eastwood canon. He revealed: 'It was suggested that Billy come back at the end and punch this guy out. That would have ruined the picture, the whole theme of loyalty. Billy doesn't approve of this kid being a deserter, and he doesn't know enough to intellectualize what his friend's feelings were about the war in Vietnam. He just knows that he doesn't approve but he's going to stick by his friend. Now if Billy had come back and kicked the crap out of the sheriff at the end, it would have ruined all that.'

Strangely *Bronco Billy* is one of the few films that he permits himself to intellectualize about, just a little, probably because it is a favoured child. 'If I ever had a message to get across, you'll find it in *Bronco Billy*. It's about the American dream and Billy's dream that he fought so hard for. And it's all in the context of this outdated Wild West show that has absolutely no chance of being a hit. But it's sweet, it's pure.' And justifying why he made this story, which was more personal than successful: 'There's no real excuse for being successful enough as an actor to do what you want and then selling out. You do it pure. You don't try to adapt it, make it commercial. It's not Dirty Bronco Billy.'

Clint Eastwood totally at home by the shores of the Pacific.

However, next time round he *did* make it commercial. No-one in their right mind – and least of all Clint Eastwood – was likely to kill off the ape that brings box-office gold. After the success of *Every Which Way But Loose,* Eastwood remarked: 'I'm not sure whether this is the end of an old career or the beginning of a new one.' Clyde had given Clint his biggest financial success and, although the first orang-utan died (a secret that was well preserved from the press, who were even prepared to believe that Clyde went on to star in Bo Derek's *Tarzan*), Clyde II romped back on to the screen in 1980 in *Any Which Way You Can,* with a new writer, Stanford Sherman, and a new director, Buddy Van Horn. Like James Fargo before him, he had worked his way up the Eastwood crew and now the Captain was giving him a chance at the helm.

But the old quartet in front of the camera remained the same, with Clint as the brawling Philo Beddoe, Sondra Locke as his initially estranged girlfriend, Lynn Halsey-Taylor, Ruth Gordon as his Ma, and Geoffrey Lewis as his slightly awry buddy, Orville. At the start of the film, Philo decides to retire from prize-fighting after an initial bout, but other people have other ideas. A ruthless gambler named James Beekman (Harry Guardino), whom we first encounter at a Mafia meet for a mongoose and a snake, wants to stage a fight between Philo and the unbeaten East Coast champ, William 'Big Bill' Smith (Jack Wilson).

But, before we get to that, romance intervenes. Phil just happens to go into a bar where lovely Lynn is singing and he wins her back—she wakes up in the morning arm-in-arm with him and Clyde. Soon Clyde gets a mate of his own when they borrow a female orang-utan from the zoo—although the two of them behave with less than good manners by wrecking their hotel room. And even octogenarian Ma is on the receiving end of an advance from a hotel clerk who imagines that she has the body of the aforementioned Bo Derek. Ma, in the family tradition, repulses his initial overtures with her right knee. 'The first live one in twenty years and I disable him,' she notes, ruefully.

Although the neo-Nazi motorcyclists from the first film are just as tedious as before, Clint and Clyde are, if anything, funnier. One of them lays a precise turd on the seat of a police car and the other sings the title song with Ray Charles. It is a film about independence and the value of friendship—'hand-outs are what you get from the government, a hand-up is what you get from a friend'. The movie did what a movie's gotta do at the box-office and even received a surprisingly warm review from the *New York Times*: 'Mr Eastwood's comic timing is a marvel, and the film capitalizes on his talent for getting the most done with the least effort. His dry, dry humour works to hold the movie together, because it's the one thing that unites its disconnected elements. When the movie finally gives way to a long, concluding fight sequence between Mr Eastwood and William Smith it turns a little dull despite all the huffing and puffing. Mr Eastwood is best when his tiny, understated mannerisms are given their full chance to register.'

Sondra Locke also managed to bring a nice combination of independence and affection as the other creature in Clint's life. Although she had been nominated for an Academy Award back in 1968 for her juvenile role in *The Heart Is A Lonely Hunter*, her career had not then immediately taken off. 'In those days hardly any roles were available for adolescents, unlike today where there are many opportunities for kids,' she said. 'Although I had a terrific part in the film, it was a one-of-a-kind role for an actress that age. Landing that part was a fairy-tale experience. In my naivety I was so confident, thinking I could just go to an audition and the person who gave the best reading would get the part. But that's not what happens.'

'Although I was totally different from the part of Mick Kelly [in *The Heart Is A Lonely Hunter*] no one was interested in my doing waifs or innocents. Ironically, several years later when I worked with Clint and had the opportunity to play some tough women, I picked up an English guide to film actors. It described me as "American leading lady of the tough variety" [the author was movie-buff, Leslie Halliwell]. It struck me as really funny because it had absolutely nothing to do with me whatever. It was the exact opposite of what I had faced before I played parts with Clint. And if he hadn't given me that chance I'd probably still be stuck with my naive image.'

He didn't give her the chance to begin with. He had seen her performance in *The Heart Is A Lonely Hunter* and as a result had given her the script of *Breezy* to read. Then they met to discuss the film but the part finally went to Kay Lenz. Sondra was not best pleased by this: 'I've never forgiven him for not casting me in that part.' But he didn't forget her, personally or professionally, and three years later made her the female lead in *The Outlaw Josey Wales*. It was an opportunity she relished. 'I had been a fan of Clint for a

long time: I could see in him a certain dichotomy, a tough surface image with a little boy lurking behind it. His vulnerability gives him a multi-dimensional quality.'

She has observed and analysed Eastwood's qualities as a director. 'Like Hitchcock, Clint is happiest with professionals who show up on the set, are totally prepared and require little correction. His directing begins with casting. He chooses actors with something interesting to offer the project. He's so understated when an actor goes off track. If he says "You don't have to scratch your nose there", that really means "Don't scratch your nose." He has a laissez-faire style but one starts getting the message after a while. He also hates rehearsing. His favourite line is "shoot the rehearsal". In fact on his set we rehearse only to get down the technical aspects and I've grown a lot because of this method. Film is such an elusive entity, what is magic is often accidental. One really has to be on one's toes to capture that accident which turns out to be magic. If you're not ready, you might rehearse that moment to death and never capture it. One thing I also like about working at Clint's pace is that flaws are incorporated to become assets.'

Miss Locke was not only working with Eastwood as a director, he was acting in the films as well. 'There was one sequence in *The Gauntlet* where Clint was actually mouthing words at me. Or, right in the middle of a shot he was in as well, if he wanted another actor to

Clint and Sondra Locke on a trip to Normandy, France, for the Deauville Film Festival, which paid tribute to Eastwood with a retrospective of his films.

speed up he'd wave his arm off camera. Sometimes he would even talk to me in the middle of a shot.'

She and Clint have a place in Los Angeles and another in Monterey, near his children. 'The gardens at both places keep me busy,' she says. Initially, Sondra did not enjoy the publicity that their relationship had attracted. 'I used to get my blood pressure up over it, it always hurts. But the Eastwoods have a very good relationship and are very happy with the domestic situation they have created. Clint is sort of secret to the nth degree. It's part of his personality. He just doesn't like to tell anybody what he's doing. It extends to all parts of his life. I'm basically the same way. I don't like talking about myself.'

Left and below: Eastwood as Philo Beddoe with his mate the orang-utan in Any Which Way You Can *(1981). Right: Taking it easy with Sondra at Deauville.*

IT ISN'T ALL DARK GLASSES AND AUTOGRAPHS

I met Eastwood again in the November of 1981 in Vienna, where he had gone to shoot the location sequences of his next film, *Firefox*. This was the eighth film he had directed and something of a departure for him—not a Western, not a superhuman policeman, nothing metaphysical, but a cold war thriller. It was written by a Welsh schoolteacher, Craig Thomas, who was delighted when his publishers told him that the book had been optioned by a Hollywood studio, but could hardly believe his ears—'It was so ridiculous it was just impossible to believe,' he confessed to me later—when he heard that his fictional hero, Mitchell Gant, was going to be played by one of his real-life heroes—Clint Eastwood.

Clint told me how he hit on this particular book. 'I was skiing in Aspen with a friend of mine who is a pilot. And he started telling me this story about a mythical Russian jet. I thought "Well he's a pilot and this may be

a story that's very interesting to pilots but not particularly interesting to the overall general public." But as soon as I returned from skiing I got the book and by the time I was about halfway or three-quarters of the way through I realized there was a very good suspense story here without even getting to the flying stuff. Then when I got to the flying, that was, of course, wild and for that reason I enjoyed it. I had been looking for a good suspense film for some time. I guess since *Play Misty* days I hadn't really had one that I thought was very good. This had the combination of high adventure and the feelings of a tight suspense film.'

Major Mitchell Gant is an Air Force officer who has been scarred by Vietnam. He is trying to come to terms with a new rural life and has no desire to go back into the services. But an invitation to fly 'the fastest warplane ever built' proves irresistible. There is a catch, however: it is a Russian plane, so first he has to

Left: Major Mitchell Gant, Vietnam veteran turned space-age hero, pilot of Firefox *(1982). Above left: The author Iain Johnstone filming at Burbank Studios with Clint Eastwood and above right: Major Gant assumes the garb of a humble American businessman in order to enter East Germany (*Firefox*, 1982).*

Clint at the helm of Firefox. 'I just put my foot down and vacuumed their headlights.'

go to Moscow and pinch it. The plane can travel at more than five times the speed of sound, no radar can pick it up and, most amazing of all, its missiles can be fired by direct order from the pilot's brain. Surely a rather tall order? Clint thought not.

'No. At the University College of Los Angeles they have a deal where they put a helmet on your head and, once it has been programmed through a computer, you can actually think certain things and certain images will appear on the screen. And this is just a taste of things to come in the future. It is not totally perfected yet but if it was it would be a very interesting concept. And long after the book came out they are still trying to develop these kind of anti-radar capabilities that Craig Thomas's story had.'

While work began at Van Nuys airbase building the Firefox—a full scale model that would be required to taxi, and two smaller ones that would have to fly, Eastwood flew to England to find his Russians. 'Not only did I want some very good performers but I wanted performers who could play people from the Eastern bloc, people who could play accents. And British actors are much better at this than American actors because they do it more often and because of the close proximity of Europe.'

Eastwood made an unrecognized entry into Britain—it is not hard to by-pass the airport photographers if you really want to—checked into Claridges under an assumed name—it is not hard for the staff to see a famous name every day of the week and emphatically deny that he or she is there—and started

looking for actors. He used the Warner Brothers' office in Wardour Street and also Pinewood Studios where he purposefully avoided the panelled restaurant because he knew he would be importuned by certain producers who work the room at lunchtime. Instead he went to local pubs for a pint and a pie. His English production manager, Paul Webster, who often accompanied him, was amused by the fact that people would sometimes nudge each other and say 'That guy looks just like Clint Eastwood,' but nobody ever believed that it could be the man himself, standing in a public bar in the outskirts of Slough.

He looked at lots of tapes and talked to lots of actors but never asked any to audition. 'I never "read" actors. I never liked it when I had to do it and I can't bring myself to make somebody else go through it. There is something about coming into an office and meeting somebody.' Here Eastwood began to reveal the sensitivity that endears him to the actors in the films he directs. 'Once you own the part as an actor a certain relaxation sets in and a certain ability to hide behind the character or within the character, and to bring the character within you—however you want to put it. But reading is not the same as acting. Some actors can read beautifully and can't act worth a dime and other actors can't read at all and can act beautifully. There is really no correlation; reading is a sort of technique all of its own.'

This same sensitivity extends to his work on the set. How often one sees a director, heady with the number of men and mass of equipment at his disposal, bark 'Action' at an actor and hope for a totally natural performance. Eastwood never does this. Watching him at work I noticed he just would murmur 'When you're ready' or just 'Okay'. Again, having been on the receiving end himself, he told me that the shout of 'Action' tends to make people seize up rather than loosen up. Clive Merrison, one of the English actors who was finally cast, recalled his personal experience as Major Lanyev in a delightful article in *Event* magazine:

'Los Angeles, September 1981. A night shoot at Van Nuys Airport. Take one and I'm in what they call FBCU (fucking big close up). Sound is running, camera has speed and all I get from Clint is a grunted "In your own time, friend." Take two. "Do it, Clive" Take three. "Let's go, amigo." Then: "Cut it here." He rolls up to me sucking on an "Interdens". "Clive, could you do a little less on the shot?" I've had that note before. "Certainly Clint." As he moseys back to the camera I blurt out "But we don't all have your talent for economy." He slowly turns back to me, a classic Clint burn, a paradigm for doing a little less. He comes back, comes close. "Clive, you and the other English guys, you bring me a big bag. Some of us"—he points to his chest—"were born with"—he mimes an eighth of an inch with his thumb and forefinger—"just this".'

The other English guys, who included Kenneth Colley, Ronald Lacey, Nigel Hawthorne and Freddie Jones, were more than content with their American master. Especially Mr Jones. 'Clint Eastwood is a fucking saint. He must be canonized.'

When we reached Vienna, Warren Clarke, who plays a Russian dissident who helps Eastwood and accordingly has most of his scenes with him, was modest enough to confess that even a star television actor like him could still feel intimidated. 'There are times when you are standing next to Clint, the fellow that you saw in the Spaghetti Westerns when you were a young kid, and you look up to him and you think "My God, it's Clint Eastwood."

Vienna, home of the Hapsburgs, residence of the Holy Roman Emperor, a city ornate with the Hofburg, the Cathedral of St Stephen, the Opera House and the Burgteater and rich with the music of Haydn, Mozart, Beethoven, Schubert and the Strauss family, was not chosen for any of those reasons. The film unit went there because it looked a bit like Moscow at night. In fact the elegant tradition of the city ran counter to the modern style of Clint and his crew. They were banned from the dining room of their five star hotel for not wearing jackets and ties. Clint pointed out that after a day's shooting he was just too tired to get dressed up so a compromise was reached. He could eat his dinner in his tee shirt and jeans but he would have to sit behind a specially erected screen in the elegant room.

Much of the filming was at night. Eastwood staged

Freddie Jones, as Kenneth Aubrey, plays Q to Eastwood's James Bond in Firefox *(1982).*

A piece of the action as Major Gant in the stolen Firefox wards off an attack by the Russians.

fights by the murky waters of the Danube Canal with the art department on the other bank cleverly masking out the gaudy advertisements which were very un-Russian. Then they had to wait for the last underground train to stop at 1 am and sneak down with Soviet posters and pictures of Lenin to convert the place into the Moscow underground. Eastwood's first assistant, Steve Perry, a man who had done much to help Robert Redford win his directing Oscar for *Ordinary People*, told me he had never worked quite so hard. Eastwood had so much confidence that his material would cut together that he would rely on just one take where other directors would hedge their bets with other angles and master shots. But behind the lens he had the practised eye of his favourite cinematographer, Bruce Surtees—the prince of darkness.

There is always a problem when someone directs himself in the leading part in a film and it is rarely resolved. Warren Beatty got an Oscar for directing *Reds* but the film might have proved more popular if he had given a bigger, more captivating performance. Charlton Heston, about to direct himself as Antony in *Antony and Cleopatra*, had the modesty, and the wisdom, to go to Laurence Olivier for advice how best to do it. 'Get yourself a stand-in who can really act in rehearsal', suggested the noble lord. Eastwood should probably have done that for, despite his command and energy on the set, he slightly underplayed Gant in some of what should have been the most tense scenes in the film. His direction was gently decisive. 'I see the film completed before I start shooting it. I might vary the camera position from here to there but basically the

thing is laid out in your mind when you're planning on shooting. Otherwise I'd be guessing around. I might be in trouble. Don't want to paint myself into a corner, very easy to do.'

Very often actors will rightly request that there should be no-one other than the minimum crew behind the camera in their line of sight during a take since it could distract them. Nothing seemed to distract Clint and he was quite happy to have me and my documentary crew there. 'Are you sure that doesn't bother you?' I inquired. 'If I'm not used to cameras and people by now, I never will be,' came the dry reply. Equally laconically, after a long, long night of intense shooting, when everybody was rubbing their eyes in the Viennese dawn, ready to go back to the hotels for some sleep, Eastwood came across and whispered: 'You see, it isn't all dark glasses and autographs.'

Nor was it back in Burbank a few months later, when Eastwood was putting the finishing touches to the film in the cutting room with his long-time editor, Ferris Webster. Eastwood had had a new experience in making a movie that had a Special Effects climax and had gone to the best in the business, John Dykstra— the man who did *Star Wars*. 'The frustrating part of a film like this is waiting for the visual effects. There were so many different ways in which this plane had to fly. All of a sudden you go to the special effects people and say: "Now this time we're not in outer space, where nobody knows what it looks like, and we're not on a black back-drop so all the matte lines disappear. I want him to fly into clouds and over ice and snow and the Arctic", and everybody's going: "Oh my God, there's no way this is going to happen". But it did happen and I think they did a very nice job.'

Dykstra thought that the job was '*Star Wars* multiplied by a factor of 10'. He had great difficulty in getting rid of the black line on the matte shots where the two pieces of film, one of model Firefoxes chasing each other, the other of frozen Arctic wastes, were imposed on each other. He had more fun flying around the Arctic in a Lear jet to shoot the backgrounds. 'We shot at a frame a second so it meant we covered 150 miles or so for just ten seconds of film and pretty soon we were running out of places to go.' The final result, black lines or not, packed plenty of punch.

We flew east to Washington, D.C. for the premiere. Eastwood admitted to nerves. 'I don't know if I'd ever enjoy it. You're sitting there watching the film and your stomach's got to be screwed up like a knot.' The elegant Madison Hotel has played host to kings, presidents and prime ministers but the number of people on duty at reception waiting for Clint was several times the required amount.

Warner Brothers threw an intimate dinner for sixty at the Pisces Club for their favourite son, who circulated the tables with grace. Then at 4.00 pm on Sunday 13 June 1982 the doors of the Diplomatic Reception Rooms at the Department of State were thrown open to the boys from Hollywood, with Defense Secretary, Caspar Weinberger, and the President's top aide, Edwin Meese, and their wives, as hosts. Mrs Meese was proud to reveal that she and Edwin grew up in the same town as Eastwood—Oakland, California— although they didn't actually meet until Ronald Reagan became Governor of California. Then on to the Kennedy Center where Steve Ross, President of Warner Communications, was anxious to have his daughters photographed with Clint, and others shelled out $1000 a plate just to be there.

Mr Weinberger was happy to pose with the fictional hero, and he gave the film a rave review. '*Firefox* was exciting and good for morale. We won.' Other critics were less favourable. 'Cold war actioner never gets off the ground' headlined *Variety*. In fact it was the twelfth most popular film of the year. Vincent Canby in *The New York Times* was less than enthusiastic: 'It's a James Bond movie without girls, a Superman movie without a sense of humour . . . Eastwood treats himself with such solemnity that he seems to forget that action must be demonstrated, not just talked about.' Richard Schickel in *Time* magazine probably took the public pulse a little more accurately. 'It is fun to see the future zinging and skittering through our own

airspace. Eastwood's laconic professionalism plays off amusingly against the high-tech complexity of his flying machine . . . *Firefox* the movie is, on balance, rather like Firefox the plane: it is, at its best a clean, well-designed, fast-moving machine, at once practical, fanciful and capable of stunt flights that verge on the ecstatic.'

'Ecstatic . . . *Time* Magazine'—what publicist could resist it? After a trip to New York for a premiere to benefit the Museum of Modern Art's film archive, where Barbara Walters congratulated herself on her two long interviews with Clint, who himself dismissed them as "two long pauses", he fled back to the peace of his ranch. 'Now I've got to go hide out in the hills for a while. I want to see my kids, get this character out of my mind and start thinking about the next one. I've put so much into this that it's hard to unwind.'

Mitchell Gant in another disguise which may not fool us but appears to have done the trick with the Russian soldier behind him. (Firefox, 1982).

ACTING WITH THE FAMILY

He did spend more time with his children, or "the squirts" as he calls them. Kyle was now fourteen and Alison eleven, and since his separation from Maggie, Eastwood went out of his way to remain close to them. Over the next three years he gave both of them major roles in his films, the first being Kyle as his nephew in his next picture, *Honkytonk Man* (1982).

In some indefinable psychological way I think Eastwood needed his son in the film for two reasons. First, he was about to play the weakest character of his career, Red Stovall, a drunken, dying country singer in the Depression who wants to perform at The Grand Ole Opry in Nashville before he goes to the one in the sky. If Eastwood Senior was going to disappoint the fans by being such a sad and feckless character, at least Eastwood Junior should be seen to be the assertive new generation, not least in an excursion to a whorehouse. And second, when Eastwood bought Clancy Carlile's novel, he must have seen in the itinerant Red shades of his own father who moved about California during the Depression, unable to hold on to a job for

long but nobly trying to provide for Clint and his mother, Ruth and sister, Jean. Eastwood gives away very little about those days, but significantly keeps a picture of his father at the gas station on Highway 1 and Sunset Boulevard where his father was lucky to get a job just before the war.

The setting for *Honkytonk Man* was familiar from Steinbeck's *The Grapes of Wrath*. Uncle Red comes to stay at his sister's bankrupt Oklahoma farm (the sister was movingly played by Verna Bloom, whom Eastwood hadn't used since he raped her in *High Plains Drifter*). She sees that he is even worse off than they are (booze, TB) so she permits her son Whit (Kyle Eastwood) and Grandpa (John McIntire), who wants to get back to Tennessee, to go off in the Lincoln convertible with Red in search of the musical grail.

The film is the sum of their adventures. It doesn't just involve a whorehouse; they also get mixed up in a robbery, attacked by a bull, have various brushes with the law and are joined by a waitress (Alexa Kenin) whose rendering of 'My Bonnie Lies Over The Ocean' would have made the composer wish he had never written it. Red makes it to the Opry but not through his songs, due to the tuberculosis, and spends the end of the film, like Camille, passing on.

Left: Like father, like son. Clint and Kyle Eastwood as Red Stovall and his nephew, Whit, at the Grand Ole Opry in Honkytonk Man *(1982). Below left: Red Stovall has a penchant for strong women and drink. Here he tries to tempt Whit with the latter. (*Honkytonk Man, *1982). Below right: Like father like daughter. Alison Eastwood at breakfast with her father, playing homicide detective, Wes Block in* Tightrope *(1984).*

Uncle Red along with Kyle Eastwood, Bob Ferrera, John McIntire, Verna Bloom, Tracy Shults and Matt Clark.

Here I must confess that *Honkytonk Man* is my least favourite Eastwood film although young Kyle did give a remarkably naturalistic performance. 'You look at kids in TV commercials and see them being put through their paces by adults, it's kind of embarrassing,' noted Eastwood. 'I think Kyle is awfully good. He grew up as a normal, everyday kid— that's one reason I moved up the coast, away from Hollywood in the first place. But he's always been crazy about films. At an age when other kids just wanted to watch TV, Kyle would want to see some old classic movie. That's what gave me the feeling he could carry off the part. He took it very seriously, thought about what he was doing, and when he didn't, I was there to remind him. When he was younger he would make up characters, keep himself entertained, play on his own all day long, just as I used to do as a kid. I don't know if that has anything to do with becoming an actor or not.' Kyle observed of the experience: 'I enjoyed stealing the chickens and I really liked driving the car in the film.'

The film did have its critical champions, however, notably Richard Schickel in *Time*, who asserted 'Clint Eastwood has fashioned a marvellously unfashionable movie, as quietly insinuating as one of Red's honkytonk melodies. It is a guileless tribute not only to plain values of plain people in Depression America, but also to the sweet spirit of country and western music before it got all duded up for the urban cowboys. As both actor and director Eastwood has never been more laconic than he is in this film.'

Kathleen Carroll of the *New York Daily News* put her finger on the problem when she pointed out that Red Stovall was 'an appealingly good natured but rather dull character'. Indeed he did at times appear to be Bronchial Billy. Eastwood was happy to defend Red— 'I like to take a chance with a vulnerable character', — and to poke fun at himself. 'I'm 52 but I have the body of a nine-year-old. Kyle has dimples; I've got pleats.' Undoubtedly their father-son relationship benefitted from the experience; Clint had taken Kyle to the movie-brothel for the first time.

Honkytonk Man was not a hit and afterwards Eastwood felt the need to re-establish himself with a big, popular film. So he did something he told me he thought he would never do again: he returned to the sure-fire role, in every sense of the phrase, of Dirty Harry. *Sudden Impact* was to be the fourth outing for that character, but the first that Clint would actually direct himself, and his tenth film as a director.

The film begins with a couple necking in a car. A female (Sondra Locke) opens the door and gives the man what Harry later calls 'a .138 calibre' vasectomy, before shooting them both dead. We cut to Lt. Harry Callahan, somewhat dejected after a judge has given him a ticking off about his battle tactics. Things soon look up however. Harry stops for his morning coffee and, as luck would have it, stumbles across a robbery. With his new .44 Magnum auto-mag he kills three of the robbers and when the fourth attempts to go for his gun,

Harry utters the soon-to-be-immortal line: 'Go ahead, make my day.'

The action is where Harry is. If he passes a bank there is sure to be a hold-up. When he goes to give a Mafia chief a tongue lashing the old guy chokes to death in rage. The three men sent to avenge this outrage riddle the bunker where they think Harry is hiding with more bullets than were unleashed on D-Day. Not enough though; Harry wasn't there. He was behind them and three economical shots later they are horizontal. Truly, his day has been made.

But not that of the police department. Annoyed by his methods of instant justice and fearing that juries in San Francisco are going to become as obsolete as the dinosaur, 'It's a whole new ball game, Callahan,' his boss tells him. 'I didn't know it was a game,' comes the terse reply. But they send him to work with the local police in the small Californian town of San Paulo, which is the home of one of the victims of the vasectomy murderer.

It is also the home of the vasectomy murderer herself, Jennifer Spencer, who lives alone painting tortured canvasses. A grudging romance grows between them. 'I don't want to be alone tonight, Callahan,' she informs him, less than romantically. 'Neither do I,' he responds with minimal enthusiasm. Nevertheless he is still copper before lover, as he gets out of bed in the middle of the night to ascertain from her car number plates that she is probably his quarry.

It is revealed she is avenging a gang rape visited on her and her sister ten years previously. Her sister

has been in a catatonic state since and so has the son of the local police chief (Pat Hingle) who was one of the rapists. The gang was led by a loud-mouthed lesbian and, in a typical piece of Eastwood crowd pleasing, she is punched in the mouth for her truculence.

Harry is faced with a moral conundrum. He still respects the law and he is required to bring Jennifer to justice. In a deserted funfair at night three remaining rapists set on Harry and Jennifer. In a fist fight they knock him into the sea and hold her hostage. Echoing the surreal street scene in *High Plains Drifter*, Eastwood marches, backlit, along the boardwalk to rescue her. The auto mag rings out and all are dead, one landing on the horn of the carousel unicorn. Clint and Sondra walk into a new dawn together.

If I have been slightly tongue-in-cheek in describing the film, it is because Clint was decidedly tongue-in-cheek in making it. In many ways it is as much a parody of his Dirty Harry persona as Bronco Billy was of his 'man with no name' persona. If that needed to be underlined, Eastwood provided himself with a bulldog named Meathead, which farted with the frequency of Sorrow in *The Hotel New Hampshire*. With more guile than he was given credit for, except by the massive audience response, he managed to counterpoint this rough humour with the dark drama of Jennifer's genuine tragedy and thus have his cake and eat it. It wasn't a wholly new technique to mix violence and tragedy with a droll superhero: a man called Sergio Leone had

Eastwood as homicide detective, Wes Block in Tightrope.

Sondra Locke as vengeful Jennifer Spencer imitating her mentor in Sudden Impact *(1983).*

already made some successful Westerns that way.

Eastwood was only too aware of how he was playing with light and shade. 'It's a film with a lot of action and it has a dark, almost sinister quality to it at times. We shot most of our chase and special effects sequences at night, and both the boardwalk and the San Francisco waterfront areas open all sorts of possibilities. Locations like these take the story out of a conventional setting and give it a perspective. I like that.'

The success of Dirty Harry films is measured in queues rather than reviews. Eastwood knows this only too well and rarely promotes them with the nurturing care of *Honkytonk Man* or the proud premieres of *Firefox*. He goes to ground and lets the critics' salvoes sail overhead. 'A disquisition on the justice of revenge written with a spray can'—*Newsweek*. 'The picture is like a slightly psychopathic version of an old Saturday-afternoon serial'—*New Yorker*. 'Morose, lurid, filled to the brim with the depressing sadness of sadism,'—*New York* Magazine. Let it never be said that the critics can take a joke, however sick. Some appreciated Miss Locke's tantalizing Veronica Lake presence, but the greatest appreciation probably came from Clint's bank manager. In terms of box office it re-established him as the world's number one star, a position he seemed able to recapture by the flick of the right script.

He was by now divorced from Maggie. It was not his favourite topic of conversation but Lorenzo Carcaterra, interviewing him in the *New York Sunday News* on 12 August 1984 published the following exchange:

'Q: Does it bother you that the whole world knows about your divorce settlement of $25 million?

A: Yeah, but there's nothing you can do about it. It's a large sum of money, but my wife helped me a great deal in those early years, working and all. I don't begrudge the amount, but I wasn't comfortable with the attention it received.

Q: Was Sondra Locke the main reason for the separation and the later divorce?

A: There's never any one reason for anything. It was just an accumulation of things. Sondra and I are very close. She's a good friend. In fact, when the idea of my daughter Alison appearing in *Tightrope* was first mentioned, I asked Sondra for her advice. She talked to Alison, ran through some things with her and said she'd be okay.'

Although at the time of *Honkytonk Man*, Clint had said that Alison seemed less interested in acting than her brother, clearly nobody was better prepared to play the twelve-year-old daughter of New Orleans detective, Wes Block, played by Clint Eastwood, than his own twelve-year-old daugher.

Eastwood has always nurtured young talent, not just among members of his family, and had spotted Richard Tuggle after reading his screenplay of *Escape From Alcatraz*. When Tuggle wrote *Tightrope* (1984) it was with inside knowledge of Eastwood's desire to ring the changes. 'I don't just want to be remembered as the man who played Dirty Harry and 100 Westerns,' he would tell interviewers. But when Eastwood veered sharply away from his popular personae the audience stayed away—although he was anxious to point out that *Bronco Billy* took $30 million which was more than *The Natural*, starring Robert Redford—and Tuggle cleverly came up with a story that made a 'Harry' character less superhuman, more rounded and consequently more intriguingly vulnerable. Eastwood liked it and agreed to do it. But Tuggle attached a condition to his script: he wanted to direct it himself. Eastwood finally agreed; after all he was to be in nearly every scene himself, his man Bruce Surtees would shoot it and Joel Cox, whom he had brought up from cutting room assistant, would edit it. There was little likelihood of it not turning out the way he liked it.

Wes Block is a New Orleans homicide detective. He is somewhat embittered—at least as far as women are concerned. His wife left him for a richer man and he looks after their daughters Amanda and Penny (Alison Eastwood and Jennifer Beck). At home he is a gentle and caring father but at work he is tracking down a serial sex killer. It takes him to the sleazier areas of New Orleans, massage parlours and brothels and he is himself tempted by the ladies there, on one occasion using his handcuffs for his greater gratification (surely against police procedure).

This pursuit brings him in contact with Beryl (Genevieve Bujold) who is in charge of the city's rape prevention centre. Her feminist views run counter to

Wes's attitude to the fairer sex, with the exception of his daughters. But their common cause brings them closer together and so does a growing mutual attraction. Wes is shocked to discover that the latest victim of the rapist murderer is a girl he has just had sex with. He begins to wonder whether he could be the murderer himself, but he is being framed. His tie is found at the next murder and he rushes home, fearing for the safety of his daughters. Rightly so, as the baby sitter has been killed and Penny has been handcuffed to her bed (giving food for considerable thought). The killer has left some vital clues as to his identity and the final combat comes down to man-to-man, as it does so often in Eastwood films, and if you think Richard Tuggle is going to ruin his commercial chances by letting the wrong man win, you're as crazy as the one who loses.

This *film noir* ventures into Hitchcock territory. Eastwood was anxious to emphasize that more strongly than the original script suggested. He even spoke the lines of the killer at the beginning with a disguised voice to heighten this possibility. The audience is left wondering if there is just a chance they are one and the same man and, if not that, certainly gets the message that they are similar men. Even the murderer voices the thought that Wes is just as screwed up as he is. And as Wes gets deeper and deeper into his quest, he comes face to face with some unacceptable realities about himself. If Wes were played by a little known actor the audience might be more likely to catch the mythic pass; with Eastwood in the role, however, they know that there is a repository of ultimate honour somewhere within him.

Free from the chores of directing, the part of Wes was an exceptionally fine piece of acting by Clint. His face changed remarkably; he seemed sadder, less in command of himself and more tortured. He doesn't use any make up but, as he says, 'you've got to donate yourself to the character'. The early domestic scenes with Alison were beautifully natural, she and her dad are clearly pals and this transferred affectingly to the screen. Miss Bujold was chosen, not least, for her grit. 'It's a selfish reason,' he said. 'If any of the characters I play just came in and had some coy little angelic creature acting as a sort of female symbol to work against, it would not only be unbelievable, it would be a major drag. The thing that's made movies throughout history was that the leading man—Bogart, Gable, Cooper—always had someone strong to play off.'

It was interesting to note that in his early fifties and in this his fortieth film, Eastwood now felt confident enough to speak of himself in association with those three men. He knew that some of his audience might be disappointed by the film 'if they come expecting to see twenty people blown away in the first reel', but as ever he was exploring new audiences. He got them. David Denby, the film critic of *New York* Magazine for one. 'I've resisted Clint Eastwood for years,' he wrote at the end of an admiring review, 'but it's time to stop making jokes.' Even the *New York Times* acknowledged '*Tight-*

Richard Tuggle who wrote and directed Tightrope *in conference with his star.*

rope isn't quite top level Eastwood but it's close', the unwritten compliment being that 'top level Eastwood' was now a mark of quality.

Eastwood made a second film in 1984, a romp for Christmas with Burt Reynolds. Originally it was called *Kansas City Blues* and had been scheduled to be directed by Blake Edwards. But both the title and the director changed and by the time Clint climbed on board it was *City Heat*, directed by the ex-actor Richard Benjamin, who had demonstrated a nifty comic touch behind the camera with *My Favorite Year*, starring Peter O'Toole. Details of any behind the scenes rows were not vouchsafed to the press but it seems fair to assume that since Mr Edwards, who also wrote the film, had his name changed to Sam O. Brown (the initials of one of his own movies) in the credits, he was not exactly delighted to find himself on the sidelines.

Eastwood and Reynolds had expressed the desire to work together for several years and this period piece, set in the thirties during Prohibition seemed to have a certain satiric potential. In the movie the two of them are old cop buddies who have gone their separate ways—Burt has become a most maladroit private detective and Clint has remained lethally within the force—but they team up again for some wacky confrontations. The satiric potential certainly shows at the start when Lt Eastwood solemnly sips his coffee while Reynolds is being beaten up in the same diner, only being riled into action when one of the hoodlums is careless enough to make him spill it. The plot thereafter owes a little to *The Sting* and a little to *The Maltese Falcon* and a lot to the undeniable charms of Clint and Burt playing off each other with ribald insults—'See

you around, Shorty'; 'Not if I see you first, Flatfoot.'

Burt's henchman, Richard Roundtree, has tried to pit two gang leaders against each other with disastrous results, especially for his own boss. Clint is cool on Burt but hot for his secretary, Jane Alexander. It is the era of the speakeasy and the even easier murder. Irene Cara, she of *Flashdance*, is a singer who witnesses a murder and Madeline Kahn is an heiress who is Burt's girlfriend and turns a hostage to fortune. Rip Torn and Tony Lo Bianco make credible criminals but it is the war between Burt and Clint that is the more enjoyable contest. 'I didn't hear you knock,' says Burt disdainfully as Clint enters his office. 'That's a relief,' replies the droll detective, 'I thought I was going deaf.' The film ends with an overdose of fists and bullets which deliver rather less punch than the better lines.

However it did achieve the distinction of a *Time* cover of the two actors, with the description 'Hollywood's Honchos'. Off the screen it had been revealed that Eastwood had been considerably more honcho with another actor, William Shatner, alias Captain Kirk of *Star Trek*. They had helped subsidize a fifteen-man raid into Laos, to try and find American servicemen held there since the end of the Vietnam war. While Sylvester Stallone was putting *Rambo* on the screen, another actor, probably better suited to the part, was making a more realistic attempt to do the same thing behind it.

Above: Genevieve Bujold as Beryl Thibodeaux, director of the New Orleans Rape Crisis Centre, tries on Detective Block's bracelets in Tightrope *(1984). Right: Hollywood Honchos. Burt Reynolds as Mike Murphy and Clint Eastwood as Lieutenant Speer* (City Heat, *1984).*

MAYOR AND MOVIEMAKER

Although New York's Museum of Modern Art ran an Eastwood retrospective in 1980, America had been the place where he had made a profit without honour. But in Europe things were different and in January 1985 he, and various senior Warner Brothers executives, climbed into the company's Gulfstream jet and set off to collect some of these honours. First stop was Paris where Clint was to be made a *Chevalier des Arts et Lettres*. Clint had always had a soft spot for the French; one of the accompanying plane-load told me that the star liked the way they referred to 'the body of his work'. And indeed at the glittering ceremony at the Cinemathèque in the Palais de Chaillot, Pierre Viot, who was about to take over the Cannes Film Festival, referred to 'the abyss of perplexity' that Eastwood had created for film intellectuals.

He was undoubtedly pleased at the accolade: 'When I first went to Europe they wouldn't give me the time of day. Now they're giving me medals. It's taken twenty years.' He spoke with greater freedom than he

Left: Clint in London. A happy moment from Clint Eastwood's European tour of 1985. Below left: 'Behold a pale horse; and his name that sat on him was Death, and Hell followed with him. (Pale Rider, 1986). Below right: Telling it to the Marines. Eastwood directing Heartbreak Ridge *in 1986.*

might have done in his native America, where he thought there should be less government and lower taxes. He observed that in the last Presidential campaign Walter Mondale was paying too much attention to the fringe groups at the expense of middle America, who might well say, 'What is this about? We don't care about that. What about us?'

Even in the cathedral city of cinema the tone was occasionally lowered but Clint, as ever, was able to fend off the nonsense with a little wit. 'Did you once describe yourself as a bum and a drifter?' inquired one interviewer. 'No,' came the stonewall reply. 'Then what are you?' followed the philosophical French supplementary. Eastwood barely paused. 'A bum and a drifter,' he smiled.

By the time they got to Munich things had become a little worse. A Spanish countess came to interview him and asked, 'Would you have liked to make movies with Greta Garbo?' 'Who me? I don't have a foot fetish,' was Eastwood's comeback, which many of those who were with him are still trying to interpret to this day. Someone had booked him on a German variety show hosted by a compère whom Eastwood's agent, Leonard Hirshan, described as 'the kind of guy Dirty Harry would have shot if he had the opportunity'. Eastwood appeared between a child who was about to see how long he could stay in an icy river and a rock group called the Kane Gang. Eastwood was given a plaque; what the person who booked him on the show got remains unrecorded.

'I'm very close to the Western. That's where my roots are.' And his bullets. (Pale Rider, 1986).

So the entourage breathed a sigh of relief when their jet touched down in the icy and insalubrious surroundings of Britain's Luton Airport. They knew they had arranged a photographic session with someone who was near-royal, a fact that was revealed to the star in a confidential briefing paper. 'As you know Lord Snowdon is one of the most respected portrait photographers working today. His family connections on his wife's side (his first wife's side) are not to be sneezed at.'

By 7.00 am on Sunday 13th January a queue had formed outside London's National Film Theatre in the slender hope of getting tickets for the Guardian Lecture that Eastwood was to give there at 3.00 pm. Like the Cinemathèque, the National Film Theatre is a place where some come to revere rather than enjoy movies, but at least one of the crowd was dressed as a cowboy with several days' stubble on his chin and chewing on a black cheroot. His hero looked slightly different: a plain blue shirt, smart tie and corduroy jacket adorned the Stranger on this occasion. Clint rehearsed the familiar details of his career with good grace but never really had cause to think until Chris Auty, a former *Variety* reporter, asked from the back of the auditorium how he reconciled his two sides: the man who dispensed frontier justice and the laid back liberal. Eastwood paused and scratched his head and, to his credit, did not try to escape by saying these were merely different parts he played, not him. 'One thing I've always fought against is being aligned politically,' he answered. 'I have liberal approaches to some things and maybe conserva-

tive approaches to other things. People who are aligned aren't much fun. I guess I prefer the individual. An individual can change his mind. There are certain things you feel at one point in your life that you don't feel at another and that's just one of the facts.'

Throughout his flit through Europe he was asked if he would consider running for President. He normally deflected the question but hinted that he might be able to look the part, then hastily retracted it: 'If I've got the presidential face [something that Norman Mailer had said he had] I'm lacking in a lot of other areas. I don't feel that I could get up and say a lot of things that I know I couldn't perform on. Yet you have to do that to win. The ones who are honest about what they can or cannot do don't have a chance. I just have a look that might inspire some sort of credibility with the public. It's just thinking out loud, I don't think it's meant to say I am the best prepared. I am probably the least prepared.'

In both Britain and France he was asked about Bernard Goetz, the man who shot his potential muggers on a New York subway train. He observed that there was something pretty significant in the wave of public sympathy for the vigilante, but emphasized that in *Magnum Force* Dirty Harry said that taking the law into your own hands would end up with shooting someone whose dog had urinated on your lawn. In London he asserted: 'Audiences are more intelligent than people give them credit for. Regardless of their education they instinctively know it's a film and a fantasy as they go out. Maybe some kid would think he was Dirty Harry for five minutes. But if they did an act of violence it would be a highly unusual thing. You wouldn't make any form of entertainment if you thought anybody was going to be affected. I wouldn't make a film if I thought it was going to cause one violent act. I'm very anti-violence.' Then he added, 'Maybe he's gone to see Mary Poppins or something', and the audience laughed with relief.

Proof that some people in audiences are less intelligent than people give them credit for came in the shape of an Irish questioner who wanted Clint to say 'Make my day' in a Dirty Harry voice. Poor Clint did everything to avoid it but found, eventually, that it would provide him with his most immediate avenue of escape. He had a much better time on TV, on the Michael Aspel Show who, after the tumultuous applause that greeted Clint's arrival, quipped: 'I think you're among friends', and the programme spun amusingly along from there.

More privileged friends attended a select dinner in the star's honour at London's Arts Club. Apart from Charlton Heston pinching the veteran critic Dilys Powell's place next to Clint, it went without a hitch. Terry Semel, the President of Warners, said how proud he was of his star and the star said how proud he was to be there. In front of such luminaries as Walter Matthau, Faye Dunawaye and Dudley Moore, the *filet de boeuf* Wellington was duly piped in. And when most of the limousines had snaked into the early hours of the January morning, Clint was still there, beer can in hand, listening to Dudley extemporizing magnificently on the piano. 'Why didn't you bring Sondra?' I asked him. 'She's on a diet,' he replied with a smile, 'and she figured the trip would involve a lot of eating.' Why had he bothered to do this long distance tour? 'They're pretty nice people and I hadn't been to Europe in a while.'

Then he went back to his roots in more ways than one: to the West and to the Western. During 1984 Eastwood once again swam against the tide by making *Pale Rider* at a time when the Western had become distinctly unfashionable. He finished shooting before he came to Europe and now had to add the final touches in the cutting room and dubbing theatre. *Pale Rider* had been written four years previously by Michael Butler and Dennis Shryack, who had scripted *The Gauntlet*. Eastwood had liked it but put it in his desk drawer. In the summer of 1984 he took it out again. 'I'd like to say I picked the moment but I'm not that smart. All of a sudden it just hit me that I'd like to see a Western. Everything I've always done has been that way, something I'd like to see. I hate to play to the preconceived idea of the audience. I just like to make the project. I've done this all the way along. If you go with a pre-conceived idea you get into a bind of second-guessing the audience, which is dangerous. It would affect the film and the way you make it. I'm sure if I had wanted to make *Bronco Billy* a more commercial picture I could have found all sorts of ways. I could have

tossed in action scenes but that would have ruined the film. Somewhere down the line I would have paid for it since it wouldn't be as good quality. I guess the studios feed stuff into computers and poll people, but that's nonsense.'

However, Eastwood had done some market research of his own, always keeping a weather eye open on the younger generation. 'There is a whole youthful audience that hasn't seen me in a Western for nine years and whose only exposure to the genre has been through television re-runs. I've been very lucky: *High Plains Drifter* and *The Outlaw Josey Wales* keep getting good ratings every time they're on. So somebody out there wants to see Westerns. Look at the so-called space movies. Aren't they really just spin-offs of the Westerns? In *Star Wars*, they talk about the Force, but Westerns use all those same elements.'

Pale Rider became his forty-second film, his first Western in nine years and his eleventh film as director. On 17th September Eastwood and his faithful team— Fritz Manes, production manager, Bruce Surtees, Director of Photography, Edward Carfagno, production designer, and Joel Cox, film editor—assembled at Sun Valley, Idaho to start shooting. The film might well have been called *Behold A Pale Horse*, if Fred Zinnemann and Gregory Peck had not already used the title. The same biblical quotation, from Revelations 6:8, informed both films: 'And I looked, and behold a pale horse; and his name that sat on him was Death, and Hell followed with him.' It might equally have been called *High Plains Rider*, since the mythic elements of Ernest Tidyman's script for *High Plains Drifter* were also much in evidence here.

The time is the Gold Rush. The livelihood of a small community of struggling gold miners is being threatened by the neighbouring mining baron Coy LaHood (Richard Dysart) who, not content with using the high pressure water hoses of hydraulic mining to put them out of business, also wants their land. LaHood's men harass the small community and beat up Hull Barret (Michael Moriarty) when he is unwise enough to set foot in town to get some supplies. Enter The Man With No Name or, in this instance, the Preacher With No Name (Eastwood sports a dog collar), who wields a plank of wood as deftly as Babe Ruth to see off the assailants. 'There's nothing like a nice piece of hickory,' he observes as the gang are sprawled over the main street.

He returns to the camp, proving to be the answer to young Megan's prayers. He bunks with her mother Sarah (Carrie Snodgress) and rolls up his sleeves and helps in the dig, pausing only to give one of LaHood's hoods a boot in the testes when he comes to cause trouble. Gold is duly struck and LaHood offers to buy out their claims. The preacher encourages them not to but then disappears. They think he has forsaken them but he has merely gone to get his guns and is back in time to save Megan (Sydney Penny) from rape, dynamite LaHood's workings and annihilate the perverted lawman, Marshal Stockburn and his six deputies in a high street showdown. This is especially annoying to Stockburn as he thought he had killed the preacher some years previously and the preacher adds insult to injury by drilling a pattern of bullets into the Marshal that correlate to the scars on his own back. 'Who are you?' asks the infatuated Megan. 'It doesn't really matter, does it?' replies the stranger as he rides into the echoing mountains.

It was a film very dear to Clint's heart. 'I feel very close to the Western, that's where my roots are.' He claims that he is not a writer: 'The written thing is the creative work. As an actor, you're just interpreting. I've never been smart enough to write it from scratch, to take a blank piece of paper and make a story. If I could have done that, that would be a great thing to do.' But on *Pale Rider* he was possibly more involved with the script than with any other and insisted on the mythic elements in it. 'I ended up making it a little more supernatural than it was written, getting into parallels with the Bible. I felt my character needed a prior relationship with the Marshal. That would give the Pale Rider an added dimension. It also tied in with the image of the horseman of the Apocalypse. I'm not a Biblical scholar but I've always been fascinated by the mythology of those Biblical stories and how they relate to the mythology of the Western.'

The down-to earth territory was also familiar to Clint, in more ways than one. 'I'd been raised with a little bit of history, having lived in some smaller California towns that had been affected by the Gold Rush. Naturally, I'd read a lot of Western stories about pioneering in this particular part of the country. My grandmother used to live in Angels Camp, the centre of the Gold Rush country, in fact right near where we filmed. I had also done some episodes of *Rawhide* in the area, and that's where we filmed the train station, in Sonora.'

The last words of the original script had the preacher 're-ascending into the mighty fortress of the heavens' but, that mythic element apart, many critics saw the film as something of a lift from *Shane*. The public was less worried and the $40 million taken in *Pale Rider's* first few weeks of release underlined that Eastwood's hunch was, once again, on target. And his boldness in that regard caused some critics to temper their reservations about the film with a new found respect for the star. Andrew Sarris wrote in the *Village Voice* 'Clint Eastwood has become the biggest star around not through one or two boffo freak hits but through a steady stream of semi-magical, semi-lyrical, semi-mystical, semi-nihilistic incarnations in a variety of moods and genres. He hasn't been consistently successful either critically or commercially, but he keeps moving in fair weather and foul with a seemingly indestructible star persona. His now grizzled countenance hasn't lost any of the teeth-clenched tenacity and implacability that seethed in the salad days of his Spaghetti Westerns for Sergio Leone.' Even more flattering Vincent Canby in the *New York Times* deemed it 'the first decent Western in a very long time' and observed of Eastwood's actor-director performance, 'this veteran movie icon handles both jobs with such intelligence and facility that I'm just now beginning to realize that, though Mr Eastwood may have been

improving over the years, it's also taken all these years for most of us to recognize his very consistent grace and wit as a film maker'.

Others who had recognized it a little earlier were rewarded with a lunch with Clint on board the M.Y. *Broka*, tied up in the Old Port at Cannes in May 1985. Clint was pretty tied up, too. He had been advised that it would be impossible for him to stay in any of the hotels during the film festival, so great was his popularity. As a result he remained on the yacht which was easily spotted since it resembled an embassy in a state of siege. He braved the crowd in the evenings in order to jump into a car and sample some of the local culinary delights at the Festival's traditional watering holes, L'Oasis and Le Moulin de Mougins, guided by Warners' French associate, Pierre Rissient, and sometimes accompanied by Fritz Manes and Joe Hyams who, unencumbered by fame, were able to stay at the Gray D'Albion.

Pale Rider was in competition that year and the night before it was shown Eastwood saw the French subtitled print for the first time at 3.00am in the Palais de Cinema. To his disappointment he found that the subtitles lightened the deliberately dark interiors which he and Bruce Surtees had striven for. 'I tried to get the mood of how it would be to live with two or three little lamps lighting a whole house. They really just make pools of lights.' He told me how he had been anxious to make it look different from television and by using these 'make or break interiors' he had hoped to bring the audience a little more to the edge of their seats.

He duly fielded questions at the press conference after the first screening. To the philosopher who suggested that the pattern of bullets he drilled into Marshal Stockburn was really Eastwood killing the image of his own father, Sergio Leone, he pointed out that this was unlikely since he and Leone were almost the same age (Leone is only nine years older). Asked about capital punishment he said he had had mixed feelings about it over the years, contrary to some of the films he had been in, but now felt there were some circumstances in which it was valid.

No such absurdity or seriousness was present at the small lunch where Eastwood, sipping a beer but declining to eat, was more relaxed than I had ever seen him before. He talked about his skiing career: 'They put me in some celebrity race and I had never been on skis before, I got down face down with bamboo all over the hill.' He revealed he had taken a worse spill in *Pale Rider*. 'A horse and I took a little egg beater into the ground on the last day. I'd actually finished shooting and I was in this long, snowy field, probably riding him too fast considering there was no way of knowing the ground with snow covering it. We hit a ditch that had ice on it, his front feet when through the ice and he just turned over. I was lucky that he didn't come down on top of me. The shoulder was broken in about five places. But I was skiing a month later — very carefully.'

He revealed that Kyle was thinking of going to film school and had taken a summer job as a cleaner in the Carmel cinema. 'He saw *Star Wars* 33 times or something and can tell you all the flaws and mismatches. Give us a break, I told him, nobody's supposed to see a movie 33 times.'

He had heard that I had given Alison a good review for *Tightrope* on the BBC's *Film '84* and said that there was a lot of interest in her as an actress. She was going to be thirteen later in the month. 'She has cut her hair real short and stylish. As a child she would always come on the set and do the clapper. She would mug and ham it up in front of camera. She's had some offers for movies of the week or some films which weren't very good material. She has the same agents as me and if they had something really good I'd discuss it with her and talk to her mother about it.' It was evident that he was very close to both children, pretending that now he had to make an appointment to see them since they preferred hanging out with friends of their own age group.

Eastwood revealed his next assignment: to work for Steven Spielberg. 'I'm directing one of his "Amazing Stories" on television, one that he wrote. It's terribly romantic and I'm not really interested in romantics but Steven thinks my films are romantic. It's a lark—six days shooting, 24 minutes and a million dollar budget. If I was using my own crew I could probably do it in half the time for half the money.' He only was half joking.

The Cannes jury failed to give any prizes to *Pale Rider* but the French critics were more appreciative. 'At the height of his art' said *Le Matin*. The film soon earned its keep in America, making $42 million in the first few weeks of its release. So Eastwood returned contentedly to Carmel, no longer to the spacious home and twelve acres by the ocean where Maggie and the children lived, but to a much smaller stone house which he bought complete with its furniture. He also had a substantial property in Northern California. 'He never spent any money on toys,' Fritz Manes remarked, 'it's only recently he's opened up and bought sports cars and ranches, but he uses them.'

His next role was to be, in many ways, the most challenging one he had ever tried. Eastwood has always insisted that he sees himself as a character actor rather than a leading man and was keen to build on the unusual experience of playing a loser as Red Stovall. It was the very complexity of Gunnery Sergeant Tom Highway's character that drew him to *Heartbreak Ridge*. 'He was a man at a crossroads, in life and in his career. He's approaching mandatory retirement, and he's trying to come to terms with the world he'll be facing after the service. He's been a problem soldier, too. He's a brawler, he drinks too much, by this time he probably should have been promoted to the maximum rank, especially being a Congressional Medal of Honor winner. But he's a little bit of a screw-up.'

So are many of the members of the 2nd Marine Reconaissance Platoon to whom he is assigned. Let me quote their problems from the production notes: 'Stitch is a jive-talking hustler who would prefer being a rock and roll star; Aponte is a distant brooding individual with family problems; Profile is a good natured flake; Johanson is a huge mountain of a man who can't seem to stay out of the brig; Fragetti is a hard boiled instigator who becomes a Marine to stay out of jail; Quinones is a

Marine Gunnery Sergeant Tom Highway training by example in Heartbreak Ridge *(1986)*.

competitive lifer who has always been a discipline problem. Only Collins is a young, fresh recruit, out to prove himself.' The Marines are looking for a few good men, their sergeant informs them, 'and you ain't them.'

Indeed they are hardly the men to win a war but, drilled by the battle hardened Highway, they play a winning part in America's most proficient military action since the Korean War: the invasion of the island of Grenada. It was intuitive of Clint to stay away from Vietnam—the sort of movies that were to profit from that war (generally negative in tone) were not the sort that carried his personal point of view.

Highway's personal life plays as big a part in the film as his professional one. He cannot understand what has gone wrong, and although he can communicate with the barmaid Little Mary (Eileen Heckart) he cannot get through to his ex-wife Aggie (Marsha Mason). She says to him: 'The only reason you want to come together now is because it's all coming to an end.' Eastwood relished this aspect of the character: 'He's a sort of a lost soul, an empty soul. He's never really understood women at all. The sort of guy who's very hard-boiled but, at the same time, searching for the sensitivities of his own soul. In a way he's like a lot of men. There's a lot of very macho guys who are that way, because they don't realize there's something else there. They've matured in some ways but not in others.'

The very title of the film, *Heartbreak Ridge*, communicated the duality of its content. It refers to a

Clint swops his .44 Magnum for an M-16 rifle to serve his country in Heartbreak Ridge *(1986).*

Korean battle where Highway distinguished himself, and also to the turning point in his personal life. The sentimentality was well balanced by the humour, as Highway can deliver a nice, sarcastic line or two in his gravelly voice, and Eastwood found himself on the end of some unaccustomedly good reviews for what was essentially an action movie. 'Pure entertainment. Eastwood's best performance since *Dirty Harry*—tough, funny, credible, even tender,' raved *USA Today*. The *New York Times* deemed it 'impressive ... Clint Eastwood's performance is one of his richest, funny and laid back'. *Time* Magazine hinted at the icon Clint was now becoming: 'Nobody does it with greater conviction, energy and unpatronizing affection for the grand old forms than Eastwood. His toughness is all the tougher.'

His worst review came from the officer who claimed he was the spokesman for the Marines themselves. 'There is an excessive amount of profanity, which we object to. As a matter of fact drill instructors are not permitted by regulations to swear at recruits. We especially objected to a scene in which the Clint Eastwood character shoots a wounded Cuban soldier in the back.' The official view was that it depicted a hard-bitten way of military life that was no longer prevalent.

Didn't they read the script, one wonders. After all, they had supplied an adviser, Lt. Col. Fred Peck, allowed Clint to shoot at their base in Camp Pendleton in Oceanside, California, given him some helicopters and ships to play with and permitted off-duty Marines to work on the film. They couldn't provide the Caribbean

island of Grenada so the Puerto Rican island of Vieques had to be dressed to look like it, right up to the lighthouse. Eastwood had an argument with a general and a civilian lady in the Pentagon who wanted the film to represent the new, high tech army, rather than the different eras of World War II and Korea. As Eastwood pointed out to them, 'I imagine that people who served in World War II and in Korea and Vietnam might resent that. Are you putting down all those people who fought and died for their country? That was all crap and this is all so great and new now?'

But he failed to heal the rift. The US Defense Department withdrew their official support and approval and a benefit performance in aid of the San Diego County Armed Forces YMCA had to be cancelled. Eastwood gave the proceeds from the premiere at the Manns Oceanside Theater to the YMCA anyway. Needless to say, regular Marines, loved the movie. It was his thirty-third major film and his twelfth as a director.

Clint, in the meantime, had been fighting a more intransigent foe than the Marines: the city council in Carmel. He wanted to build a three-storey office building next to the Hog's Breath Inn and they refused him planning permission. One can imagine his brow lowering, mouth tightening, the familiar squint. What does the loner do against the forces of bureaucracy? In this instance he did the democratic thing: if you can't

The mayor of Carmel-by-the-Sea samples the first of what will be two years of chicken salads.

beat them, replace them. He was persuaded to stand for mayor himself. The incumbent, Mayor Charlotte Townsend, had been less than helpful in his modest quest for expansion and after fifteen years in Carmel he felt the time had come to bring the place a little more up to date.

In January 1986 he paid for a phone survey to see if a majority of the 4700 residents would be willing to vote for him. The results looked favourable. 'I wanted to make sure the constituency out there felt as I did,' Eastwood said outside the Hog's Breath, now adorned with an 'Eastwood for Mayor' sign. He submitted a nomination paper signed by twenty residents and wrote in his candidate's filing statement: 'Our village faces some fundamental problems which are not being re-solved by our current mayor and city council.'

These no longer included his office; the city had settled out of court on a compromise development plan. Ice cream was one of the main issues. A city ordinance prohibited the eating of cones on the town's well-groomed streets. Also women needed a permit before they could wear high heels in town—and presumably men, too. Mayor Charlotte, who had been returned unopposed at the last election, had not only hampered Clint's new building but tourists' parking, people playing frisbee and even, it is said, children playing in the park. She was a 60-year-old former librarian.

Eastwood noted that even the retired were not immune from the busy-body rules. Some of them depended on renting out part of their houses to tourists for their income, but to prevent this the city rules said that each home could only have one kitchen. Spot checks which became known as 'Gestapo busts' were made by inspectors. The overall intention was to keep Carmel in its pristine perfection. If they were going to start shooting people for letting their dogs deface the side-walk anywhere in America, this precious town was the most likely place.

If elected, Eastwood promised that he would take a hiatus from films for his two years in office—an expensive gesture since the Mayor's salary was $200 a month and Clint's films had by then earned nearly $2 billion. But then, he probably had some savings in the bank, and 55 is a good age for reflection.

The campaign hotted up. Eastwood knocked at doors, attended coffee mornings and spoke at meetings with a new-found relish. Mrs Townsend stood against him, accusing him of having an ex-directory phone number and being inaccessible, a charge she could equally have laid at another of the candidates, Tim Grady, who had given up dentistry to live in a tent on the dunes four years previously. The fourth candidate, Paul Laub, owned shops selling T-shirts with familiar sayings like 'Do you feel lucky?' and 'Make my day', not to mention frilly knickers with 'Make my night' in-scribed on them.

Clint enjoyed the campaign: 'It was a great experience. I liked meeting a lot of people within the community. I got to know the town.' He insisted that it

161

was a form of altruism that was driving him. 'I've lived in Carmel for fifteen years now and I felt the need to give some of myself back to this town. I mean it—to give. Politics is certainly the route to power or money, or both at once. But I don't need money and I don't want power.' What he did want was to preserve individual freedoms and to see the community, and the country, run more like a business. 'My soul is in Carmel,' he said.

As polling day drew closer the world descended on the town. The tiny election was followed on every television set from Seoul to Sydney. Eastwood neither welcomed nor helped such presidential coverage but there was little he could do to stop it. On 8th April 1986 he was elected Mayor by an overwhelming 72 per cent. He got 2166 votes, Mrs Townsend got 799 and the other two got 37 votes between them. In answer to the question on the world's lips, he replied: 'My ambitions begin with Carmel and they end there. Let Reagan do his job and I'll do mine.'

And he stuck to his words. He solved the problems of the lavatories, the ice creams, the frisbees and the parking—and it is unlikely that any prosecutions for high heels would have happened during his term of office. He put new blood on the council, including, prudently, the editor of the local paper. Even his opponents had to concede that his pragmatic solution to the Mission Ranch problem was most effective. There was a danger that developers would put new and ugly faults on the Ranch but a mysterious company, Tehama, thwarted them by buying it. It was discovered subsequently that Eastwood owned the company. A year after his election he told Time, 'If someone had told me two years ago that I'd be spending time in someone else's garage, deciding if it could be moved three inches to the north, I would have said he'd lost it.'

Most people now concede he has done a good job. The businessmen of the local Rotary Club gave him an award for 'having substantially contributed to the quality of life in Carmel'. His only crime was to attract more ice cream licking tourists to the town than there is room for. On the first Tuesday of every month, wearing his new spectacles, he presided over the Council meeting. Since it is open to the public—not just the residents, people traveled for hundreds of miles to come—they had to hold it in the biggest hall available and, even then, there was usually standing room only.

Sondra Locke had not been involved in the campaign—at the time locals recall only having seen her once in Carmel. She had however embarked on her first film as director, Ratboy. It was a Malpaso production for Warner Bros. with Clint's old friend Fritz Manes as producer and the safe hands of Bruce Surtees as director of photography and Edward Carfagno as production designer. The film was a fable about an ambitious young woman (Sondra herself) who found a boy who looked like a rat (make-up by Rick Baker) and exploited the Hollywood publicity circuit to obtain fame for him—and her. Clint only looked in on shooting for a short time but pronounced himself very pleased with the final result. 'I was the one who suggested she direct it. I'm very proud of her. The action is some of the best

stuff in the film, I think. Maybe some of the work I've done has rubbed off.' His enthusiasm was reciprocated by the French who accorded it a warm reception at the 1986 Deauville Festival. She told the London Times that this reinforced her determination to continue directing. 'I don't see marriage and children on the cards any more,' she told them, 'I think I chose this profession as a way to remain an eternal child.'

As it stands they appear to have a modern relationship—together when they're together. Eastwood has enormous respect for her—'Sondra knows much more about the history of films than I do. She'll watch a film more than once and really study it.' And she has great understanding of him—'He's so self-effacing it's almost funny. He is so equal-minded. He's the original non-threatened person.'

When the Variety Club International honoured Clint Eastwood at their eleventh annual salute, Sondra was there with his children, his mother, his step-father, his sister and her husband. Alison and Kyle actually introduced the ceremony, pointing out that the previous year the Variety Club had honoured the President of the United States, but that this year they had gone over his head to honour the Mayor of Carmel, California. Cary Grant in his last appearance on this televised show read out a letter from the President which began: 'Dear Clint, When Variety Club International asked me to send a message in honour of an actor who holds public office and plays with a chimp I had a strong sense of deja-vu.' Jimmy Stewart put his finger on Eastwood's art: 'Don't act—be.' Bob Hope, on good form, teased that Carmel was the only town to send out a S.W.A.T. team to collect overdue library books.

Following these three legends, Eastwood was clearly overwhelmed. 'None of you are Carmel voters in this room so this is going to be real short,' he joked. But it was. He never believed when he was a young child watching their movies that one day he would be in the same room as them. 'I've had a fantastic life,' he said.

Nobody expected that Eastwood would give up films completely during his reign as Mayor of Carmel. It was, after all, only a part-time job. However he did use the opportunity to check his pace, if only slightly, and then set about what for him was a labour of love and respect. He had always had a passion for jazz—indeed he was and remains an adept piano player—and in 1945 he saw his idol Charlie Parker play in his native Oakland. Parker, nicknamed Yardbird, further refined to Bird, was, along with Dizzie Gillespie, the originator of 'bop' in the forties. This was a reaction against the swing era which brought the art of improvisation—melodic, harmonic and rhythmic—back into jazz.

Parker and his saxophone ventured into territories few other players would dare enter. He would speed up the tempo, descant on the melody, counter the beat, improvise brilliantly and seemingly casually as he veered vertiginously away from the piece only to return to the basic work with magnificent control. He was a musical genius and he lived like one and died like one at the same age as Mozart—35. At 15 he was a heroin addict, at 16 he was married and by the time of his

'He breathes in air. He breathes out light. Charlie Parker was my delight.' (Adrian Mitchell). Clint directs Forest Whitaker in Bird *(1988).*

death from alcohol and drugs in 1955 he was regarded as the greatest jazz player of all.

The script for *Bird*, written by Joel Oliansky, had been around for many years. Ray Stark owned it and entertained hopes of making it a Columbia vehicle for Richard Pryor. Eastwood wanted it, while Stark wanted *Revenge*, a Warner Brothers script that Clint had turned down, so they did an amicable deal. But whereas Stark had perceived the need for a major star to support the venture, Eastwood was of a different opinion. 'I thought this should be a small project with unknown people,' he said, 'using names clutters it up.' Warner Brothers approved a $7 million dollar budget and no stars—save the one behind the camera. Not since *Breezy* in 1973 had Eastwood directed a film in which he did not appear but he was prepared to take the risk with this, his thirteenth as director. However Eastwood's value as a publicist for the film must not be underestimated. That in itself would be worth several million dollars.

He had seen Forest Whitaker as a pool hustler who took on Paul Newman in *The Color of Money* and thought him right for Parker. For much of Bird's short life a girl called Chan played a supportive role, although he never married her since he failed to disentangle himself from his teenage marriage. Diane Venora who made her name as Joe Papp's female Hamlet was given her cinema break and Sam Wright played Dizzy Gillespie.

Aljean Harmetz of the *New York Times* visited the set—Burbank was standing in for 52nd Street, New York—and Clint confided: 'I'd love to go back in time, to Bourbon Street in the twenties, to 12th Street in Kansas City in the thirties and to 52nd Street in the late forties'. In a way he was achieving the third as he wandered past the neon signs of the Club Samoa, Jimmy Ryan's, Leon and Eddie's and the 3 Deuces.

Harmetz met Lennie Niehaus, who had actually been in the army with Eastwood at Ford Ord and who had scored his last four movies. Niehaus rated Eastwood's piano playing skills high enough to persuade him to perform on the *City Heat* album. Niehaus may well have been instrumental in getting the *Bird* venture off the ground since he had played alto sax at Birdland with Stan Kenton's band. His complex challenge was to use Bird's original saxophone recordings in the film, while fading out the other instruments.

Eastwood managed to combine shooting with his mayoral duties. One morning he filmed in a cemetery from 6 to 8 am and then took the Warners jet to Carmel for the monthly city council meeting. But he decided not to run for office again. Like the loner in so many of his films, he just got the job done and then said goodbye. Pundits have pinned higher political ambitions on him, but he is a man who, above all, likes to control every aspect of his own existence and in politics life has an inevitable habit of controlling you.

In early 1988 he returned once again to the streets of San Francisco to make the fifth Dirty Harry film. The pressure from Warner Bros. and the incalculable remuneration for doing so would not have been easy to withstand and, more than either, it is what his public wants. He is in the enviable position of being able to subsidize projects dear to his heart by doing those dear to his bank manager—that way he can make everybody's day. Indeed when in his official capacity Eastwood met the Pope in Monterey, Paul Laub had the temerity to suggest that the Pontiff might have been equally blessed. He produced a T-shirt for the occasion with the inscription: 'Thou Makyth My Day.'

163

FILMOGRAPHY

FRANCIS IN THE NAVY (1955)

Director: Arthur Lubin
Producer: Stanley Rubin
Screenplay by Devery Freeman
Based on the character 'Francis The Talking Mule'
created by David Stern
Music by Joseph Gershenson
Director of Photography: Carl Guthrie
Universal-International Picture

Cast: Donald O'Connor (*Lt. Peter Sterling/Bosun's Mate Slicker Donevan*), Martha Hyer (*Betsey Donevan*), Richard Erdman (*Murph*), Myrna Hansen (*Helen*), David Janssen (*Lt. Anders*).

REVENGE OF THE CREATURE (1955)

Director: Jack Arnold
Producer: William Alland
Screenplay by Martin Berkeley
Music by Joseph Gershenson
Director of Photography: Charles S. Welbourne
Universal-International Picture

Cast: John Agar (*Clete Ferguson*), Lori Nelson (*Helen Dobson*), John Bromfield (*Joe Hayes*), Robert B. Williams (*George Johnson*), Nestor Paiva (*Lucas*).

LADY GODIVA (1955)

Director: Arthur Lubin
Producer: Robert Arthur
Screenplay by Oscar Brodney and Harry Ruskin
Music by Joseph Gershenson
Director of Photography: Carl Guthrie
Universal-International Picture, Technicolor

Cast: Maureen O'Hara (*Lady Godiva*), George Nader (*Lord Leofric*), Eduard Franz (*King Edward*), Victor McLaglen (*Grimald*).

THE FIRST TRAVELLING SALESLADY (1956)

Director: Arthur Lubin
Producer: Arthur Lubin
Screenplay by Devery Freeman and Stephen Longstreet
Music by Irving Getz
Director of Photography: William Snyder
RKO-Radio Picture, Technicolor

Cast: Ginger Rogers (*Rose Gillray*), Barry Nelson (*Charles Masters*), Carol Channing (*Molly Wade*), James Arness (*Joel Kingdom*), Clint Eastwood (*Jack Rice*).

TARANTULA (1955)

Director: Jack Arnold
Producer: William Alland
Screenplay by Robert M. Fresco and Martin Berkeley
Music by Joseph Gershenson
Director of Photography: George Robinson
Universal-International Picture

Cast: John Agar (*Dr. Matt Hastings*), Mara Corday (*Stephanie Clayton*), Leo G. Carroll (*Professor Deemer*), Nestor Paiva (*Sheriff*).

NEVER SAY GOODBYE (1956)

Director: Jerry Hopper
Producer: Albert J. Cohen
Screenplay by Charles Hoffman
Based on a screenplay by Bruce Manning, John Klorer and Leonard Lee
Music by Joseph Gershenson
Director of Photography: Maury Gertsman
Universal-International Picture, Technicolor

Cast: Rock Hudson (*Dr. Michael Parker*), Cornell Borchers (*Lisa*), George Sanders (*Victor*), Ray Collins (*Dr. Bailey*), David Janssen (*Dave*), Shelley Fabares (*Suzy Parker*).

STAR IN THE DUST (1956)

Director: Charles Haas
Producer: Albert Zugsmith
Screenplay by Oscar Brodney
Music by Frank Skinner
Director of Photography: John L. Russell, Jr
Universal-International Picture, Technicolor

Cast: John Agar (*Bill Jorden*), Mamie Van Doren (*Ellen Ballard*),
Richard Boone (*Sam Hall*), Leif Erickson (*George Ballard*),
Coleen Gray (*Nellie Mason*).

ESCAPADE IN JAPAN (1957)

Director: Arthur Lubin
Producer: Arthur Lubin
Screenplay by Winston Miller
Music by Max Steiner
Director of Photography: William Snyder
RKO-Radio Picture, Technicolor and Technirama

Cast: Teresa Wright (*Mary Saunders*), Cameron Mitchell (*Dick
Saunders*), Jon Provost (*Tony Saunders*), Roger Nakagawa (*Hiko*),
Philip Ober (*Lt. Col. Hargrave*), Clint Eastwood (*Dumbo*).

AMBUSH AT CIMARRON PASS (1957)

Director: Jodie Copeland
Producer: Herbert E. Mendelson
Screenplay by Richard G. Taylor and John K. Butler
Based on a story by Robert A. Reeds and Robert W. Woods
Music by Paul Sawtell and Bert Shefter
Director of Photography: John M. Nickolaus Jr.
20th Century Fox Picture, Regalscope

Cast: Scott Brady (*Sgt. Matt Blake*), Margie Dean (*Teresa*),
Clint Eastwood (*Keith Williams*).

LAFAYETTE ESCADRILLE (G.B. *HELL BENT FOR GLORY*)
(1957)

Director: William A. Wellman
Producer: William A. Wellman
Screenplay by A.S. Fleischman
Based on a story by William A. Wellman
Music by Leonard Rosenman
Director of Photography: William Clothier
Warner Bros Picture

Cast: Tab Hunter (*Thad Walker*), Marcel Dalio (*Drillmaster*),
Etchika Choureau (*Renee*), David Janssen (*Duke Sinclaire*),
Paul Fix (*US General*), Veola Vonn (*Madame Olga*), Will Hutchins
(*Dave Putnam*), Clint Eastwood (*George Moseley*).

PER UN PUGNO DI DOLLARI
(A FISTFUL OF DOLLARS) (1964)

Director: Sergio Leone
Producers: Arrigo Colombo and Giorgio Papi
Screenplay by Sergio Leone and Duccio Tessari
Music by Ennio Morricone
Director of Photography: Massimo Dallamano
A Jolly Film (Rome)/Ocean (Madrid)/Constantin Film (Munich)
Production, released by United Artists, Technicolor and Techniscope

Cast: Clint Eastwood (*The Stranger*), Gian Maria Volonté (*Ramon
Rojos*), Marianne Koch (*Marisol*), Pepe Calvo (*Silvanito*),
Wolfgang Lukschy (*John Baxter*).

PER QUALCHE DOLLARI IN PIU
(FOR A FEW DOLLARS MORE) (1965)

Director: Sergio Leone
Producer: Alberto Grimaldi
Screenplay by Sergio Leone and Luciano Vincenzoni
Based on a story by Fulvio Marzello and Sergio Leone
Music by Ennio Morricone
Director of Photography: Massimo Dallamano
A PEA (Rome)/Arturo Gonzales (Madrid)/Constantin Film
(Munich) Production, released by United Artists, Technicolor and
Techniscope

Cast: Clint Eastwood (*The Stranger*), Lee Van Cleef
(*Col. Mortimer*), Gian Maria Volonté (*Indio*), Klaus Kinski
(*Hunchback*), Mara Krup (*Hotel Manager's Wife*).

IL BUONO, IL BRUTTO, IL CATTIVO
(THE GOOD, THE BAD, AND THE UGLY) (1966)

Director: Sergio Leone
Producer: Alberto Grimaldi
Screenplay by Age-Scarpelli, Luciano Vincenzoni and Sergio Leone
Music by Ennio Morricone
Director of Photography: Tonino Delli Colli
A Produzioni Europee Associate (Rome) Production, released by
United Artists, Technicolor and Techniscope

Cast: Clint Eastwood (*Joe*), Eli Wallach (*Tuco*), Lee Van
Cleef (*Setenza*).

LE STREGHE (*THE WITCHES*) (1966)

Directors: Luchino Visconti, Pier Paolo Pasolini, Mauro Bolognini,
Franco Rossi, Vittorio de Sica
Producer: Dino de Laurentiis
Screenplay for segment in which Eastwood appeared: 'Una Sera
Come Le Altre' by Cesare Zavattini, Fabio Capri and Enzo Muzzi
Director: Vittorio de Sica
Music by Piero Piccione and Ennio Morricone
Director of Photography: Giuseppe Rotunno
A Dino de Laurentiis (Roma)/Les Productions Artistes
Associés (Paris) Production

Cast: Clint Eastwood and Silvana Mangano.

HANG 'EM HIGH (1967)

Director: Ted Post
Producer: Leonard Freeman
Screenplay by Leonard Freeman
Music by Dominic Frontière
Director of Photography: Leonard South and Richard Kline
A Leonard Freeman Productions/Malpaso Production, released
by United Artists, De Luxe Colour

Cast: Clint Eastwood (*Jed Cooper*), Inger Stevens (*Rachel*),
Ed Begley (*Captain Wilson*), Pat Hingle (*Judge Adam Fenton*),
Arlene Golonka (*Jennifer*), James MacArthur (*Priest*).

COOGAN'S BLUFF (1968)

Director: Don Siegel
Producer: Don Siegel
Screenplay by Herman Miller, Dean Riesner and Howard Rodman
Based on a story by Herman Miller
Music by Lalo Schifrin
Director of Photography: Bud Thackeray
A Universal Production, Technicolor

Cast: Clint Eastwood (*Walt Coogan*), Lee J. Cobb (*McElroy*),
Susan Clark (*Julie*), Tisha Sterling (*Linny Raven*), Don Stroud
(*Ringerman*), Betty Field (*Mrs. Ringerman*).

WHERE EAGLES DARE (1969)

Director: Brian G. Hutton
Producer: Elliot Kastner
Screenplay by Alistair McLean
Based on his own novel
Music by Ron Goodwin
Director of Photography: Arthur Ibbetson
A Winkast Production, released by Metro-Goldwyn-Mayer,
Metrocolor and Panavision

Cast: Richard Burton (*John Smith*), Clint Eastwood (*Lt. Morris Shaeffer*), Mary Ure (*Mary Ellison*), Patrick Wymark (*Col. Turner*).

PAINT YOUR WAGON (1969)

Director: Joshua Logan
Producer: Alan Jay Lerner
Screenplay by Paddy Chayefsky
Based on the musical play, book and lyrics by Alan Jay Lerner
Music by Frederick Loewe
Director of Photography: William A. Fraker
A Paramount Production, Technicolor and Panavision

Cast: Lee Marvin (*Ben Rumson*), Clint Eastwood (*Pardner*),
Jean Seberg (*Elizabeth*), Harve Presnell (*Rotten Luck Willie*).

KELLY'S HEROES (1970)

Director: Brian G. Hutton
Producers: Gabriel Katzka and Sidney Beckerman
Screenplay by Troy Kennedy Martin
Music by Lalo Schifrin
Director of Photography: Gabriel Figueroa
A Warriors' Company (Hollywood)/Avala Films (Belgrade)
Production, released by MGM-EMI, Metrocolor and Panavision

Cast: Clint Eastwood (*Kelly*), Telly Savalas (*Big Joe*),
Don Rickles (*Crapgame*), Donald Sutherland (*Oddball*).

TWO MULES FOR SISTER SARA (1970)

Director: Don Siegel
Producers: Martin Racin and Carroll Chase
Screenplay by Albert Maltz
Based on a story by Budd Boetticher
Music by Ennio Morricone
Director of Photography: Gabriel Figueroa
A Universal/Malpaso Production, Technicolor and Panavision

Cast: Shirley MacLaine (*Sara*), Clint Eastwood (*Hogan*), Manolo Fabregas (*Colonel Beltran*), Alberto Morin (*General Le Claire*).

THE BEGUILED (1971)

Director: Don Siegel
Producer: Don Siegel
Screenplay by John B. Sherry and Grimes Grice
Based on a novel by Thomas Cullinan
Music by Lalo Schifrin
Director of Photography: Bruce Surtees
A Universal/Malpaso Production, Technicolor

Cast: Clint Eastwood (*John McBurney*), Geraldine Page (*Martha Farnsworth*), Elizabeth Hartmann (*Edwina Dabney*), Jo Ann Harris (*Carol*), Darleen Carr (*Doris*), Mae Mercer (*Hallie*).

PLAY 'MISTY' FOR ME (1971)

Director: Clint Eastwood
Producer: Robert Daley
Screenplay by Jo Heims and Dean Riesner
Based on a story by Jo Heims
Music by Dee Barton
Director of Photography: Bruce Surtees
A Universal/Malpaso Production, Technicolor

Cast: Clint Eastwood (*Dave Garland*), Jessica Walter (*Evelyn Draper*), Donna Mills (*Tobie Williams*), John Larch (*Sgt. McCallum*).

DIRTY HARRY (1971)

Director: Don Siegel
Producer: Robert Daley
Screenplay by Harry Julian Fink, Rita M. Fink and Dean Riesner
Based on a story by Harry Julian Fink and Rita M. Fink
Music by Lalo Schifrin
Director of Photography: Bruce Surtees
A Warner Brothers/Malpaso Production, Technicolor and Panavision

Cast: Clint Eastwood (*Harry Callahan*), Harry Guardino (*Lt. Bressler*), Reni Santoni (*Chico*), John Vernon (*Mayor*),
Andy Robinson (*Killer*).

JOE KIDD (1972)

Director: John Sturges
Producer: Sidney Beckerman
Screenplay by Elmore Leonard
Music by Lalo Schifrin
Director of Photography: Bruce Surtees
A Universal/Malpaso Production, Technicolor and Panavision

Cast: Clint Eastwood (*Joe Kidd*), Robert Duvall (*Frank Harlan*),
John Saxon (*Luis Chama*), Don Stroud (*Lamarr*), Stella Garcia (*Helen Sanchez*), James Wainwright (*Mingo*).

HIGH PLAINS DRIFTER (1972)

Director: Clint Eastwood
Producer: Robert Daley
Screenplay by Ernest Tidyman
Music by Dee Barton
Director of Photography: Bruce Surtees
A Malpaso/Universal Production, Technicolor and Panavision

Cast: Clint Eastwood (*The Stranger*), Verna Bloom (*Sarah Belding*),
Mariana Hill (*Callie Travers*), Mitchell Ryan (*Dave Drake*).

MAGNUM FORCE (1973)

Director: Ted Post
Producer: Robert Daley
Screenplay by John Milius and Michael Cimino
Based on a story by John Milius, using the characters
created by Harry Julian Fink and Rita M. Fink
Music by Lalo Schifrin
Director of Photography: Frank Stanley
A Malpaso/Warner Brothers Production, Technicolor and Panavision

Cast: Clint Eastwood (*Harry Callahan*), Hal Holbrook (*Lt. Neil Briggs*), Mitchell Ryan (*Charlie McCoy*), David Soul (*Ben Davis*),
Felton Perry (*Early Smith*).

BREEZY (1973)

Director: Clint Eastwood
Producer: Robert Daley
Screenplay by Jo Heims
Music by Michel Legrand
Director of Photography: Frank Stanley
A Malpaso/Universal Production, Technicolor and Panavision

Cast: William Holden (*Frank Harmon*), Kay Lenz (*Breezy*),
Roger C. Carmel (*Bob Henderson*), Marj Dusay (*Betty Tobin*).

THUNDERBOLT AND LIGHTFOOT (1974)

Director: Michael Cimino
Producer: Robert Daley
Screenplay by Michael Cimino
Music by Dee Barton
Director of Photography: Frank Stanley
*A Malpaso Production, released by United Artists, Colour
De Luxe and Panavision*

Cast: Clint Eastwood (*John 'Thunderbolt' Doherty*), Jeff Bridges
(*Lightfoot*), George Kennedy (*Red Leary*), Geoffrey Lewis
(*Goody*), Catherine Bach (*Melody*).

THE EIGER SANCTION (1975)

Director: Clint Eastwood
Producer: Robert Daley
Screenplay by Warren B. Murphy, Hal Dresner, and Rod Whitaker
Based on a novel by Trevanian
Music by John Williams
Director of Photography: Frank Stanley
Photographers, mountain sequences: John Cleare,
Jeff Schoolfield, Peter Pilafian, Peter White
*A Universal/Malpaso Production, released by C.I.C., Technicolor
and Panavision*

Cast: Clint Eastwood (*Jonathan Hemlock*), George Kennedy
(*Ben Bowman*), Vonetta McGee (*Jemima Brown*), Jack Cassidy
(*Miles Mellough*), Heidi Bruhl (*Anna Montaigne*).

THE ENFORCER (1975)

Director: James Fargo
Producer: Robert Daley
Screenplay by Stirling Silliphant and Dean Riesner
Based on characters created by Harry Julian Fink and
Rita M. Fink
Music by Jerry Fielding
Director of Photography: Charles W. Short
A Malpaso Production, released by Columbia-Warner, Panavision

Cast: Clint Eastwood (*Harry Callahan*), Harry Guardino
(*Lt. Bressler*), Bardford Dillman (*Capt. McKay*), John Mitchum
(*DiGeorgio*), Tyne Daly (*Kate Moore*).

THE GAUNTLET (1976)

Director: Clint Eastwood
Producer: Robert Daley
Screenplay by Michael Butler and Dennis Shryack
Music by Jerry Fielding
Director of Photography: Rexford Metz
*A Malpaso Production, released by Columbia-Warner, Panavision
and Technicolor*

Cast: Clint Eastwood (*Ben Shockley*), Sondra Locke (*Augusta
Mally*), Pat Hingle (*Josephson*), Blakelock William (*Prince*),
Bill McKinney (*Constable*).

THE OUTLAW JOSEY WALES (1976)

Director: Clint Eastwood
Producer: Robert Daley
Screenplay by Alan Kaufman, Sonia Chernus
Based on the novel *Gone to Texas* by Forrest Carter
Music by Jerry Fielding
Director of Photography: Bruce Surtees
*A Malpaso Production, released by Columbia-Warner,
Colour De Luxe*

Cast: Clint Eastwood (*Josey Wales*), Chief Dan George (*Lone
Watie*), Sondra Locke (*Laura Lee*), Bill McKinney (*Terrill*),
John Vernon (*Fletcher*), Paula Trueman (*Grandma Sarah*).

EVERY WHICH WAY BUT LOOSE (1977)

Director: James Fargo
Producer: Robert Daley
Screenplay by Jeremy Joe Kronsberg
Music by Snuff Garret
Director of Photography: Rexford Metz
*A Malpaso Production, released by Warner Bros, Technicolor
and Panavision*

Cast: Clint Eastwood (*Philo Beddoe*), Sondra Locke (*Lynn Halsey-
Taylor*), Geoffrey Lewis (*Orville*), Beverley D'Angelo (*Echo*),
Ruth Gordon (*Ma*), Bill McKinney (*Dallas*).

ESCAPE FROM ALCATRAZ (1978)

Director: Don Siegel
Producer: Don Siegel
Screenplay by Richard Tuggle
Based on the book by J. Campbell Bruce
Music by June Edgerton
Director of Photography: Bruce Surtees
A Paramount Picture, Colour De Luxe, Panavision

Cast: Clint Eastwood (*Frank Morris*), Patrick McGoohan (*Warden*),
Roberts Blossom (*Doc*), Jack Thibeau (*Clarence Anglin*), Fred
Ward (*John Anglin*), Paul Benjamin (*English*), Bruce Fischer (*Wolf*).

BRONCO BILLY (1980)

Director: Clint Eastwood
Producer: Dennis Hackin, Neal Dobrofsky
Screenplay by Dennis Hackin
Music by Snuff Garret
Director of Photography: David Worth
A Malpaso Production, released by Warner Bros., Colour De Luxe

Cast: Clint Eastwood (*Bronco Billy McCoy*), Sondra Locke
(*Antoinette Lily*), Geoffrey Lewis (*John Arlington*), Scatman
Crothers (*Doc Lynch*), Bill McKinney (*Lefty Le Bow*), Sam Bottoms
(*Leonard James*), Dan Vadis (*Chief Big Eagle*), Sierra Pecheur
(*Lorraine Running Water*).

ANY WHICH WAY YOU CAN (1980)

Director: Buddy Van Horn
Producer: Fritz Manes
Screenplay by Stanford Sherman
Based on characters created by Jeremy Joe Kronsberg
Music by Snuff Garret
Director of Photography: David Worth
A Malpaso Production, released by Warner Bros, Colour De Luxe

Cast: Clint Eastwood (*Philo Beddoe*), Sondra Locke (*Lynn Halsey-
Taylor*), Geoffrey Lewis (*Orville*), William Smith (*Jack Wilson*),
Harry Guardino (*James Beekman*), Ruth Gordon (*Ma Boggs*).

FIREFOX (1982)

Director: Clint Eastwood
Producer: Clint Eastwood
Screenplay by Alex Lasker & Wendell Wellman
Based on the novel by Craig Thomas
Music by Maurice Jarre
Director of Photography: Bruce Surtees
A Malpaso Production released by Columbia-EMI-Warner Dist. Ltd.
Colour by Deluxe

Cast: Clint Eastwood (*Mitchell Gant*), Freddie Jones (*Aubrey*), David Huffman (*Buckholz*), Warren Clarke (*Pavel Upenskoy*), Nigel Hawthorne (*Baranovich*), Ronald Lacey (*Semelovsky*).

HONKYTONK MAN (1983)

Director: Clint Eastwood
Producer: Clint Eastwood
Screenplay by Clancy Carlile (based upon his novel)
Music by Snuff Garrett
Director of Photography: Bruce Surtees
A Malpaso Production released by Warner Brothers
Colour by Deluxe

Cast: Clint Eastwood (*Red Stovall*), Kyle Eastwood (*Whit*), John McIntire (*Grandpa*), Alexa Kenin (*Marlene*), Verna Bloom (*Emmy*), Matt Clark (*Vergil*).

SUDDEN IMPACT (1984)

Director: Clint Eastwood
Producer: Clint Eastwood
Screenplay by Joseph C. Stinson
Based on characters created by Harry Julian Fink and R.M. Fink
Story by Earl E. Smith & Charles B. Pierce
Music by Lalo Schifrin
Director of Photography: Bruce Surtees
A Malpaso Production released by Warner Brothers
Colour by Technicolor

Cast: Clint Eastwood (*Harry Callahan*), Sondra Locke (*Jennifer Spencer*), Pat Hingle (*Chief Jannings*), Bradford Dillman (*Capt Briggs*), Paul Drake (*Mick*).

TIGHTROPE (1984)

Director: Richard Tuggle
Producer: Clint Eastwood & Fritz Manes
Screenplay by Richard Tuggle
Music by Lennie Niehaus
Director of Photography: Bruce Surtees
A Malpaso Production released by Warner Brothers
Colour by Technicolor

Cast: Clint Eastwood (*Wes Block*), Genevieve Bujold (*Beryl Thibodeaux*), Dan Hedaya (*Det Molinari*), Alison Eastwood (*Amanda Block*), Jennifer Beck (*Penny Block*).

CITY HEAT (1985)

Director: Richard Benjamin
Producer: Fritz Manes
Screenplay by Sam O. Brown & Joseph C. Stinson
From a story by Sam O. Brown
Music by Lennie Niehaus
Director of Photography: Nick McLean
A Malpaso/Deliverance Production released by Warner Brothers
Colour by Technicolor

Cast: Clint Eastwood (*Lt Speer*), Burt Reynolds (*Mike Murphy*), Jane Alexander (*Addy*), Madeline Kahn (*Caroline Howley*), Rip Torn (*Primo Pitt*).

PALE RIDER (1985)

Director: Clint Eastwood
Producer: Clint Eastwood
Screenplay by Michael Butler & Dennis Shryack
Music by Lennie Niehaus
Director of Photography: Bruce Surtees
A Malpaso Production released by Warner Brothers
Colour by Technicolor

Cast: Clint Eastwood (*Preacher*), Michael Moriarty (*Hull Barret*), Carrie Snodgress (*Sarah*), Richard Dysart (*LaHood*), Sydney Penny (*Megan*).

VANESSA IN THE GARDEN (1985)

Director: Clint Eastwood
Producer: Steven Spielberg
A production for the US TV series of Amazing Stories

Cast: Sondra Locke (*Vanessa*) with Harvey Keitel and Beau Bridges

HEARTBREAK RIDGE (1986)

Director: Clint Eastwood
Producer: Clint Eastwood
Screenplay by James Carabatsos
Music by Lennie Niehaus
Director of Photography: Jack N. Green
A Malpaso Production released by Warner Brothers
Colour by Technicolor

Cast: Clint Eastwood (*Highway*), Marsha Mason (*Aggie*), Everett McGill (*Maj Powers*), Mario Van Peebles (*Stitch*).

BIRD (1988)

Director: Clint Eastwood
Producer: Clint Eastwood
Screenplay by Joel Oliansky
Music by Lennie Niehaus with original Charlie Parker compositions
Director of Photography: Jack N. Green
A Malpaso Production released by Warner Brothers
Colour by Technicolor

Cast: Forest Whitaker (*Charlie 'Bird' Parker*), Diane Venora (*Chan*), Keith David (*Buster*), Sam Wright (*Dizzy Gillespie*), Damon Whitaker (*Young Charlie 'Bird' Parker*).

THE DEAD POOL (1988)

Director: Wayne Van Horne
Producer: David Valdes
Screenplay by Steve Sharon from a story by Steve Sharon, Durk Pearson and Sandy Shaw
Music by Lalo Schifrin
Director of Photography: Jack N. Green
A Malpaso Production released by Warner Brothers
Colour by Technicolour

Cast: Clint Eastwood (*Harry Callahan*), Patricia Clarkson (*Samantha Walker*), Evan Kim (*Al Qan*), Liam Neeson (*Peter Swan*), David Hunt (Harlan Rook).